Pro Communione

Pro Communione

Theological Essays on the Anglican Covenant

Edited by
Benjamin M. Guyer

PICKWICK *Publications* · Eugene, Oregon

PRO COMMUNIONE
Theological Essays on the Anglican Covenant

Pickwick Publications
A Division of Wipf and Stock Publishers
199 W. 8th Ave., Suite 3
Eugene, OR 97401

www.wipfandstock.com

ISBN 13: 978–1-61097–361-8

Cataloging-in-Publication data:

Pro communione : theological essays on the Anglican covenant / edited by
Benjamin M. Guyer.

xxx + 214 p. ; 23 cm. Includes bibliographical references.

ISBN 13: 978-1-61097–361-8

1. Anglican communion—Doctrines. 2. Theology. I. Guyer, Benjamin M. II.
Title.

BT28 P59 2012

Manufactured in the U.S.A.

My work on *Pro Communione* is lovingly dedicated to
The Rev. B. E. and Beth Palmer
Simus unum!

Contents

Abbreviations

The Anglican Communion website maintains "An Anglican Covenant" page which links all documentation concerning the Anglican Covenant: http://www.anglicancommunion.org/commission/covenant/index.cfm.

THE ANGLICAN COMMUNION COVENANT

CDG	Covenant Design Group (2007–09)
Covenant	The Anglican Communion Covenant, Final Text (2009); frequently shortened as the Anglican Covenant; cited by section (e.g., Covenant, 1.1.1)
Declaration	Declaration to either SADC, RCDC, or Covenant; cited as draft, Declaration (e.g., Covenant, Declaration); Declaration to NDC is cited as NDC, 7
Introduction	Introduction to either SADC, RCDC, or Covenant; cited as draft, Introduction, and para. (e.g., Covenant, Introduction, para. 8)
NDC	Nassau Draft Covenant (2007); cited by section (e.g., NDC, 2.1)
Preamble	Preamble to either SADC, RCDC, or Covenant; cited as draft, Preamble (e.g., RCDC, Preamble); Preamble to NDC is cited as NDC, 1
Report CDG	Report of the Covenant Design Group (2007)
RCDC	Ridley Cambridge Draft Covenant (2009); cited by section (e.g., RCDC, 1.1.1)

SADC	St. Andrews Draft Covenant (2008); cited by section (e.g., SADC, 1.1.1)
TAAC	Towards an Anglican Covenant (2006); cited by para. (e.g., TAAC, para. 16)

OTHER

39 Art.	Thirty-Nine Articles of Religion (1571); cited by Art. (e.g., 39 Art., Art. 1)
ACC	The Anglican Consultative Council; cited by meeting, resolution, and year (e.g., ACC-4, Res. 6 (1979)); Resolutions Archive online: http://www.anglicancommunion.org/communion/acc/
ARCIC	Anglican-Roman Catholic International Commission
Art.	Article
BCP	Book of Common Prayer; cited by year and page (e.g., BCP 1662, 3)
Doe, *Covenant*	Norman Doe, *An Anglican Covenant: Theological Considerations for a Global Debate* (Canterbury Press, 2008); cited by page
FLE	W. Speed Hill (ed.), *The Folger Library Edition of the Works of Richard Hooker*, seven vols. (The Belknap Press of Harvard University Press and Medieval & Renaissance Texts & Studies, 1977–98); cited by volume and page number (e.g., FLE I, 231)
JSC	Joint Standing Committee of the Anglican Communion
LC	Lambeth Conference; cited by year and resolution (e.g., LC 1968, Res. 69); Resolutions Archive online: http://www.lambethconference.org/index.cfm
IASCER	Inter-Anglican Standing Commission on Ecumenical Relations
IASCUFO	Inter-Anglican Standing Commission on Unity, Faith, and Order

IATDC	Inter-Anglican Theological and Doctrinal Commission
para.	paragraph
Res.	Resolution
ST	St. Thomas Aquinas, *Summa Theologiæ*, 61 vols. Edited and translated by the English Province of the Order of Preachers (Cambridge: Cambridge University Press, 1964–81)
TWR	The Windsor Report (2004); cited by § (e.g., TWR, §§117–20); Online: http://www.aco.org/windsor2004/
TVR	The Virginia Report (1999); cited by para. (e.g., TVR, para. 1.1); Online: http://www.lambethconference.org/1998/documents/report-1.pdf

Contributors

Jeff Boldt is a doctoral student at Wycliffe College, University of Toronto.

Augustine Casiday is Lecturer in Historical Theology in the School of Theology, Religion and Islamic Studies at University of Wales Trinity Saint David. He is the author of *Tradition and Theology in the Writings of John Cassian* (Oxford University Press, 2006) and has edited and translated several volumes, most recently with Tim Vivian, *St. Mark the Monk: On the Spiritual Life* (St. Vladimir's Seminary Press, 2009).

Neil Dhingra is Assistant Professor in the Department of Humanities at Carroll Community College.

Andrew Goddard is Tutor in Christian Ethics at Trinity College, Bristol, and has previously taught at Wycliffe Hall, Oxford. He has been editor of the journal *Anvil* and a member of the Church of England's Faith and Order Advisory Group. He previously contributed to Mark D. Chapman (ed.), *The Anglican Covenant: Unity and Diversity in the Anglican Communion* (Mowbray, 2008).

Benjamin M. Guyer is a doctoral student in the Department of History at the University of Kansas. He is editor of *The Beauty of Holiness: The Caroline Divines and Their Writings* (Canterbury Press, 2012).

N. J. A. Humphrey is scholar-in-residence at Saint Paul's Parish, K Street, Washington, DC, in the Episcopal Diocese of Washington. He is a graduate of St. John's College, Annapolis, Maryland, and Yale University Divinity School.

Nathan G. Jennings is the J. Milton Richardson Associate Professor of Liturgics and Anglican Studies at the Seminary of the Southwest. He is a priest in the Episcopal Church (USA) and has most recently authored *Theology as Ascetic Act: Disciplining Christian Discourse* (Peter Lang, 2010).

Evan Kuehn is a doctoral student at the University of Chicago Divinity School. He has previously published in the *Ecclesiastical Law Journal*, *International Journal of Systematic Theology*, and *History of Political Thought*.

Edmund Newey is vicar of St. Andrew's, Handsworth, in the Church of England. He is the author of *Children of God: Theological Anthropologies of the Child in the Work of Traherne, Rousseau, Schleiermacher and Péguy* (Ashgate, 2012), has published in journals such as *Modern Theology* and *Anglican Theological Review*, and has contributed most recently to *Fear and Friendship: Anglicans Engaging with Islam* (Continuum, 2012).

Matthew S. C. Olver is a priest in the Episcopal Church (USA). A graduate of Wheaton College (IL) and Duke University Divinity School, he serves at Church of the Incarnation, Dallas, Texas, and is a member of the Anglican-Roman Catholic Consultation in the United States (ARC-USA).

Ephraim Radner is Professor of Historical Theology at Wycliffe College, University of Toronto, and was a member of the Anglican Communion's Covenant Design Group. He is a priest in the Episcopal Church (USA) and the author of several books, including *The End of the Church: A Pneumatology of Christian Division in the West* (Eerdmans, 1998), *The Fate of Communion: The Agony of Anglicanism and the Future of a Global Church* (Eerdmans, 2006), and, most recently, *The World in the Shadow of God: An Introduction to Christian Natural Theology* (Cascade Books, 2010).

Christopher Wells is Executive Director of the Living Church Foundation and editor of *The Living Church*. He has taught at the College of the Transfiguration in Grahamstown, South Africa, and published in *Ecclesiology*, *Journal of Anglican Studies*, and *Anglican Theological Review*. He serves as a theological consultant to the Anglican-Roman Catholic Consultation in the United States (ARC-USA).

Acknowledgments

I AM INDEBTED TO MANY people for the production of this volume. First and foremost, I thank Katharine L. Silcox. Originally my co-editor, her withdrawal from this project due to reasons of health was a matter of considerable disappointment. She helped me fine tune the original ideas behind *Pro Communione*, offered insightful critiques on the original proposals for each essay, and contributed final editorial comments on the completed essays by Evan Kuehn and myself. Without her, this volume would be far less developed. I am immensely appreciative to Christopher Wells for offering Katie and myself a number of helpful suggestions early on. In particular, he pushed for the inclusion of ecumenical perspectives—an encouragement which has greatly enriched the scope of our work. I am no less indebted to Ephraim Radner for support and insight at every step, and for agreeing to write the introduction. I thank the following people for introducing me to several of our contributors: to Peter Bouteneff for placing me in contact with Augustine Casiday, to Benjamin King for referring me to Edmund Newey, and to Graham Kings for connecting me with Andrew Goddard. I am grateful for the patience extended to our project by Christian Amondson and K. C. Hanson at Wipf and Stock. I thank Rachel, as always, for her constant support. Finally, I thank the contributors themselves. Here I am, on every page, surrounded by my betters. For this I am both humbled and most grateful.

Foreword

The Covenant Way

EPHRAIM RADNER

WHAT WOULD IT LOOK like for Anglican churches to be bound to-gether by a covenant of common life and commitment? The pro-posed Anglican Covenant that is now before the various churches of the Anglican Communion remains something of a mystery in this regard, for no one is really sure of its practical effects. And this mystery has drawn to it the projections of many, born of both optimistic and fearful imagina-tions. One can argue either the theoretical parameters of provincial au-tonomy or the ideal character of interdependence—both key categories in Anglican ecclesial life—but how a covenant, and how *this* particular covenant, might shape these realities in fact remains uncertain, as with all future historical elements of a relational kind, whose forms are subject to so many contingent dynamics.

The present collection of essays by and large moves beyond such speculative performances by considering the Anglican Covenant in a manner that is more than institutionally bound. Instead, the authors here explore elements of the dynamics of covenantal life itself. Anglicanism, after all, has often been understood as a kind of "way," and not simply as a set of institutional collectives whose frames and gears must be care-fully meshed. The phrase *via media* is of course a standard description of this way, that is, as a "middle way." And, generally speaking, this *via media* has been described in terms of a place "in between" the "extremes" of Catholic papalism and Calvinist Puritanism of one kind or another. Edmund Newey's essay in this volume, however, points out how this description is, from a historical perspective, misleading. Rather, many of the seventeenth-century framers of the notion of an Anglican *via media* saw the phrase as describing a "way" between earth and heaven, not between ecclesial or theological traditions, institutionally settled; it was a way, in fact, that might provide the Christian in the Church a passage from earth *to* heaven. In this sense, the Anglican *via media* was understood in the context of the long Western tradition of the Church (and the Christian) as *viator*, the pilgrim *along the way* from the gift of birth, through the struggles of a difficult and sinful self and world (even a recalcitrant Church), to the promised glories of life with God.[1] It is bound to the way who is Christ himself, who is *mediator* in the midst of just this passage. Thus, the Anglican *via media* is the life on this earth that takes us to our promised and fulfilled end in and through Christ. It is shaped—and often re-shaped—by certain convictions, promises and hopes, practices and struggles, graces and joys, and, of course, a certain kind of "life together."

A "way," however, is not given in a limited set of rules. It is bound to uncertainties and strewn with obstacles and ordered by a range of often readjusted decisions. But a "way together" is nonetheless *shaped*, and so shaped by one another. Part of the argument of this volume is that this way can be properly seen today as a "covenanted" way among Anglicans. But this is a complicated argument. Essays in this book rightly struggle with questions of history, both the history particular to Anglicanism (see Andrew Goddard) and history particular to the larger Christian tradition, Western and Eastern (see Matthew S. C. Olver and Augustine Casiday). Matters of ecclesiology on a broader scale necessarily come into view (see the essays by Neil Dhingra, Christopher Wells, and Evan Kuehn and, from the direction of liturgical ecclesiology, Nathan Jennings; so too more fundamental matters of ecclesial presupposition, as in N. J. A. Humphrey's reflection on Rowan Williams's moral personalism). Rather tricky issues of political order and constitutionalism are addressed, and in ways that touch upon a broad range of contemporary concerns (see Jeff Boldt's and Benjamin Guyer's contributions). Over all of them, on some more explicitly than others (Wells's is the most pointed in this respect), hovers the shadow of a deep desire for the wider Christian Church's healing

---

1. The classic consideration of this tradition is Gerhard Ladner, "*Homo Viator.*"

and unity, the lack of which has been underscored by Anglicanism's late travails, and the glory of which these essays lift in yearning hope. And it is just here, all the authors argue, however cautiously at times, that covenanting in the form of the proposed Anglican Covenant is a "way" worth pursuing, indeed perhaps even a divinely demanded way, for it is a "way through" these assaults, and not only a suffering of them.

But what in fact is such a way? Is it political? Liturgical? An ecumenical strategy or a form of faithfulness to heritage? None of this volume's contributors is so narrow; rather they see their task as one of uncovering aspects of a deeper reality at the center of Christian existence, which the Anglican Covenant itself only opportunistically provides. One way to get a grasp of this center is through a method of contrast. Is there such a thing as the "uncovenanted way"? And what, in such a light, is the "covenant-way" itself? In what follows, I offer a brief Scriptural outline, which I hope can offer a few lines for a framework in which to place some of the interests of the essays that follow. To look for the contrasting "ways" of covenant and its lack, we might first gaze at Israel and her own division, as described in the Books of Kings. The division itself, as I and others have argued elsewhere,[2] is rightly taken in part as an "ecclesial figure," a way of gauging the Church's form and life itself. And to this degree, the question of Israel's internal and external "covenanting" is ecclesiologically illuminating.

The covenanting of the Israelites among themselves, in a way that goes beyond or in some sense renews, in a practical way, the initial covenant with God at Sinai, is a practice that we see already in Joshua 23–24 (see 24:25), as the tribes, following their allotments of the land, gather at Shechem on this basis. More particularly, we see the Israelites, as in Judges, make covenants among themselves for the sake of pursuing and establishing justice among their members. The language of unity and vowing before God falls within this category (cf. Judg 20:8, 11), and it appears as if this kind of gathering through and for the sake of common commitments is well known. By David's time, we see "covenanting," in its literal form, taking place in the face of civil war, in this case, between Saul's followers and the ascendant David. So, in 2 Samuel 3, we hear of the "long war" between the two groups that is devastating the people, and see how Saul's general, Abner, now seeks to make a "covenant" (*berith*)

---

2. Cf. Congar, "Reflections on the Schism of Israel." See also Radner, "The Cost of Communion."

with David to bring peace and to unite the two hostile factions (3:12). By 5:3, this covenanting has embraced "all the tribes of Israel" who come to David and seek to form an agreement that will formally make him their king and bring an end to the prolonged bloodshed and insecurity within the land. "Covenanting," then, refers to a set of commitments made internally among the Israelites, in this case, for the restoration of peace, and the reordering of the nation. Its violation—as in the case of Abner's murder by Joab, in the face of the promises made—is also presented in its paradigmatic destructiveness, a figure that envelopes the kingship of David and his successors in the most comprehensive fashion.

Indeed, the covenant of renewed peace within Israel, together with its repeated collapse, becomes a shadow cast over Israel's later life as a whole, the history of which in the Books of Kings displays a repeated and spiraling descent into the breaking of promises, and a desperate search for their restoration in new and ever less stable forms. Israel herself divides into two kingdoms, the result of Rehoboam's political oppression, and in the course of this major division between Judah and northern Israel over the next several centuries, parties are realigned in ever encroaching violence. Covenants are made with other nations, as Judah and Israel seek to strengthen themselves against the other, and covenants are made even amongst themselves, for shorter periods of time as each reacts against the dangers posed by former foreign friends. (Cf. 1 Kgs 15, and v. 19, on the making and breaking of covenants by Judah with Syria in her struggle with Israel; or 1 Kgs 22:44, which refers to a formal peace between Judah and Israel.) Without a lasting covenanted peace among themselves, as bound through the Covenant of God at Sinai, the Israelites gradually impoverish themselves by staking their resources upon passing and constantly shifting treaties with the nations, that reduce her bit by bit into vassalage and finally destroy her altogether.

The terrifying accounts of the Israelites' gradual religious, moral and political disintegration, that are given in 2 Kings, culminate in chapter 17. Having reached the final point of their internecine hostilities, the crushing judgment upon Israel's own political survival is given. This chapter presents a litany of unfaithfulness, of which the division (17:21) constitutes one key element in a process that will swallow both Samaria and Judah to the dregs (17:19–20), as each "hangs separately," as it were. In the retrospective summary given here, the various covenanting ways of Israel are revealed as insufficient in their overriding goal, unfaithful in their disparate and transitory commitment, and finally overwhelmed by the self-regarding concerns of nations and peoples set on their own way, fulfilling the summary assessment of Israel given at the close of Judges (21:25). Israel cannot keep her covenants.

The casualty in all this, in addition to the people's survival, is the founding Covenant that God made with them. For the failure of Israel's own covenanting represents an attack upon the divine Covenant of Sinai. The text itself outlines this failure on a number of fronts: adopting the customs of the nations; permitting the abominable customs of individual kings (2 Kgs 17:8, 15, 22); the internalization of deceit by the people (17:9). This undermines the fundamental relationship with God (17:15, 35) that is bound up in divine law, and the dilution of religion itself proves the inexorable consequence as Israel plunges into local syncretism (17:24–41). As covenants crumble and increasingly disappear altogether, and as the Covenant is thereby assaulted, Israel marks out its own "way," one rightly understood as the "uncovenanted way" that moves into the rising current of confusion, injustice, woe, destruction, and the disappearance of a people. It is driven by territorial possessiveness and division, localized cultures of irresponsibility, individual self-assertions and avarice, and conflicting interests that never mesh. The figure is powerful and all-consuming in historical terms.

By contrast, it is important to see that the individual covenants themselves, as they emerge in the midst of this current, are presented often as moments of renewal. So the priest Jehoiada, in 2 Kings 11 and 12, reestablishes Judah's religious life through a new covenant among people and king (11:17), and it is on this basis that the land enjoys some limited blessing and peace (12:2). It is this kind of covenanting renewal that Ezra will later lead in establishing (cf. Neh. 9:38). At their best, these renewed mutual commitments are aimed at focusing on the Lord's Covenant (or "Covenants" in the plural, as Paul will have it), and hence their interest consistently involves matters relating to worship, obedience, and common action. These are commitments that arise in the midst of a history, usually a negative one, or at least one of difficult challenge. They regather, reaffirm, and reorient for the sake of the larger realities of God's promises. This too marks a certain "way."

And it is one that, in its limited scope, bears some similarities with New Testament covenanting among the early Christians. For here too we see individual covenants being made. Thus, Paul in Galatians 2:9 speaks of having received, along with Barnabas, the "right hand of fellowship" (*koinonia*) from the apostolic leaders in Jerusalem; this seems to be a technical form of covenant, in this case based on an agreement regarding their shared mission and common responsibilities within the Church.[3] More individually, one has something like Paul's Nazirite "vow" (Acts 21:23–24; cf. 18:18), a kind of "covenant" derivatively in the form of a sacred promise, aimed at restoring and aiding the common life of the Jerusalem Church, both with him and with its Jewish neighbors. Even the letter from the apostles in Jerusalem to the church in Antioch includes some covenanting language of shared and consecrated responsibilities (Acts 15:28).

In all these contrastive cases, human covenanting is meant somehow to support, perhaps expressively, the originating covenantal work of God. God's ways are "faithfulness" with respect to the Covenant in which Israel is engaged (Ps 25:10), and this becomes the basis for the dozens of instances in the Scriptures where God's epithet is given in terms of "steadfast love and faithfulness [truth]" (e.g., Exod 34:6; Ps 146:6). Paul builds on this in Romans 3:3, and ranges God's covenantal faithfulness over and against human disobedience. From the Church's side, of course, it is the Covenant of Christ that is fundamental to her own covenantal ways. This is the "new Covenant" established on the Cross and represented in the Eucharist as first enacted at the Last supper (cf. Mark 14:24). Its own meaning, to be sure, remains that covenant whose shape is promised, out of the foundation of Sinai, in Jeremiah 31:31–34 (cf. Heb 8:8). If Christians themselves "covenant," then they do so only in a way that, just as in Israel's many re-covenantings, attaches somehow to this more basic covenant of divine faithfulness given in Christ.

The great debate over baptism as a "covenant" is reflective of this relation between human and divine covenants. By the time of the Reformation this had become a standard trope, among all Protestants (although it was Catholics who, in the mid-16th-century, seem first to have spoken of baptism as a "covenant"). Anglicans, in line with theologians like Hooker,[4] will, by the early seventeenth century, speak of the "baptis-

3. Cummins, *Paul and the Crucified Christ in Antioch*, 132. The interpretation of this act as a formal covenant rather than as a simple sign of friendliness or good-will is now well-established.

4. *Lawes*, V.64. The notion that any Christian "vow" or "promise" is a covenant was already implied in the first Book of Common Prayer marriage service, and quickly

mal covenant" quite distinctly, and those of a more Calvinistic bent will associate it with the "covenant of Grace"—in the emerging "covenant" or "federal" theology of the Puritans—while others will tie it, in their defense of infant baptism, to the covenant of circumcision now fulfilled. In the eighteenth century, the Evangelical Samuel Walker, whose sermons so influenced Charles Simeon, gathers a number of these elements together in lifting up the "covenant-way" itself as a kind of general figure by which baptism and other Christian responsibilities and privileges are lived out.[5] The point in all these debates, however, is that there is a Covenant that is Christ's, and that this Covenant stands behind all covenanting of the Christian Church and her members. At the same, however, such covenanting owes its very real integrity and ineluctability to its foundation in Christ's original covenant.

But how are we to understand such Christian covenanting? The key chapters of Hebrews on Christ's Covenant (chaps. 6–9) speak to this, as this central theological section is made to inform the following chapters on the Church's historical life. The "new covenant," the writer insists, is indeed the form of Christ's own self-offering (9:23–26). But just this form is spoken of in terms of a "way," in what is probably a quite distinct choice of words that draws on the earliest Christian understandings of the prophetic fulfillment of the Messiah's coming (cf. Mark 1:2–3), now refashioned in terms of his specific life and passion (Mark 10:32; 11:8). Jesus' own declaration that he *is* "the way" (John 14:6) becomes the clear point of origin for the earliest churches' own self-identity as "the Way," in the words of Luke and Paul, that comes in Jesus' wake (Acts 9:2; 16:17; 19:23; 22:4; 24:14, 22).

In Hebrews, then, the new covenant opens up a "way," indeed just *this* way (10:20) which leads us to God's own final "rest." It is, furthermore, and as later writers well noted, something that includes baptism and that informs the breadth of Christian behavior within the Church:

> Having therefore, brethren, boldness to enter into the holiest by the blood of Jesus, By a new and living way, which he hath consecrated for us, through the veil, that is to say, his flesh; And having an high priest over the house of God; Let us draw near with a true heart in full assurance of faith, having our hearts sprinkled from

shifted to vows and promises of baptism.

5. Cf. Walker, *Fifty-Two Sermons*, vol. 1, 7–8. For a Reformed perspective on this history, see Jewett, *Infant Baptism and the Covenant of Grace*.

an evil conscience, and our bodies washed with pure water. Let us
hold fast the profession of our faith without wavering; (for he is
faithful that promised;) And let us consider one another to pro-
voke unto love and to good works: Not forsaking the assembling
of ourselves together, as the manner of some is; but exhorting one
another: and so much the more, as ye see the day approaching.
[Heb 10:19–25, AV]

The way that is opened here is given through Christ's "flesh"—the curtain
pierced—and this makes possible the writer's final movement into a description of the Christian Church's life in chapters 10–13, with all of its
quite specific detail. Here, just as in earlier outlines of covenanting, we see
engaged the elements of worship, obedience, and common action in the
form of mutual support and suffering (cf. 10:33, which uses the cognate
of *koinonia* as the frame for such common suffering).

The human covenants of God's people are, then, shadows and figures
of the one covenant that is Jesus. This is a properly theological assertion,
and it is a central one for the Church, and for her scattered members.
And the proper manner of looking at these ecclesial covenants is as a
form of ordering, as "ways" along the "Way." In the medieval framework,
such covenants—whether they are about common life or formation or
mission, among monks or within the lay apostolate—constitute the shape
of *stabilitas* for the *peregrinus*, a formative consistency of life for the pilgrim or wayfarer as he or she journeys across the rugged and dangerous
landscape of the world. Christian covenants are not permanent or eternal
in themselves; rather, they are gathered to serve this larger and eternal
purpose that is the movement through earthly life towards God in the
embrace of Jesus' own passage. This is why chapter 11 of Hebrews, with
its notion of the distant land (11:14–16; cf. Phil 3:20) to which the faithful
aim in the midst of their journey to God, founds the following discussion
on discipline and common life. The order here is important and its comprehensive vision is taken up by Gregory the Great with his influential
description, following Augustine, of the life of the Christian *viator*. Thus,
although relative to and in service of the Christian Church's Lord, such
covenanting—with its common commitments, promises and vows—takes
up precisely the forms of such active life as seek to renew faithfulness and
order conformance to the great gifts of grace. The practical character of
such *stabilitas*—even its "political aspects," as Guyer shows us—is central, not somehow debased in comparison to the goal; for only thus can

the elements of worship and obedience, of mission and faithfulness be given form within the passage of time. Even if it cannot do so consistently and unchangeably, the "covenant way" almost inevitably gives shape to the "way of Christ" within the world in which he himself first passed. The way *without* covenant is simply another way altogether. When *The Windsor Report* famously spoke in terms of the contrast between "walking together" and "walking apart," it was not to juridical constitutions or their lack that it referred, but to the movements and directions that pass along such contrasting "ways."[6]

It is, I believe, possible to fruitfully engage the intrinsically difficult discussion over "autonomy" and "interdependence" in the Anglican Communion[7] with respect to local ecclesial existence and self-determination, a question that seems to be lodged as a great barrier to healing among Anglican churches. But it will only be as part of a willingness to go together along this covenant-way first. As one of the original members of the Covenant Design Group that first began meeting in 2007, it proved a surprising privilege to see just how this could work. After all, the members of the Group, nominated as they were by very different interest groups within the Communion, came together with quite diverse commitments and indeed with mutual suspicions. But these differences were indeed transformed, not simply by willed changes of heart, but rather by the prior commitments to the purposes of covenanted renewal itself, even if without any shared preconceptions of what such renewal might mean. That is to say, our work was governed by a founding set of commitments simply to search for a way that might covenantally bring new life to a broken Church. It should be understood that such a founding framework itself functions as its own covenantal figure, its own "covenant-way." The initial "vow," if you will, was given in the Group's brief, and in each person's willingness to serve for such a purpose. This was not "dialogue," but rather a mission ordered by several forms of common life, including worship and prayer over a long period. And in this sense, covenanting preceded a Covenant, as Nathan Jennings implies in his essay; a certain "way" revealed a new way, for the sake of the one Way. That work was certainly not without challenges and even stumbling. But just in this, the need for such a way is made manifest and its value demonstrated.

6. Cf. TWR, §157.
7. Cf. TWR, §76.

The "uncovenanted way," as a principled form of ecclesial existence, seems, by contrast, not only to preempt the discussion from the start, but even to have made a decision for a form of existence whose past lies within the realm of terrible journeys, relations, and judgments attending, a past of broken nations, false hopes, weak alliances, squandered patrimonies, and finally violence. This stands as the Scriptural evidence, supported by centuries of unfortunate epigones. Is it really possible to claim that there is a way without covenant that is still on the way of Christ? One of the great gifts of this volume, which brings together the disciplined reflections of a range of scholars, many of them younger Anglicans, is how they demonstrate the richness of the "covenant way." This richness is both real and potential at once, for it promises not solutions but precisely a range of faithful but also challenging responses to the *vita terrena* of the Church, challenges which are not simply blots upon Christian existence to be expunged by proper ecclesial strategy and polity, but rather elements that frame the *via media* of Christian existence itself, where mystery and uncertainty are to be expected and engaged. In considering this rich way, the volume also points out that seriousness and eagerness about its inevitability and engagement can be healing. Precisely because it is a "way," and not a proposition or an institution, it can be joined by others, it is companionable at its center, and hence open to being met by the Lord who has traveled it already and travels it yet again, as on the way to Emmaus. Hence, it is a way that is owned by no one but its Lord, that gathers together in commonality. The Covenant is a gift, then, not only to Anglicans, but to all Christian churches. It is a gift, though, only if set out upon, in the same way that perfection is given, not as a condition, but as a movement with Another: "Come, follow" (Mark 10:21).

BIBLIOGRAPHY

Congar, Yves M.-J. "Reflections on the Schism of Israel in the perspective of Christian Divisions" (1951), translated and reprinted in his *Dialogue Between Christians*, 160–83. London: Chapman, 1966.

Cummins, Stephen Anthony. *Paul and the Crucified Christ in Antioch: Maccabean Martyrdom and Galatians.* Society for New Testament Studies Monograph Series 114. Cambridge: Cambridge University Press, 2001.

Jewett, Paul K. *Infant Baptism and the Covenant of Grace.* Grand Rapids: Eerdmans, 1978.

Ladner, Gerhard. "*Homo Viator*: Medieval Ideas on Alienation and Order." *Speculum* 42/2 (April 1967) 233–59.

Radner, Ephraim. "The Cost of Communion: A Meditation on Israel and the Divided Church." In *Inhabiting Unity: Theological Perspectives on the Proposed Lutheran-Episcopal Concordat*, edited by Ephraim Radner and R. R. Reno, 134–52. Grand Rapids: Eerdmans, 1995.

Walker, Samuel. *Fifty-Two Sermons on the Baptismal Covenant, the Creed, the Ten Commandments, and other Important Subjects of Practical Religion*, Vol. I. London: Mathews & Leigh, 1810.

Additional Note

BENJAMIN M. GUYER

These essays were completed at the end of 2011 and therefore could not discuss the failure of the Anglican Covenant in the Church of England in late March, 2012. At a diocesan level, the Covenant appears to have been decisively defeated: 26 dioceses voted against it, while only 18 dioceses voted for it. Yet analyzing the distribution of votes yields a very different portrait:[8]

	For	Against	Abst.	Total	% For	% Against	% Abst.
Bishops	75	14	5	94	79.79%	14.89%	5.32%
Clergy	738	774	61	1573	46.92%	49.21%	3.88%
Laity	951	860	96	1907	49.87%	45.10%	5.03%
Total	1764	1648	162	3574	49.36%	46.11%	4.53%

These numbers proclaim no resounding defeat. Only among clergy was direct opposition greater (and just marginally) than direct support for the Covenant. Among laity, abstentions ultimately determined the negative vote, but here too deeper inquiry is informative. When adding the percentage of votes against the Covenant together with the percentage of those in abstention, we find that for the laity, 50.13% of the vote was negative against a positive vote of 49.87%—a difference of merely .26%. Bishops supported the Covenant overwhelmingly, at a ratio of nearly 4:1.

---

8. These figures are computed from the *Modern Church* webpage "C of E Diocesan Synod Debates on the Anglican Covenant": http://www.modernchurch.org.uk/resources/mc/cofe/2012-1.htm.

Eight other Anglican provinces have already adopted the Covenant. For them, covenanted interdependence is a fact of existence. It is expected that the Church of England will vote on the Covenant again, and the above numbers do not indicate that a re-vote will necessarily be negative. Nothing is inevitable; the past itself is never final. We dare to hope. It is one unseen who hymns, "take up and read."[9]

9. St. Augustine, *Confessions*, Book VIII, 29, 12.

Introduction

A Covenantal Horizon[1]

BENJAMIN M. GUYER

"Come now, and let us reason together."

Isa 1:18 (AV)

T HE ANGLICAN COMMUNION IS currently struggling, both loudly and painfully, with a wide variety of matters. There are disputes over human sexuality and the place of women in holy orders; there are disputes over the unity of the Communion and the reliability of its authority structures. These and other debates converge—and sometimes collide—at a single point: the proposed Anglican Communion Covenant, which offers a procedural framework for working through these issues and any others that will arise in the future. The Anglican Covenant offers historical and theological rationales for why the Anglican Communion should pursue—rather than flee from—Christian interdependence. The present introduction seeks to perform four distinct tasks. I first offer a historical outline of the use and development of ecclesial covenants in the Anglican tradition. I then mark the ways that the proposed Anglican Covenant draws upon this same history. In the third section, I consider several criticisms of the

---

1. I thank Ephraim Radner, Graham Kings, and Christopher Wells for helpful comments on an earlier draft of this essay.

Covenant, raising formal questions about the perspicuity, and thus the viability, of such critiques. I conclude with some brief comments on the shared aspirations and thematic harmonies of the essays that comprise this volume. In the pages and chapters that follow, it is our goal to touch both hearts and minds.

ANGLICANS AND COVENANTS

Ecumenical Covenants

The Anglican use of ecclesial covenants may be traced to 1948, with the First Assembly of the World Council of Churches. Because of these origins, the Anglican Communion Covenant reflects concerns for global unity and peace that developed in the aftermath of the First World War, culminating in the founding of the United Nations in 1945 and the World Council of Churches in 1948. During this quarter century, *covenant* became and remained a key theme in those secular and religious discourses concerned with attaining political concord. We see this as early as 1920, when the Covenant of the League of Nations was enacted. Its stated aim was "to promote international co-operation and to achieve international peace and security."[2] The creation of the League the previous year had been a matter of widespread interest and support by secular and religious leaders, and consequently provided a sharp impetus for the development of Christian ecumenism. In January 1920, in an encyclical addressed "Unto the Churches of Christ everywhere," the Ecumenical Patriarchate of Constantinople followed the lead provided by the League of Nations and urged the founding of an international body of churches that might call itself the League of Churches.[3] This encyclical became the first, albeit unintentional, step toward creating the World Council of Churches, although it must be underscored that the Orthodox were concerned not only with politics but with evangelical witness. The penultimate paragraph of the Encyclical reads, "Finally, it is the duty of the churches which bear the sacred name of Christ not to forget or neglect any longer his new and great commandment of love. Nor should they continue to fall piteously behind the political authorities, who, truly applying the spirit of the

2. *The Covenant of the League of Nations*, Preamble.

3. Visser 't Hooft, *Genesis and Formation*, chap. 1; the text of the encyclical may be found in ibid., 94–97. See also Ware, *Orthodox Church*, 322–24.

Gospel and the teaching of Christ, have under happy auspices already set up the so-called League of Nations in order to defend justice and cultivate charity and agreement between the nations."[4] The creation of a League of Churches first demanded an admonished and repentant Christendom.

Concerns for international stability, both within and beyond the Church, were also discussed in earnest at the 1920 Lambeth Conference, which began several months later on 2 July.[5] The bishops supported the founding of the League of Nations in Resolutions 3–6. Resolution 3 reflected both ecumenical and political concerns in its conclusion, which stated that the bishops were "of the opinion that steps should immediately be taken, whether by co-operation or concurrent action, whereby the whole Church of Christ may be enabled with one voice to urge the principles of the League of Nations upon the peoples of the world." At the same time, the bishops received a delegation from the Ecumenical Patriarchate of Constantinople and devoted the single largest bloc of their resolutions to what they termed "The Reunion of Christendom."[6] The most important of these was Resolution 9, the lengthy "Appeal to all Christian People." Its text still rings with notes of urgency; the bishops recognized "the responsibility which rests upon us at this time," and wrote of the need "to associate ourselves in penitence and prayer with all those who deplore the divisions of Christian people." Only a truly united Church, they argued, could give "a common service to the world." Like the Ecumenical Patriarchate, the Lambeth Fathers believed that the well-being of the world was secured through Christian penitence, the necessary precursor of Christian unity.

In the ensuing decade, Anglican support grew for the League of Nations and the burgeoning ecumenical movement. Like its predecessor, the Lambeth Conference of 1930 supported both. With a bloc of seventeen resolutions, ecumenism was clearly the more important of the two, although three resolutions endorsed the League of Nations and its work.[7] By this point in time, however, a number of Anglicans were also personally involved in the ecumenical movement and were directly contributing

---

4. In Visser 't Hooft, *Genesis and Formation*, 97.

5. Stephenson, *Anglicanism and the Lambeth Conferences*, 133.

6. For information on the Orthodox delegation at Lambeth 1920, see Geffert, *Eastern Orthodox and Anglicans*, 72–75.

7. The League of Nations is referred to in LC 1930, Res. 21, 26, and 30; Res. 31–47 discuss ecumenical relations.

to the formation of the World Council of Churches (WCC). Most well known today is perhaps William Temple, who participated in the Faith and Order conferences of 1927 and 1935, the Committee of Thirty-Five, which drew up plans for the WCC in 1936, and the Committee of Fourteen, which drafted the WCC constitution in 1938 and which Temple also chaired.[8] Following Adrian Hastings, Stephen Spencer speculates that had Temple lived, he would have been the WCC's first president.[9] If so, he would not have been the only high-ranking Anglican in the WCC; other ecumenically-devoted Anglicans also involved themselves in pre-WCC ecumenical bodies, laying the foundation for ecumenism as it now stands. The founder of Faith and Order was Charles Henry Brent, bishop of Western New York in the American Episcopal Church, and bishops George Bell and Charles Gore were among those who participated in both the Faith and Order and the Life and Work conferences.[10]

The Second World War profoundly disrupted the momentum of the previous decade on both ecumenical and political fronts, but *covenant* remained an important concept in both spheres. Despite the failure of the League of Nations to prevent the outbreak of another world war, the United Nations was founded in 1945 and soon began drafting its Covenant on Human Rights. This became the basis for the two covenants contained in the International Bill of Human Rights: the International Covenant on Economic, Social and Cultural Rights, and the International Covenant on Civil and Political Rights.[11] When the World Council of Churches held its First Assembly in 1948, it too used the language of covenant to express its intentions. In the "Message" released at the conclusion of the Assembly, the WCC stated: "Here at Amsterdam we have committed ourselves afresh to Him, and have covenanted with one another in constituting the World Council of Churches. We intend to stay together. We call upon Christian congregations everywhere to endorse and fulfill this covenant in their relations one with another. In thankfulness to God we commit

8. Visser 't Hooft, *Genesis and Formation*, 48; for Temple's Memorandum on the Constitution, see ibid., 107–11 (Appendix IV).

9. Spencer, *William Temple*, 82–85.

10. Vidler, *The Church in an Age of Revolution*, 260–61; Geffert, *Eastern Orthodox and Anglicans*, esp. chap. 9; Visser 't Hooft, *Genesis and Formation*, 26, 47.

11. United Nations Office of the High Commission for Human Rights, "Fact Sheet No.2," no pages.

the future to Him."[12] The 1948 Lambeth Conference, the first Lambeth Conference since before the start of World War II, endorsed the United Nations Covenant on Human Rights in Resolution 8 and embraced the WCC in Resolution 76. The final lines of the latter resolution read, "The Conference hopes that the results of the Assembly at Amsterdam may be made widely known throughout the Anglican Communion, and that an active interest in the World Council of Churches may be encouraged in all dioceses and parishes." Archbishop of Canterbury Geoffrey Fisher intended for the first post-war Lambeth Conference "to revive the whole idea of the Lambeth Conference as the great family gathering of the Anglican Communion."[13] These resolutions, which reveal the strong thematic continuity between earlier Lambeth Conferences and that of 1948, indicate that the Archbishop attained his goal. With the WCC at the center of Anglican, Orthodox, and Protestant ecumenical endeavors,[14] 1948 marked the definitive entry of *covenant* into both Anglican and ecumenical discourse, just as its presence in international politics had already been secured by the United Nations Covenant on Human Rights.

A British Covenant

The hope that fired the World Council of Churches quickly burned itself into the Anglican imagination. A number of Anglican leaders attended the 1948 Assembly, including Archbishop Fisher, bishop Stephen Neill, future Archbishop of Canterbury Michael Ramsey, and Oliver S. Tomkins, then Assistant General Secretary of the WCC but future Bishop of Bristol.[15] Tomkins provides the direct link between the covenanting of the WCC and that which was later taken up into Anglican ecumenical ecclesiology. In "Regional and Confessional Loyalties in the Universal Church," his speech to the 1948 Assembly, Tomkins identified the problematic which ecumenical covenanting was intended to address by outlining various forms of ecclesiastical affiliation. He surmised that Scripture only recognizes the mystical body of Christ and its local manifestation.

12. World Council of Churches, "Message," in *Man's Disorder and God's Design*, vol. 4, 231.

13. Cited in Hein, *Geoffrey Fisher*, 60.

14. In distinguishing Anglican from Protestant, I am following the distinction made by Visser 't Hooft, "The Significance of the World Council of Churches," 178.

15. Chadwick, *Michael Ramsey*, 64; Hastings, *Oliver Tomkins*, 65–74.

Thus any other definition of the Church—whether regional, national, denominational, or international—has only a "temporal legitimacy" because it has been produced by "the division of Christendom."[16] Tomkins began his speech with a discussion of regional and national churches, arguing against both nationalism and the reduction of any church to national—and thus secular—borders. This allowed him, in turn, to propose that churches which define themselves either regionally or nationally are far more likely to reproduce within themselves those patterns of sin that are most prevalent in the surrounding culture.[17] Such churches have a place within the scheme of salvation because human beings are defined by regional and national identities. But if any church is content with such a limited identity, it stands in the way of Christian unity.[18] Tomkins was evidently less concerned with international confessions and particular denominations; he spent the bulk of his address speaking to the problem posed by regional and national churches. The problem which he and the World Council of Churches faced was that of uniting diverse churches, so frequently and complacently defined by the boundaries of the secular nation-state, into an ecumenical whole. With the covenanting that concluded the 1948 Assembly, Tomkins was given his answer.

In his key 1952 article "Implications of the Ecumenical Movement," Tomkins proposed that the covenanting of the WCC carried five implications for all churches. The first and second implications are most important for our present concerns.[19] First, Tomkins perceived that "this covenant relationship brings us to the end of . . . *mere comparative ecclesiology*."[20] Like many others, Tomkins recognized that by mid-century, the ecumenical movement had produced points of confessional convergence which rendered null and void any lingering belief that ecclesial division was exclusively theological. However, amidst this convergence was a lingering danger; in comparing belief systems, he continued, "we are tempted by

---

16. Tomkins, "Regional and Confessional Loyalties," 136.

17. Ibid., 140–41.

18. Ibid., 140.

19. The third implication was that the covenanted churches needed to develop new forms of shared life; the fourth concerned the need for liturgical convergence; the fifth dealt with Christian witness, a perennial theme in the post-war years, by emphasizing that the churches could not claim to have unity in Christ without having visible unity in the Church.

20. Tomkins, "Implications," 19, emphasis original.

the same process to justify them."[21] Discussing confessional differences should serve only as a first step toward greater unity, and never as an excuse for eliding commitment to Christian unity. The second implication followed immediately upon this: "the essence of our covenant with each other is to deny that our denominations are enough."[22] Here Tomkins pushed for "international confessions," which he discussed only briefly in 1948, to engage themselves in the pursuit of greater unity. Those familiar with the work of Michael Ramsey will recognize a similar theme—and it is not surprising, given Ramsey's presence at the 1948 Assembly and his own deep, ecumenical commitments. Like Tomkins, Ramsey envisioned the progressive dissolution of denominational identities as churches traveled the road to ecumenical wholeness.[23] But each also believed that churches could not simply escape the realities of denominational division here and now.[24] As with his 1948 speech, Tomkins recognized the facts of historical existence and confessional commitment, even as he proclaimed the limitation of any commitment that shirked the interdependent, twofold need for Christian unity and Christian witness.

In Britain, these aspirations came to fuller fruition twelve years later at the 1964 British Conference on Faith and Order. Christians from many denominations participated, although the Roman Catholic Church only sent observers. As bishop of Bristol, Tomkins chaired the Conference and led it in adopting the covenantal model of 1948 as the guiding pattern for British ecumenism. The Conference resolved: "United in our urgent desire for One Church Renewed for Mission, this Conference invites the member churches of the British Council of Churches, in appropriate groupings such as nations, to covenant together to work and pray for the inauguration of union by a date agreed amongst them."[25] Of 474 voting conference members, 329 of whom were official church delegates, only 5 voted against the resolution and merely 12 abstained. Inspired by this, the Conference continued in its next resolution: "We dare to hope that this date should not be later than Easter Day, 1980. We believe that we

21. Ibid., 19–20.
22. Ibid., 20.
23. Ramsey, *The Gospel and the Catholic Church*, 220–21; *The Anglican Spirit*, 125–26.
24. Tomkins, "Implications," 21.
25. British Council of Churches, *Unity Begins at Home*, 77 (Res. V.A.1).

should offer obedience to God in a commitment as decisive as this."[26] This "dare to hope" formed the immediate background of two Anglican developments later in the decade. The first was Resolution 47 of the 1968 Lambeth Conference, which encouraged covenanting proposals at the provincial level insofar as they included "agreement on apostolic faith and order" and took place "under the general direction of the bishop." Second was the development of Local Ecumenical Projects (LEPs).[27] In less than three years, 170 LEPs had been initiated as a direct response to the 1964 Conference[28] and by 1998 there were 837 LEPs across Britain.[29] Notably, one form of LEP today is the "Covenant Partnership," which is entered into through a Declaration of Intent and maintained by a Constitution.[30] In 1964, the era of covenanting had dawned.

The late-1960s and 1970s saw the rapid development of grassroots covenanting. At a national level, however, similar developments ensued throughout Britain. In Wales, five churches, including the Church in Wales, covenanted together in 1975. In 1978, the British Council of Churches established the Churches' Council for Covenanting, which produced the 1980 report *Towards Visible Unity: Proposals for a Covenant*. This was intended to fulfill the resolutions from 1964. The bulk of the report was a series of liturgies, ranging from those for the ordination of bishops, presbyters, and deacons and other ministers, to those for the celebration of the Eucharist and confirmation. The most important liturgy was entitled "The making of the Covenant," and it culminated with a vow of common decision making.[31] The report contained an entire chapter devoted to this topic, elucidating that, "If the Covenant is to be an effective instrument of common action for mission and a means of growth into greater unity, commitment to common decision making will be crucial."[32] In the liturgy, the presiding minister was to declare: "Within this Covenant, we bind ourselves to develop methods of decision making in common, to act together for witness and

26. Ibid., 78 (Res. V.A.2).

27. The acronym LEP was revised in 1994 to denote *Partnerships* rather than *Projects*. See Welch and Winfield, *Travelling Together*, 17.

28. Hastings, *Oliver Tomkins*, 127.

29. Tovey and Waller, *Worship in Local Ecumenical Partnerships*, 3.

30. Welch and Winfield, *Travelling Together*, 18–21.

31. Ibid., 67 (8.1.3); Cf. Appendix Three, 74–81.

32. Ibid., 66 (8.1.2).

service, to aid one another in Christian growth, and to honour the authority of shared decisions." When the people were then asked, "Do you so bind yourselves?" they were to respond: "By God's grace, we do."[33] The Churches' Council for Covenanting elaborated: "This enterprise, like the Covenant itself, must depend on a growth of trust between the Churches as they move towards each other."[34] This was indeed a "dare to hope," and to many it appeared attainable.

Despite broad support across Britain, the Church of England did not accede to the British Covenant. Signs pointing to the possibility of such an outcome had already appeared on the horizon but they had been ignored. *Towards Visible Unity* included a Memorandum of Dissent composed by three of the Council's Anglican members. Their fundamental point of contention concerned episcopacy; although ordinations to the episcopate were part of the British Covenant, *Towards Visible Unity* read: "It is recognized that as Churches are accepting one another in this Covenant, so they are accepting one another's ministers, including those persons carrying out functions analogous to those of bishops."[35] Against this, the Memorandum called for "the total and invariable adoption of episcopal ordination," which it claimed had been the original intent of the Council. The much weaker understanding of the episcopate which emerged in the final text of the report missed "a fundamental principle of Catholic order" and erected "a further barrier to our closer associations with other parts of the Church Catholic."[36] This point is important, given that the Roman Catholic Church had refused membership in the British Council of Churches. Robert Runcie, then only recently elevated to the See of Canterbury, emerged as a strong critic of the Covenant's ecumenical viability for these same reasons, although he voted for its ratification in the end.[37] The Covenant nonetheless failed in General Synod by a slight majority. Adrian Hastings later described the results of this upset as "numbed uncertainty" and "a sort of ecumenical despair."[38] Only in 1982, with the World Council of Churches report *Baptism, Eucharist and*

33. Churches' Council for Covenanting, *Towards Visible Unity*, 15.
34. Ibid., 69 (8.4.5.i) and 70 (8.6.2).
35. Ibid., 49 (5.4.4.3)
36. Ibid., 86–87 (paras. 14–15).
37. Hastings, *Runcie*, 128.
38. Ibid., 131.

Ministry and the first report by the Anglican Roman Catholic International Commission, did ecumenism again appear viable in Britain—but even here a change had taken place. Borrowing again from Hastings, these reports together provided "the ground for a new kind of ecumenical doctrinal orthodoxy" in the Church of England, which involved ecumenical commitment to both the British Council of Churches and those outside of it, above all Roman Catholics.[39] It was no longer clear that covenanting had a future.

Anglicans, Covenants, Communion

The failure of ecumenical covenanting proved to be short lived when the 1988 Lambeth Conference returned covenanting to the forefront of Anglican ecumenism. In its thirteenth resolution, the Conference declared that "the withdrawal of Anglicans from several previous covenanting proposals and schemes of unity with Methodist, Reformed and other Churches is a cause for sorrow and repentance." By calling for "sorrow and repentance" in particular, the Lambeth Conference gave its strongest endorsement yet to covenanting as *the* way forward for ecumenical reconciliation. Such language also echoed those earlier Lambeth Conferences which saw repentance as the hard but necessary road to Christian unity. The restoration of covenanting played out in several other resolutions from the same conference. Resolution 12.3 encouraged the covenanting between Welsh Anglicans and other churches in Wales, and in Resolution 17 the bishops restated their ecumenical-covenantal commitments: "This Conference recognises that the growth of Christian unity is a gradual and costly process in which agreement in faith, sharing in prayer, worship and pastoral care, and co-operation in mission all play their part and recommends to the Churches in their own particular situations that they progress from mere coexistence through to co-operation, mutual commitment or covenant and on to full visible unity with all their brothers and sisters in Christ." This basic outlook indicates why Anglican provinces such as South Africa, England, Australia, and New Zealand have each pursued ecumenical covenants, thereby joining many other Anglican provinces in developing clearly stated ecumenical commitments.[40]

---

39. Ibid., 132 and 137.

40. Norman Doe notes that insofar as covenant is approached as a legal category, a number of other arrangements, although variously entitled concordats or compacts,

The history of Anglican ecumenical covenanting since 1988 draws together a number of the threads already touched upon. Four examples should suffice. First, covenanting in Southern Africa, as elsewhere, has a fairly complex history. South African Anglicans withdrew from a covenanting scheme in 1983 due to arguments over episcopacy, although questions concerning the ordination of women also played a role.[41] In 1993, however, amidst the crumbling of apartheid, concern with Christian unity again arose and discussions of covenanting proceeded apace.[42] Resolution IV.4 of the 1998 Lambeth Conference subsequently noted "with interest the Covenant Agreement on Mutual Recognition of Ministers of the Church Unity Commission in Southern Africa." Although the development of covenantal union has not yet been realized in Southern Africa, it is still being sought after. Second, in 2001, the Church of England and the Methodist Church of Great Britain entered into *An Anglican-Methodist Covenant*, which identified the goal of covenanting as "full visible unity."[43] This covenant consists of seven affirmations and six commitments, which are defined as "interdependent."[44] The Common Statement which prefaces *An Anglican-Methodist Covenant* recalls the breakdown of covenantal negotiations in the 1980s; the Anglican-Methodist Covenant is then described as "a new opportunity to discover and make visible the unity of the Church."[45] The "dare to hope" of 1964 clearly echoes in these aspirations.

Third, in 2004 the Anglican Church of Australia joined eighteen other Australian churches in *Australian Churches Covenanting Together*. The preamble of this covenant notes that the language of covenanting "has been found to be helpful and used widely in an ecumenical context," and then cites the invitation of the 1964 British Conference on Faith and Order for churches "to covenant together to work and pray for the inauguration

---

are nonetheless covenantal because they bind their respective parties together through stated commitments. Thus a much larger number of Anglican provinces than those discussed here have entered into *covenantal* relationships with other churches, even if these are not explicitly termed *covenants*. Various Anglican-Lutheran compacts, such as the Porvoo Agreement and the Episcopal-Lutheran Concordat, are therefore *covenantal*. See Doe, *Covenant*, ch. 2.

41. Duncan, "The Church Unity Commission," 5.

42. Best, et. al., "Survey of Church Union Negotiations 1999–2002," esp. 373–78

43. *An Anglican-Methodist Covenant*, para. 194

44. Ibid.

45. Ibid., para. 25.

of union . . . so that all in each place may act together forthwith in mission and service to the world."[46] Like the 2001 *Anglican-Methodist Covenant*, the Australian covenant consists of stated commitments and agreements. Throughout the text, the goal of "full visible unity" is time and again re-iterated, and its concluding Affirmation of Commitment describes the "covenanting process" as a "journey towards visible unity."[47] Finally, in 2009, an Anglican-Methodist covenant was signed in New Zealand. Like its English predecessor, the New Zealand covenant contains both affir-mations and commitments. The first affirmation states that "the unity of the church is not incidental to God's purpose"; the fourth commitment reiterates the need for common decision-making, with each church vow-ing "to take account of each other's concerns, especially in areas that affect our relationship as churches."[48] As with other covenants, this *Anglican-Methodist Covenant* aspires to interdependence and the visible unity of the covenanted churches. In sum, since 1964 the Anglican vision of covenanting has become international in scope. Far from treating cov-enants as a less rigorous form of ecumenical obligation, Anglicans have consistently pledged themselves to achieving the highest and most sac-rificially demanding of ecumenical ideals: full visible unity, understood and defined by interdependence.

THE ANGLICAN COMMUNION COVENANT

The Anglican Communion Covenant draws upon a number of themes and overlaps with several of the developments found in the preceding historical narrative. The *Anglican-Methodist Covenant* between the Church of England and the Methodist Church of Great Britain was signed 1 November, 2003. Less than a month before this, Archbishop of Canterbury Rowan Williams created the Lambeth Commission to deal with two points of conflict within the Anglican Communion: debates over human sexuality and debates over provincial autonomy. The fol-lowing year, the Lambeth Commission produced *The Windsor Report*

46. National Council of Churches in Australia, *Australian Churches Covenanting Together*, Preamble.

47. E.g., ibid., Preamble; Part A: Declaration of Intent; Part C: The Future Pledge; Affirmation of Commitment.

48. *The Anglican-Methodist Covenant* (New Zealand), no pages.

in response to these issues. Robin Eames, Chairman of the Lambeth Commission and Archbishop of Armagh, explained that the Lambeth Commission was established to find "ways in which communion and understanding could be enhanced where serious differences threatened the life of a diverse worldwide Church."[49] *The Windsor Report* therefore did not attempt to resolve the debate over human sexuality. Instead, and in keeping with its mandate, it dealt with procedural matters in the Anglican Communion. One of its suggestions was the creation of an Anglican covenant, "which would make explicit and forceful the loyalty and bonds of affection which govern the relationships between the churches of the Communion."[50] Born in the wake of the 2003 ecumenical watershed between Anglicans and Methodists, the 2004 Windsor Report directed the Anglican Communion to consider its future in the light of its ecumenical past.

Two responses to the suggested covenant came in 2005. The first was from the Joint Standing Committee of the Anglican Communion. After noting the use of covenants in both Scripture and Church history, they drew attention to the 1964 British Conference on Faith and Order. The Joint Standing Committee recognized that although the British Covenant failed, it had nonetheless "become the model for many ecumenical covenants by separated parties seeking greater union, voluntarily submitted in a covenant for a common purpose."[51] The second response was issued by the Inter-Anglican Standing Commission on Mission and Evangelism (IASCOME), which produced *A Covenant for Communion in Mission* in 2005 in direct response to the Windsor Report. The introduction to the IASCOME covenant notes that "As Anglican churches, we have a tradition of covenants that help to clarify our relationships with other ecumenical churches."[52] After nine pledges, *A Covenant for Communion in Mission* culminates with the words, "We make this covenant in the promise of our mutual responsibility and interdependence in the Body of Christ." The

49. TWR, Foreword, 5.

50. TWR, para. 118. It is worth noting that NACC, "Ten Reasons," misconstrues the meaning of the word "forceful" to imply the use of force and coercion. Quite obviously, this is not the meaning of the word; "forceful" is synonymous with words such as "compelling," "effective," and "satisfying." It has no connotations of violence or compulsion.

51. Joint Standing Committee of the Anglican Communion, "An Anglican Covenant," para. 15.

52. IASCOME, *A Covenant for Communion in Mission*, no pages.

phrase "mutual responsibility and interdependence in the Body of Christ" is of no small importance; it was originally the title of the ecumenical statement released at the 1963 Anglican Congress in Toronto, Canada, by the Primates and Metropolitans of the Anglican Communion.[53] It has been part of Anglican ecumenical ecclesiology ever since.[54] By the end of 2005, the Joint Standing Committee and IASCOME had paved the way for the drafting of a second Anglican covenant, the former by emphasizing the importance of the 1964 British Conference on Faith and Order, and the latter by again articulating the vision of mutual responsibility and interdependence in Christ. Both of these were subsequently incorporated into the text of the Anglican Communion Covenant.

In 2006, the Covenant Design Group was established by Archbishop Williams. Between 2007 and 2009, three drafts were completed and subsequently revised, leading to the fourth and final draft, the proposed Anglican Communion Covenant. The first, Nassau Draft Covenant (NDC), contained both affirmations and commitments.[55] In this it followed the general pattern of ecumenical covenants that Anglicans have entered into. Like other covenantal agreements, both ecumenical and Anglican, the NDC also affirmed "interdependence"[56] and "shared discernment"[57] as necessary for the wellbeing of the Communion. The covenant drafts of 2008 and 2009, the St. Andrews and Ridley Cambridge drafts respectively, refined but did not change the scope of NDC. With the Ridley Cambridge draft, however, the structure of the Anglican Communion Covenant finally took its current fourfold shape. The first three sections contained a series of affirmations followed by a series of commitments; the fourth and final section brought the affirmations and commitments together through shared procedures of adoption and conflict resolution. The Anglican

53. 1963 Anglican Congress, *Report of Proceedings*, 117–22.

54. See esp. LC 1968, Res. 67; ACC-1 (1971), Res. 32; ACC-5 (1981), Res. 20; ACC-8 (1990), Res. 21; ACC-9 (1993), Res. 43; ACC-12 (2002), Res. 32. "Mutual responsibility and interdependence in the body of Christ" has been so widely and frequently used that it is often abbreviated MRI. TWR frequently made use of the same concept; see TWR, e.g., §§8, 12–21, 40–41, 46, 49–50, 65, 67, 122–23, 151; Appendix One, para. 1; Appendix Two, Art. 4, 16, 22, 24; Appendix Three, §§5, 8, 10, esp. §§5.2, 5.4, 5.9. This list is not exhaustive.

55. NDC, 2 (affirmations), 3 (commitments), 4 (affirmations and commitments), 5 (affirmations), and 6 (commitments).

56. NDC, 3.2, 5.2.

57. NDC, 6.2; cf. 3.5, 5.2

Communion Covenant retained this structure, too, with affirmations and commitments dovetailing with one another at every point. In the final text, interdependence is stressed throughout, and Section Four, entitled "Our Covenanted Life Together," opens with the covenanting churches affirming and committing to "a readiness to live in an interdependent life."[58] In every section of the Anglican Covenant, notes of ecumenical and historic Anglican correspondence ring aloud.

It is a curious irony that the willingness of Anglicans to enter into ecumenical covenants with non-Anglicans does not map the willingness of some Anglican provinces to covenant with other Anglican provinces. Yet those who adopt the Anglican Communion Covenant affirm that "our bonds of affection and the love of Christ compel us always to uphold the highest degree of communion possible."[59] This commitment is no more exacting than the visible unity which Anglicans have consistently vowed to pursue and maintain in their ecumenical covenants. The "highest degree of communion possible" is a continued ascent that finds its *terminus* in the triune life of God, even as it is worked out here and now. Defeating the Anglican Covenant would be a sweeping rejection of the ecumenical principles that many Anglican provinces have already affirmed because these same principles are the very building blocks of the Covenant itself. Committing to the Anglican Communion Covenant reaffirms Anglicanism's own ecumenical history and the progress that this same history has brought forth in its hard, long, and as yet unconsummated labor. It is no exaggeration to claim that the Anglican Communion Covenant is composed of the ecumenical hopes and toils of many generations.

AN ANGLICAN COVENANT AND ITS CRITICS

As of late-December, 2011, the Anglican Covenant has been adopted by a growing number of provinces in the Communion: Mexico (2010), the West Indies (2010), Ireland (2011), Myanmar (2011), South East Asia (2011), Papua New Guinea (2011), and the Southern Cone (2011). No Anglican province has rejected the Covenant, and several other provinces have taken initial steps toward ratification. In 2010, the General Synod of the Church of England, in an almost-unanimous vote, approved the Draft

58. Covenant, 4.1.1; cf. Introduction, para. 2, 2.1.4, 3.2, 3.2.2, 4.1.2.

59. Covenant, 3.2.7.

Act of Synod Adopting the Anglican Communion Covenant, thereby sending it to individual dioceses for further ratification. That same year, the General Synod of the Anglican Church of Southern Africa resolved to adopt the Covenant, a decision which only awaits final approval in 2013. In 2011, the Doctrinal Commission of the Church in Wales commended the Covenant "as a theologically coherent description of the nature of the Church and the form of the Christian life as expressed in Scripture and Church tradition" which "falls within a discernable trajectory in the development of Anglican identity."[60] Through their respective synods and at the first available opportunity, each of the above-named provinces either adopted, or initiated the process of adopting, the Anglican Covenant.

Theological criticism of the Covenant comes from two directions. The first is that of the Global Anglican Future Conference (GAFCON), which formed in 2008 to resolve the "crisis of doctrine and also of leadership" in the Anglican Communion. GAFCON, in the positive elements of its self-definition, advocates returning to "Christ's authority in the Church and the authority of the Bible," applying the implications thereof to "personal morality and mission."[61] In November 2010, the GAFCON Primates Council released the *Oxford Statement*, which read in part, "we have come to the conclusion the current text [of the Covenant] is fatally flawed and so support for this initiative is no longer appropriate."[62] Regrettably, the *Oxford Statement* offers no justification for this decision; we will therefore turn to earlier GAFCON documents to construct the logic behind their rejection of the Covenant. The second line of argument is really a collection of arguments found throughout the Anglo-American world. Liberal criticisms are not the product of any single movement and are thus less focused than the criticism offered by GAFCON. However, there are shared patterns of critique across the Anglican far left—regrettably betraying a sustained logical incoherence and a reliance upon exaggerated rhetoric. Neither line of criticism explains what to do for the Communion as a whole, and neither evinces any concern to deal with the history enshrined in the Anglican Covenant. Each offers a rejection of the Covenant that is divorced from the larger ecology of Anglican history,

---

60. The Church in Wales, "Briefing Paper," no pages.
61. GAFCON, *Being Faithful*, 73.
62. GAFCON, *Oxford Statement*, para. 5.

tradition, and ecumenical commitments. But as in the realm of nature, such a witness offers no future in the realm of grace.

Lines of Criticism, I: GAFCON

The *Oxford Statement* offers no justification for its dismissal of the Covenant. In the statement's introduction, however, the signatories endorse the *Jerusalem Declaration*, an earlier GAFCON document which was published with a formal Commentary at the conclusion of GAFCON's 2008 conference in Jerusalem. According to the *Oxford Statement*, the *Jerusalem Declaration* has "theological clarity" and "offers a solid foundation on which to engage with other Anglicans in the pursuit of Gospel mission."[63] It is not entirely clear why the *Jerusalem Declaration* is held to be stronger than the Anglican Covenant. Many of its fourteen clauses— for example, its endorsement of Holy Scripture as "containing all things necessary for salvation," and its support for the normative authority of the three catholic creeds and the 1662 Book of Common Prayer—will be familiar to, and consonant with, the views of all Anglicans.[64] Clause four's endorsement of the Articles of Religion may arouse some controversy, as these have not been constitutive of Anglican identity since the 1968 Lambeth Conference.[65] The affirmation of heterosexual monogamy in clause eight—the longest clause in the *Jerusalem Declaration*—touches upon a key point of contention within the Anglican Communion at present, but this will serve as a rallying point only for those who, whether conservative or liberal, believe that the debate over human sexuality is the defining issue of our day. Only clause thirteen offers insight into GAFCON's rejection of the Anglican Covenant: "We reject the authority of those churches and leaders who have denied the orthodox faith in word or deed. We pray for them and call on them to repent and re-

63. GAFCON, *Oxford Statement*, Introduction.

64. GAFCON, *Jerusalem Declaration*, opening para., in *Being Faithful*, 6–7. I take the *Jerusalem Declaration*, because it is a product of the Jerusalem gathering, as normative for what might be termed "GAFCON orthodoxy." Earlier GAFCON documents, many of which are also published in *Being Faithful*, are, by my analysis, of secondary concern: they offer historical insight into the development of the *Jerusalem Declaration* and its Commentary, but the same normative weight should not be ascribed to them. The differences, sometimes considerable, between pre-Jerusalem GAFCON publications and the final Jerusalem Declaration may or may not point to unresolved tensions within GAFCON. This history has yet to play itself out.

65. LC 1968, Res. 43.

turn to the Lord." In and of itself this statement is hardly revolutionary, but GAFCON's 2008 Commentary on the *Jerusalem Declaration* reveals clause thirteen as the springboard for an ecclesiology which makes no place for the *procedural* aspects of the Anglican Covenant.

Although the commentary on clause thirteen begins with the clear declaration that "we break communion with those who deny the orthodox faith," and although the authority for this decision is justified with reference to Holy Scripture,[66] procedure and authority are the primary *foci* in this section. Yet readers are offered only an uneasy, unresolved, and perhaps irresolvable tension. On the one hand, the Commentary recognizes that "there is *no exact precedent* within the Anglican Communion for dealing with the present situation." It also asserts that "the breaking of communion between churches is to be applied only in extreme circumstances" and "should be exercised with *due process* over time."[67] On the other hand, the lengthy preface to the Commentary states that "There is no need to be precisely canonical at this stage."[68] Problematically, the Commentary never resolves how there can be "due process" when there is "no exact precedent . . . for dealing with the present situation." Readers are assured that "orthodox leaders" have been in "patient consultation" with one another.[69] But without precedent, one cannot hope to define any procedural matter, including "patient consultation." Only an arbitrary decision by GAFCON can determine the scope and the limits of these claims, but this cannot be called "due process." In the end, and despite its strong endorsement of evangelism in clause nine of the *Jerusalem Declaration*, it is unclear what GAFCON's witness to the wider world is because it is unclear what GAFCON wishes to signify in thought, word, and deed. The *Jerusalem Declaration* leaves much undone; the *Oxford Statement* offers no good reason for rejecting the Anglican Covenant because it offers no clear reason at all.

Lines of Criticism, II: Liberal Theologies

Liberal attacks on the Anglican Covenant are diffuse and vary in quality and coherence. Official rejections have sometimes carried wide but curi-

66. GAFCON, *Being Faithful*, 64; citing Eph 5:11; Titus 3:10.

67. Ibid., 65, emphases mine.

68. Ibid., 22.

69. Ibid., 66.

ous implications. In its response to the Covenant, the Episcopal Church's Diocese of New Jersey stated that it "strongly" objected to the very word *covenant*. They claim that it is "puffery" to "describe what is essentially a multilateral contract between earthly churches" with the same Biblical language used to denote an "agreement between God and Humankind."[70] If one applies these words to the larger history discussed above, then as a matter of logical consistency the diocese must denounce not only all ecumenical covenanting but the secular, human rights covenants promulgated by the United Nations. Far from offering a substantive analysis, the Diocese of New Jersey evinces a lack of awareness. Other American dioceses have been equally gruff towards the Covenant, and equally inarticulate in stating their reasons. The Episcopal Diocese of Quincy, for example, describes the Covenant as "gobbledygook." The diocesan response continues: "The average church person probably will have little idea what the covenant really says or means, if she or he can be induced somehow to read it. We *doubt few* have any real interest in a covenant."[71] However unintentional, such wording marks a tacit admission that *many*, within and beyond the Anglican Communion, have a "real interest in a covenant." The unfortunate but evident carelessness of the diocese's statement offers a clear, if inelegant, testimony to the incoherence that encumbers so many criticisms of the Anglican Communion Covenant.

Unofficial critiques have been no less sweeping in their condemnation, and no more logical in their execution. They are too often built upon the insecure but imaginative ground of conspiracy, and held together by little more than the force of loaded language. For example, Marilyn McCord Adams complains that TWR advances a "new authoritarian polity" overseen by a "collective papacy, an international college of primates exercising dictatorial powers."[72] Adams is not the only critic who multiplies the terms of discontent beyond what is necessary. Evidencing just as little care for the craft of argument, Tobias Haller asserts that TWR is "not a little blasphemous" in collectively denoting the Archbishop of Canterbury, the Lambeth Conference, the Anglican Consultative Council, and the Primates Meeting as the Anglican Communion's "Instruments of

70. The Diocese of New Jersey, "Response to the Anglican Covenant," no pages.

71. The Episcopal Diocese of Quincy, "Anglican Covenant Responses," para. 5; italics mine.

72. Adams, "Leaven in the Lump," no pages.

Unity."[73] And, in "Ten Reasons Why the Proposed Anglican Covenant is a Bad Idea," the No Anglican Covenant Coalition (NACC) alleges that the Covenant has been advanced "with the threat of dire consequences," and that it will "give extraordinary power to the newly enhanced Standing Committee."[74] Those who advance such "dire" threats—assuming such persons even exist—are never named. So too the "extraordinary" powers given to the Standing Committee—purportedly contained within the Covenant itself—are never identified. Incongruously, NACC complains that the Covenant is "dangerously vague,"[75] even as it construes the Covenant in the most sinister of ways.

Both individually and collectively, these arguments provide textbook examples of logical fallacies, such as the appeal to emotion and the use of loaded language.[76] The latter fallacy is especially disconcerting because, as Anthony Weston notes, it "is only a form of manipulation."[77] Cutting through such illogic is not difficult, however, and provides us with an opportunity for considering a recent observation made by anthropologists Jean and John Comaroff. They propose that conspiracy theories have become the "autonomic explanatory trope of our age" because they "fill the explanatory void" and "the epistemic black hole."[78] Dystopian visions hardly signify critical rigor, and sharp language is of little use if it points only to the vague generalities of a fantasized worst-case scenario.[79]

Lines of Criticism, III: Baptismal Ecclesiology

A different critique of the Anglican Communion Covenant has been advanced in the name of "baptismal ecclesiology."[80] This argument claims

---

73. Haller, "Anglican Disunion," no pages. For the history of the Instruments of Communion, see chapter one by Andrew Goddard below.

74. NACC, "Ten Reasons," paras. 9 and 1.

75. Ibid., para. 5.

76. The earliest discussion of logical fallacies is Aristotle, *Sophistical Refutations*. Gensler, *Introduction to Logic*, chap. 4 contains a detailed discussion of logical fallacies; Weston, *Rulebook for Arguments*, Appendix I, provides a helpful list of the same.

77. Weston, *Rulebook for Arguments*, 77.

78. Comaroff and Comaroff, "Transparent Fictions," 287–88.

79. For additional considerations of such critiques, see the essays by Edmund Newey and Jeff Boldt below.

80. Meyers, *Continuing the Reformation*, xvi. Turner, *Welcoming the Baptized*, 42, describes this as a "baptismal paradigm."

that the baptismal covenant found in the Episcopal Church's 1979 Book of Common Prayer advances a distinct theology which obviates the need for the sacrament of confirmation and bolsters the roll of the laity. It is then claimed that the baptismal ecclesiology of the baptismal covenant cannot be harmonized with the aims of the Anglican Covenant because the latter does not say enough about baptism.[81] Ruth Meyers, the most articulate American advocate of baptismal ecclesiology, roots the development of baptismal ecclesiology in the cultural shifts of the 1960s,[82] and describes it as effecting a "radical" and "revolutionary" change in the history of the American Episcopal Church.[83] Notably, Meyers also claims that the 1979 baptismal covenant is a novelty in Anglican liturgy and that far from being intended, it was a "happy accident" of liturgical revision.[84] By so binding baptismal ecclesiology to its diachronic origins, baptismal ecclesiology appears as a novelty, wistfully ensconced in the valuative language of a bygone era. Meyers thus undercuts the ability of American Episcopalians to appeal to the baptismal covenant as a form of tradition, for baptismal ecclesiology is expressly defined as untraditional.

Although Meyers portrays the baptismal covenant as a unique facet of American Episcopalianism, there is no evidence that it was intended as such. Marion J. Hatchett's 1980 *Commentary on the American Prayer Book*, the "authoritative study" of the 1979 Prayer Book,[85] contains no sustained discussion of the baptismal covenant.[86] More recent works, such as the revised version of Charles Price and Louis Weil's *Liturgy for Living*, mentions the baptismal covenant only once and only in passing.[87] The second edition of Leonel Mitchell's *Praying Shapes Believing* contains a discussion of the baptismal covenant, but unlike Meyers, Mitchell does not portray the baptismal covenant as a form of baptismal ecclesiology. He instead writes, "The Baptismal Covenant binds us to Christ in his

---

81. Meyers, "The Baptismal Covenant and the Proposed Anglican Covenant," 13; see also Thompsett, "Inquiring Minds Want to Know," 29.

82. Meyers, *Continuing the Reformation*, xv, 22–25, 40–42, 63–64, 236–38.

83. For "radical," see ibid., xv, 1, 120, 192, 227; for "revolutionary," see xv, xvi, 17, 20, 101, 145, 162, 187, 211, 226. This list is not exhaustive.

84. Meyers, "The Baptismal Covenant and the Proposed Anglican Covenant," 9.

85. Powell, "Foreword," xii.

86. Hatchett's 1995 revision of his work is no different in this regard.

87. Price and Weil, *Liturgy for Living*, rev. ed., 192.

saving death and resurrection, which inaugurated the New Covenant."[88] Mitchell explains that the baptismal covenant is a twofold set of vows; the first set contains the traditional, threefold renunciation of Satan, the world, and sin, while the second set contains a threefold vow to follow Christ.[89] Current interest in the baptismal covenant thus appears to be of rather recent vintage. Academic and popular Episcopalian literature evidence the same. The North American journal *Anglican Theological Review* did not publish an article on the baptismal covenant until 2004,[90] and the first books written on the baptismal covenant for a lay audience were not published until 2005 and 2006 respectively.[91]

Such recent developments help us understand why the baptismal covenant has been subjected to a growing number of criticisms. In 2006, in a noteworthy but less celebratory echo of Ruth Meyers, Bryan D. Spinks described the baptismal covenant as the "very reversal" of historic Anglican liturgy, because it tends towards a "semi-Pelagian" theology.[92] In 2008, Paul Avis took a slightly different approach by arguing directly against baptismal ecclesiology. He emphasizes the place of confirmation and especially the Eucharist in the process of Christian initiation as historically practiced.[93] The Church of England's Faith and Order Commission, of which Avis is a member, further developed this lead in 2011 with *The Journey of Christian Initiation*. It too disavows baptismal ecclesiology in favor of a broader and more robust sacramental wholeness. In the words of Harriet Harris, a member of the Commission, "We cannot rely on baptism alone as a basis for unity, because the Eucharist itself is instrumental in sustaining us as members of the Body of Christ."[94] Critics such as these are not rejecting the 1979 liturgy for baptism as such, but its misapplication.

Thus a more foundational question must now be asked: does the baptismal covenant contained in the 1979 Prayer Book actually teach baptismal ecclesiology? A historical discussion may be helpful. In 1969,

88. Mitchell, *Praying Shapes Believing*, 289.

89. Ibid., 96–102.

90. Thompsett, "Baptismal Living: Steadfast Covenant of Hope."

91. Morris, *Holy Hospitality*; and McLaughlin, *Do You Believe?*

92. Spinks, *Baptism*, 175.

93. Avis, "Is Baptism 'Complete Sacramental Initiation?'" 166.

94. The Faith and Order Commission of the General Synod of the Church of England, *Christian Initiation*, 68.

the Standing Liturgical Commission of the Episcopal Church produced *Prayer Book Studies* 18: *Holy Baptism with the Laying-on-of-Hands*, which proposed revising historic Anglican practice by uniting baptism and confirmation in a single liturgy.[95] The goal was to "emphasize the essential unity of Christian initiation . . . by placing Baptism with the Laying-on-of-hands within the context of a celebration of the Holy Communion."[96] The report noted that this was the practice of the early Church, and subsequent studies have also drawn attention to the influence of Eastern Orthodox liturgical models upon the 1979 Prayer Book.[97] The proposal provoked sharp controversy because it abandoned confirmation as it had been practiced in western churches since the medieval era. Confirmation was traditionally a coming of age ceremony in which personal faith and emerging adulthood were affirmed, prayed for, and blessed. It took the better part of a decade before the Episcopal Church reached a compromise on the issue. Confirmation was retained, but as a separate and now-optional liturgical rite. Similarly, and with a nod toward Eastern Orthodox and early Christian practice, priests and bishops were not required to anoint the newly baptized with oil but were only given the option of doing so.[98] The attempt to reunite baptism with confirmation thus failed. The 1979 Prayer Book merely intimated a restored rite of initiation.

None of this indicates any drive on the part of the Standing Liturgical Commission towards baptismal ecclesiology. To the contrary, the goal of liturgical revision was to set baptism within a holistic and unified framework—*unified* because it re-united baptism with both confirmation and the Eucharist.[99] This is the exact same concern recently enunciated by

95. The *Prayer Book Studies* were a series of reports, studies, and draft liturgies leading up to the 1979 Book of Common Prayer.

96. The Standing Liturgical Commission of the Episcopal Church, *Prayer Book Studies* 18, 21–22.

97. Ibid., 16; Price, "Rites of Initiation," 28; and Price and Weil, *Liturgy for Living*, 80 and 86, note Orthodox influence. I thank Victoria Heard for giving me this article.

98. Chrismation, or the anointing with oil, is the Orthodox equivalent of the western rite of confirmation. See Stevick, *Holy Baptism*, (Supplement to *Prayer Book Studies* 26) 25–25, 98–99.

99. See also Stevick, *Holy Baptism* (Supplement to *Prayer Book Studies* 26), 16–35, 48–70 for a broad, historical discussion of confirmation; 86–89, 95, 98–101 discuss the reunification of baptism, confirmation, and Eucharist; 71 and 95 describe baptism as being completed only by the Eucharist. Notably, and in keeping with other historical evidence, Stevick never discusses the baptismal covenant as such.

the Church of England's Faith and Order Commission. But when taken together, the liturgies in the current American Prayer Book for baptism, optional chrismation, and optional confirmation do not form a coherent vision of Christian initiation. They do not offer *common* prayer in the historic sense, but a collection of unresolved theological and liturgical debates set side by side within the pages of a single Prayer Book. This is not to deny that the attempt to restore the pattern of early Christian initiation was laudable, but this does raise a question concerning the universal applicability of the liturgical commonplace *lex orandi, lex credendi*—"the rule of praying is the rule of believing."[100] With two optional post-baptismal liturgies available, two interpretations of the 1979 baptismal rite are therefore possible. A *maximalist* interpretation looks upon baptism as a robust rite which, on the pattern of the early Church, ought to include anointing. From this perspective, baptism does not stand alone and the 1979 Prayer Book changed nothing other than who administered confirmation: it remained present through chrismation, which was administered by a priest. This interpretation accords with the Catechism in the 1979 Prayer Book, which describes confirmation as a sacrament. However, a *minimalist* interpretation of the rite looks upon baptism as something separable from both chrismation and confirmation, neither of which is required in the 1979 Prayer Book, although each remains widely practiced. The liturgical revisions of the 1960s and 1970s sought to restore the baptismal and sacramental maximalism of the early Church. It is a curious logic which argues that the baptismal covenant is safeguarded through a minimalist interpretation of the baptismal rite. There is therefore no reason why the baptismal covenant should be read as a form of baptismal ecclesiology, and no reason why it should be set against the Anglican Covenant.

PRO COMMUNIONE

Pro Communione: Theological Essays on the Anglican Covenant was conceived with the intent of attaining several ends in a single volume. First, it offers a distinctly Anglican theological assessment of the Anglican Covenant by using normative Anglican sources to address what is first of all a matter of Anglican ecclesiology and communion. To borrow from

---

100. See, e.g., Stevenson, "Lex Orandi—Lex Credendi."

Alec Vidler, "there are very important questions which theologians are now being called upon to face, and which are not yet being faced with the necessary seriousness and determination."[101] There are times for "ploughing, not reaping . . . for making soundings, not charts or maps."[102] The present volume offers soundings that seek to discern how and where the Covenant resonates with the Anglican tradition. The echoes may return slowly but they return nonetheless.[103] The essays in this volume propose that historic Anglicanism is not absorbed by the Anglican Communion Covenant, but instead reflects it. If earlier Anglican tradition is received as a map for interpreting the present terrain, then the horizon offered by the proposed Covenant appears significantly less foreign than some of its critics maintain.

Our second goal is to address the whole of contemporary Anglicanism by avoiding any and all attempts to entrench or vindicate the identity of a particular church party. There is a time for beating "swords into plowshares," just as there are times for reaping, embracing, and building up.[104] No author in these pages assumes that the Covenant will magically make longer-standing divisions disappear, but the Covenant does provide us with an opportunity to heed an old call still echoing—"*ad fontes!*" Indeed, the Covenant encourages us in this direction. Third, we are concerned to advance the Covenant's ecumenical interests and application. Here are responses from members of the Roman Catholic and Orthodox churches, and considerations by Anglicans within and beyond the Anglican Communion. Far from presenting an obstacle, the Covenant is seen as a decisive move beyond ecumenical stasis, and as a trustworthy guide for charting the ecumenical future. Finally, the present collection ventures to give voice to a new generation of Anglicans. Biblical covenants, although made in a particular time and place, were never limited to those who made them. The "everlasting covenant" made with Abraham included his descendents.[105] It is fitting and sweet that these essays speak this same biblical vision. The 1964 "dare to hope" still resounds; and "deep calls

101. Vidler, *Soundings*, xi.

102. Ibid., ix

103. See Thomas, *The Echoes Return Slow* (1988) in *Collected Later Poems 1988–2000*, 11–72; cf. Mascall, *Up and Down in Adria*, 14.

104. Isa 2:4; Eccl 3:2–5.

105. Gen 17:7. The covenant with Noah does the same (Gen 9:12).

unto deep" with clear and simple words: "Follow thou me."[106] So come, and let us reason together.

BIBLIOGRAPHY

Covenants

British Council of Churches. *Unity Begins at Home: A Report from the First British Conference on Faith and Order, Nottingham 1964.* London: SCM, 1964.

Churches' Council for Covenanting. *Towards Visible Unity: Proposals for a Covenant: The Report of the Churches' Council for Covenanting.* London: Churches' Council for Covenanting, 1980.

Inter-Anglican Standing Commission on Mission and Evangelism. *A Covenant for Communion in Mission* (2005). No pages. Online: http://www.aco.org/ministry/mission/commissions/iascome/covenant/covenant_english.cfm.

League of Nations. *The Covenant of the League of Nations* (1920). No pages. Online: http://avalon.law.yale.edu/20th_century/leagcov.asp.

Methodist Church of Great Britain and the Church of England. *An Anglican-Methodist Covenant* (2001). Peterborough: Methodist Publishing House and Church Publishing House, 2001.

Methodist Church of New Zealand and the Anglican Church of Aotearoa, New Zealand and Polynesia. *The Anglican Methodist Covenant* (2008). No pages. Online: http://www.ecbmethodist.org.nz/documents/AngMethCvtleaflet.pdf.

National Council of Churches in Australia. *Australian Churches Covenanting Together* (2004). No pages. Online: http://www.ncca.org.au/files/Departments/Faith_and_Unity/Covenanting/2010_July_Australian_Churches_Covenanting_Together.pdf.

General

1963 Anglican Congress. *Report of Proceedings*, edited by E. R. Fairweather. New York: Seabury Press, 1963.

Adams, Marilyn McCord. "Leaven in the Lump of Lambeth: Spiritual Temptations and Ecclesial Opportunities." No pages. Originally printed in the *Church Times*, 27 April, 2007. Online: http://www.episcopalcafe.com/lead/anglican_communion/leaven_in_the_lump.html.

Avis, Paul. "Is Baptism 'Complete Sacramental Initiation'?" *Theology* 111 (May/June 2008) 163–69.

Best, Thomas F., and Church Union Correspondents. "Survey of Church Union Negotiations 1999–2002." *The Ecumenical Review* 54/3 (July 2002) 369–419.

Chadwick, Owen. *Michael Ramsey: A Life.* London: SCM, 1990.

The Church in Wales. "The Anglican Communion Covenant: A Briefing Paper." No pages. Online: http://www.churchinwales.org.uk/resources/acc/docs/gb_paper.pdf.

Comaroff, Jean and John Comaroff. "Transparent Fictions; or, The Conspiracies of a Liberal Imagination: An Afterword." In *Transparency and Conspiracy: Ethnographies*

---

106 Ps 42:7; John 21:22.

of Suspicion in the New World Order, edited by Harry G. West and Todd Sanders, 287–99. Durham: Duke University Press, 2003.

The Diocese of New Jersey. "Response to the Anglican Covenant." No pages. Online: http://newjersey.anglican.org/News/index.html.

Duncan, Graham. "The Church Unity Commission: South African Ecumenical Perspectives on Ministry (1968–1983)." *Studia Historiae Ecclesiasticae* 37/1 (May 2011) 1–11.

The Episcopal Diocese of Quincy. "Anglican Covenant Responses." No pages. Online: http://thedioceseofquincyonline.com/Documents/Quincy%20Convenant%20 Response.doc.

The Faith and Order Commission of the General Synod of the Church of England. *The Journey of Christian Initiation: Theological and pastoral perspectives.* London: Church House Publishing, 2011.

GAFCON. *Being Faithful: The Shape of Historic Anglicanism Today.* London: The Latimer Trust, 2009.

GAFCON Primates Council. *Oxford Statement.* No pages. Online: http://www.gafcon. org/news/oxford_statement_from_the_gafcon_fca_primates_council.

Geffert, Bryn. *Eastern Orthodox and Anglicans: Diplomacy, Theology, and the Politics of Interwar Ecumenism.* Notre Dame: University of Notre Dame Press, 2010.

Gensler, Harry J. *Introduction to Logic.* 2nd ed. New York: Routledge, 2010.

Haller, Tobias Stanislas. "Anglican Disunion: The Issue Behind 'the Issue.'" No pages. Online: http://jintoku.blogspot.com/2011/11/anglican-disunion-issues-behind-issue.html.

Hastings, Adrian. *Robert Runcie.* Philadelphia: Trinity, 1991.

———. *Oliver Tomkins: The Ecumenical Enterprise.* London: SPCK, 2001.

Hein, David. *Geoffrey Fisher: Archbishop of Canterbury, 1945–1961.* Princeton Theological Monograph Series 77. Eugene, OR: Pickwick Publications, 2008.

Joint Standing Committee of the Anglican Communion. "An Anglican Covenant—Consultation Paper." No pages. Online: http://anglicancommunion.org/commission/covenant/consultation/index.cfm. 2005.

Mascall, Eric. *Up and Down in Adria: Some Considerations of* Soundings. London: The Faith Press, 1963.

McLaughlin, Nancy Ann. *Do You Believe? Living the Baptismal Covenant.* New York: Morehouse, 2006.

Meyers, Ruth. *Continuing the Reformation: Re-Visioning Baptism in the Episcopal Church.* New York: Church Publishing, 1997.

———. "The Baptismal Covenant and the Proposed Anglican Covenant." In *The Genius of Anglicanism*, edited by Jim Naughton, 9–14. Chicago: The Chicago Consultation, 2011.

Mitchell, Leonel L. *Praying Shapes Believing: A Theological Commentary on the Book of Common Prayer.* second ed. Harrisburg, PA: Morehouse, 1991.

Morris, Clayton L. *Holy Hospitality: Worship and the Baptismal Covenant.* New York: Church Publishing, 2005.

Naughton, Jim, editor. *The Genius of Anglicanism: Perspectives on the Proposed Anglican Covenant. Essays and Study Questions.* Chicago: The Chicago Consultation, 2011. Online: http://www.chicagoconsultation.org/site/1/docs/Genius_of_Anglicanism_final.pdf.

No Anglican Covenant Coalition. "Ten Reasons Why the Proposed Anglican Covenant is a Bad Idea." No pages. Online: http://noanglicancovenant.org/docs/10reasons-a4-c.pdf.

Podmore, Colin. "The Baptismal Revolution in the American Episcopal Church: Baptismal Ecclesiology and the Baptismal Covenant." *Ecclesiology* 6 (2010) 8–38.

Powell, Rt. Rev. Chilton. "Foreword." In *Commentary on the American Prayer Book* by Marion J. Hatchett, xi–xii. New York: Seabury, 1980.

Price, Charles P. "Rites of Initiation." In *The Occasional Papers of the Standing Liturgical Commission*, 24–37. New York: The Church Hymnal Corporation, 1987.

Price, Charles P., and Louis Weil. *Liturgy for Living.* Rev. ed. Harrisburg, PA: Morehouse, 2000.

Ramsey, Michael. *The Gospel and the Catholic Church*, second ed. London: Longmans, 1956.

———. *The Anglican Spirit.* New York: Seabury Classics, 2004.

Spencer, Stephen. *William Temple: A Calling to Prophecy.* London: SPCK, 2001.

Spinks, Bryan D. *Reformation and Modern Rituals and Theologies of Baptism: From Luther to Contemporary Practices.* Burlington, VT: Ashgate, 2006.

The Standing Liturgical Commission of the Episcopal Church. *Holy Baptism with the Laying-on-of-Hands. Prayer Book Studies* 18: On Baptism and Confirmation. New York: The Church Pension Fund, 1970.

Stephenson, Alan M. G. *Anglicanism and the Lambeth Conferences.* London: SPCK, 1978.

Stevenson, W. Taylor. "Lex Orandi—Lex Credendi." In *The Study of Anglicanism*, edited by Stephen Sykes, et. al., 187–202. Rev. ed. London: SPCK, 1998.

Stevick, Daniel B. *Holy Baptism Together with a Form for the Affirmation of Baptismal Vows with the Laying-On of Hands by the Bishop also called Confirmation.* Supplement to *Prayer Book Studies* 26. New York: The Church Hymnal Corporation, 1973.

Sykes, Stephen, John Booty, and Jonathan Knight. *The Study of Anglicanism.* Rev. ed. London: SPCK, 1998.

Thomas, R. S. *Collected Later Poems 1988–2000.* Northumberland: Bloodaxe, 2004.

Thompsett, Frederica Harris. "Baptismal Living: Steadfast Covenant of Hope." *Anglican Theological Review* 86/1 (Winter 2004) 9–18.

———. "Inquiring Minds Want to Know: A Lay Person's Perspective on the Proposed Anglican Covenant." In *The Genius of Anglicanism*, edited by Jim Naughton, 29–35. Chicago: The Chicago Consultation, 2011.

Thompson, David M. *Baptism, Church and Society in Modern Britain: From the Evangelical Revival to* Baptism, Eucharist and Ministry. Milton Keynes, UK: Paternoster, 2005.

Tomkins, Oliver S. "Regional and Confessional Loyalties in the Universal Church." In *Man's Disorder and God's Design*, prepared under the auspices of the World Council of Churches, Volume One, 135–46. New York: Harper & Brothers, 1948.

———. "Implications of the Ecumenical Movement." *Ecumenical Review* 5/1 (1952) 15–26.

Tovey, Phillip and John Waller. *Worship in Local Ecumenical Partnerships.* Cambridge, UK: Grove, 1998.

Turner, Timothy J. *Welcoming the Baptized: Anglican Hospitality within the Ecumenical Enterprise.* Cambridge, UK: Grove, 1996.

United Nations Office of the High Commission for Human Rights. "Fact Sheet No.2 (Rev.1), The International Bill of Human Rights." No pages. Online: http://www.ohchr.org/Documents/Publications/FactSheet2Rev.1en.pdf.

Vidler, Alec R., editor. *Soundings: Essays Concerning Christian Understanding*. Cambridge: Cambridge University Press, 1962.

―――. *The Church in an Age of Revolution: 1789 to the Present Day*. Penguin Books, 1990.

Visser 't Hooft, W. A. "The Significance of the World Council of Churches." In *Man's Disorder and God's Design*, prepared under the auspices of the World Council of Churches, Volume One, 177–95. New York: Harper & Brothers, 1948.

―――. *The Genesis and Formation of the World Council of Churches*. Geneva: World Council of Churches, 1987.

Ware, Timothy. *The Orthodox Church*. London: Penguin Books, 1997.

Weston, Anthony. *A Rulebook for Arguments*, fourth ed. Indianapolis/Cambridge: Hackett: 2009.

Welch, Elizabeth and Flora Winfield, *Travelling Together: A Handbook on Local Ecumenical Partnerships*, revised ed. London: Churches Together in England, 2004.

World Council of Churches. *Man's Disorder and God's Design: The Amsterdam Assembly Series*. Four Volumes in One. New York: Harper & Brothers, n.d.

1

Communion and Covenant
Continuity and Change

ANDREW GODDARD

I N DECEMBER 2009, FIVE years after the Lambeth Commission on
Communion proposed the idea in *The Windsor Report*, the Archbishop
of Canterbury commended the final text of the Anglican Covenant to the
Communion for adoption by churches who are members of the Anglican
Consultative Council. The aim of this chapter is to set this development
in the context of the evolution of the Anglican Communion over recent
decades in order to understand the Covenant's origins, assess the competing claims as to whether it marks a departure from Anglican patterns,
and evaluate whether it addresses the needs of the Communion that have
been identified.

The Covenant is a very significant step in the life of the Communion
but the extent to which it represents continuity or marks a fundamental
change in Anglican identity and common life is a matter of major disagreement. The Covenant Design Group, after their first Nassau meeting in 2007, claimed that the Covenant "need not introduce some new
development into the life of the Communion . . . What is to be offered
in the Covenant is not the invention of a new way of being Anglican,
but a fresh restatement and assertion of the faith which we as Anglicans
have received, and a commitment to inter-dependent life such as has

always in theory at least been given recognition."[1] Critics, however, have viewed the document quite differently. In one of the more sustained academic critiques, Bruce Kaye has argued that the Covenant is "a bad idea for Anglicans" above all because "it is against the grain of Anglican ecclesiology."[2]

Part of the difficulty in assessing such competing claims is that the Covenant proposal has been inextricably connected with the disagreements over sexuality since Lambeth 1998 and particularly since the consecration of Gene Robinson to the American episcopate in 2003. In addition, the responses to this conflict, notably *The Windsor Report* of 2004, which proposed a covenant, were shaped by *The Virginia Report*. This report, in the context of disagreements over women bishops, followed the request of Lambeth Conference 1988, Resolution 18. Although presented at the tenth meeting of the Anglican Consultative Council in 1996 and at Lambeth 1998, some felt that it was neither sufficiently discussed nor received by the Communion as a whole. Many of those critical of these two reports have also been critical of the Covenant.

Is the Covenant an at-best dubious development born out of the crises over women bishops and homosexuality? To answer this it is helpful to consider four areas in which the Anglican Communion has developed over the last half-century:

1) the developments in the Communion's institutional life,

2) the forces which produced these developments,

3) the principles which guided the developments, and

4) those issues still unresolved by these developments.

In the light of these, the Covenant can be evaluated and seen as part of a larger history of Anglican institutional growth.

1. Report CDG.

2. Kaye, "Why the Covenant Is a Bad Idea for Anglicans." On a populist level see No Anglican Covenant Coalition, "Ten Reasons Why the Proposed Anglican Covenant Is a Bad Idea."

DEVELOPMENTS IN COMMUNION STRUCTURES

Instruments of Communion

The traditional understanding of the Communion's institutional life as expressed in section 3 of the Covenant focuses on the four Instruments of Communion. This perspective was first articulated in the following statement from Archbishop Robin Eames at ACC-7 (1987): "By tradition there are four instruments for maintaining the unity in diversity of the Anglican Communion: The Archbishop of Canterbury, The Lambeth Conference, The Anglican Consultative Council, The Meeting of Primates."[3] Although described as an Anglican "tradition," I have not been able to locate any previous use of the nomenclature, enumeration and conceptualisation of "four instruments." Furthermore, the Primates' Meeting, first held in 1979, was less than ten years old and had only met four times, while the ACC, which first met in 1971, had existed for just over fifteen years.[4] Nevertheless, this has become the self-understanding of the Communion's structures, although the "instruments of unity" are now called "instruments of communion."[5]

The development of the Instruments is also far from even. The first Lambeth Conference of 1867 was partially born out of conflict over the biblical scholarship of John William Colenso, bishop of Natal, and was also viewed as a controversial development. Called neither as a Synod nor Council but as a Conference for "brotherly counsel and encouragement," the Archbishop of York was famously among those bishops in communion with the See of Canterbury who declined the invitation to attend.[6] Amidst such concerns, the initial Conference clarified its intended limits, although subsequent, regular Conferences meant that it became an established feature of Anglican common life and gained authority. As Owen Chadwick noted in 1992, "Meetings start to gather authority if they exist and are seen not to be a cloud of hot air and rhetoric. It was impossible that the leaders of the Anglican Communion should meet every ten years

3. "Unity in Diversity within the Anglican Communion," ACC-7, 129 at A.2.

4. ACC-7, 129–34.

5. This change was proposed in WR, para. 105 and agreed upon at ACC-13, Res. 2 (2005).

6. The best account remains Stephenson, *The First Lambeth Conference.*

and not start to gather respect; and to gather respect is slowly to gather influence, and influence is on the road to authority."[7]

At Lambeth 1958, in what could have been portrayed as a significant centralisation, Resolution 61 redefined the composition and duties of the Lambeth Consultative Body (hereafter, LCB). This had been established in 1897 and its advisory nature was clarified by Lambeth Conference 1920, Resolution 44. In 1958 the LCB was given financial support, sixteen named provinces were invited to participate through their Primates or a substitute bishop, and, most significantly, the post of a full-time secretary to it was created. The resolution further charged the LCB "to advise on questions of faith, order, policy, or administration referred to it by any bishop or group of bishops, calling in expert advisers at its discretion" and "to deal with matters referred to it by the Archbishop of Canterbury or by any bishop or group of bishops."

In January 1960, the first Secretary—Bishop Stephen Bayne—was appointed as the Executive Officer of the Anglican Communion. He was clear that "the whole point of the office, as I see it, is to give articulation and expression to the corporate life of our whole Communion, and to give it a new and deeper level than our present patterns afford."[8] The most significant event during his four years in office was the Anglican Congress in Toronto in 1963. Earlier Congresses in 1908 and 1954 had also brought together lay Anglicans, clergy and bishops from around the Communion. Its vision of "Mutual Responsibility and Interdependence in the Body of Christ" (MRI) marked a major paradigm shift in the Communion's self-understanding and development which in turn shaped institutional developments over the following decades.[9]

At the Lambeth Conference of 1968, Resolution 69 proposed the creation of the Anglican Consultative Council subject to approval by two-thirds of the provinces by October 1969. The proposed constitution was unanimously agreed to by the provinces and the Council first met in Nairobi in 1971. Its significance was most obvious in the very narrowly carried resolution 28 relating to the divisive issue of women's ordination: "this Council advises the Bishop of Hong Kong, acting with the approval of his Synod, and any other bishop of the Anglican Communion acting

7. Chadwick, "Introduction," xvii.

8. Cited in Howe, *Highways and Hedges*, 78.

9. Anglican Congress 1963, *Report*, 117–22.

with the approval of his Province, that, if he decides to ordain women to the priesthood, his action will be acceptable to this Council; and that this Council will use its good offices to encourage all Provinces of the Anglican Communion to continue in communion with these dioceses."[10]

The Executive Officer became the Secretary General of the ACC, a post first filled by Bishop John Howe from the Scottish Episcopal Church. In the Preface to the report on ACC-3 (1976), Bishop Howe wrote, "The Anglican Churches are steadily making more use of this servant called the Anglican Consultative Council which they created half-a-dozen years ago. Its involvement in much of what is going on in the Anglican Communion grows. The creation and the involvement seem to have happened because these are things that a family requires."[11]

Two years later, at Lambeth 1978, the fourth Instrument was established. The report from section 3 of the Conference called for more frequent meetings of the Primates and Archbishop Coggan said he hoped these would now happen "perhaps as frequently as once in two years."[12] The first Primates' Meeting—representing 25 provinces of the Communion—took place in Nov/Dec 1979. The significance of the new Instrument was made clear in 1986 when the American House of Bishops informed it that they would not refuse consent to a bishop on grounds of gender. In order to assist consultation between provinces, the Primates' Meeting then asked the Archbishop of Canterbury to appoint a small "Working Party" to collate reactions of the provinces to women bishops, and this issued the Grindrod Report (1987).

As noted above, it was also in 1987 that the language of "four Instruments" began to be used in the Communion. In the quarter-century since, a consistent question and discussion has been how the different Instruments—particularly the Primates' Meeting and the ACC—should relate to each other. Appeals for close working and co-ordination have generally not worked in practice although, beginning in the mid-1990s, the Standing Committee of the Primates met jointly with the ACC as the Joint Standing Committee, and those Primates became members with voice but no vote on the ACC.[13] However, despite the ACC claiming

10. ACC-1, Res. 28 (1971)

11. ACC-3, ix

12. LC 1978 Report, 123.

13. See Remarks of Chair of ACC at ACC-10, 18–19. See also his closing sermon in Ibid., 39–43.

to represent lay people, clergy, and bishops, both the Archbishop of Canterbury (for example, George Carey[14] at ACC-10 in 1996) and successive Lambeth Conferences [15] looked to the Primates' Meeting to take an increasingly significant role, which it sought to do in meetings from 2003 onward.

Other Communion Bodies

Although the four Instruments have become the focus of inter-provincial consultation, it is misleading to reduce institutional expressions of interdependence and accountability to them. Alongside the Instruments other important structures for sustaining the Anglican Communion have developed. They form an important historic and thematic backdrop for understanding the Covenant.

Mission Consultations and Commissions

From 1973 to 1997, the ACC oversaw the Partners in Mission consultations.[16] These had a major impact on the life of the Communion through various means including the growth of Companion Link relationships between dioceses.[17] At ACC-5 (1981), the Mission Issues and Strategy Advisory Group (MISAG) was created with representatives from across the Communion to serve the Anglican Communion's Mission Department (established in 1971). This was to be the first of a number of such Mission Commissions, the present one being the Inter-Anglican Standing Commission on Mission and Evangelism (IASCOME).[18] Shared

---

14. "I do not believe we exploit the Primates enough! We are a college of leaders, who together have key responsibilities in the leadership of the Communion; and because we are smaller in number and meet more frequently, we should have the facility for initiating action...I believe that, whilst retaining a central symbolic role for the Archbishop of Canterbury, my brother Primates should have a higher profile in the Communion." (ACC-10, 15–16).

15. LC 1988, Res. 18.2(b), reaffirmed by LC 1998, Res. III.6.

16. The fullest study of these consultations is Groves, "A Model for Partnership," esp. chap. 3.

17. See   http://www.anglicancommunion.org/ministry/mission/companion/index. cfm.

18. MISAG II was established by ACC-7 in 1987 and was followed by MISSIO (ACC-9 in 1993) and IASCOME (ACC-11 in 1999).

mission has thus been a key point of focused cooperation which has strongly nourished interdependence within the Communion.

Networks

The 1980s also saw the growth of both formal and informal Anglican Networks working in mission and ministry. At ACC-7 (1987), the Secretary General noted there were 16 such networks.[19] The report noted that "the emergence of Networks, such as *Peace and Justice* and the *Family and Community* Networks within the Anglican Communion was seen as a significant development in the last few years" and that a working party had been established to prepare guidelines for their establishment and operation.[20]

Extra-Provincial Bodies

Alongside these, other extra-provincial bodies and meetings developed such as regional groupings like CAPA (the Council of Anglican Provinces of Africa), which was established in 1979.[21] One of the most influential expressions of interdependence has been the meeting of Anglicans from "the South." The first such meeting was the Anglican Encounter in the South, which took place in Kenya in 1994. This received relatively little attention in the wider Communion, but the Second Anglican Encounter in the South meeting in Kuala Lumpur in February 1997 made clear the shape of its vision of Anglican interdependence when it called on "the Primates, the Anglican Consultative Council and the Lambeth Conference to take the necessary steps to establish such new structures (or reinforce old ones) that will strengthen the bonds of affection between our provinces, and especially, make for effective mutual accountability in all matters of doctrine and polity throughout the Communion."[22]

Inter-Anglican Commissions

As early as 1976 the ACC proposed an inter-Anglican theological and doctrinal advisory commission. Resolution 25 of the 1988 Lambeth

19. ACC-7, 19.
20. ACC-7, ix.
21. See http://www.capa-hq.org/.
22. Second Trumpet Call, para. 7.3.

Conference endorsed this and asked "the Standing Committee of the ACC to establish the commission with the advice of the primates." Named the Inter-Anglican Theological and Doctrinal Commission (IATDC), its importance quickly grew.[23] At Lambeth 1988 the bishops resolved that the IATDC or a similar body "undertake as a matter of urgency a further exploration of the meaning and nature of communion; with particular reference to the doctrine of the Trinity, the unity and order of the Church, and the unity and community of humanity."[24] This set the agenda for the theological discussion about the Communion's structures around the themes of communion and Trinity, leading first to a 1992 consultation that produced "Belonging Together." This was chaired by Archbishop Eames and also included Tom Wright and Archbishop Drexel Gomez, all of whom would subsequently play a significant role in TWR. It also led to TVR which was submitted to ACC-10 (1996), the Primates (1997), and finally to Lambeth 1998, where it was welcomed and its principle of subsidiarity affirmed.[25]

Further Commissions followed. In 1989 the Primates "endorsed the establishment of a regular Inter-Anglican Ecumenical Advisory Group"[26] but financial constraints (a constant pressure on developing new structures for the whole Communion) led the Primates to reject ACC-7's proposal for a new Inter-Anglican Liturgical Commission. Representing a further step toward integration within the Communion in relation to ecumenism, Lambeth 1998, despite the cost implications, endorsed in Res. IV.3 the proposal of the Ecumenical Advisory Group, already supported by ACC-10 (1996), that they be replaced by another new Commission—the Inter-Anglican Standing Commission on Ecumenical Relations (IASCER). The remit for IASCER included what could be interpreted as significant "centralization": "to ensure theological consistency in dialogues and conversations by reviewing regional and provincial proposals with ecumenical partners and, when an agreement affects the life of the Communion as a whole, after consultation with the ACC, to refer the matter to the Primates' Meeting, and only if that Meeting so

23. See *For the Sake of the Kingdom*.

24. LC 1988, Res. 18.1

25. LC 1998, Res. III.8 and III.3. A second IATDC began work in 2001 and finally produced *Communion, Conflict and Hope* in 2008.

26. ACC-8, 45.

determines, to the Lambeth Conference, before the Province enters the new relationship."[27]

Other developments proposed at Lambeth 1998 did not happen but signalled a growing sense of the need for new, interdependent structures. The Primates were requested "to initiate and monitor a decade of study in each province" on TVR and "in particular 'whether effective communion, at all levels, does not require appropriate instruments, with due safeguards, not only for legislation, but also for oversight' (para. 5.20)."[28] In the light of this study "the Primates should make specific recommendations for the development of instruments of communion not later than the 14th Lambeth Conference."[29] The Archbishop of Canterbury, George Carey, was expected to lead the way here, appointing "a Commission to make recommendations to the Primates and the Anglican Consultative Council, as to the exceptional circumstances and conditions under which, and the means by which, it would be appropriate for him to exercise an extra-ordinary ministry of episcope (pastoral oversight), support and reconciliation with regard to the internal affairs of a Province other than his own for the sake of maintaining communion within the said Province and between the said Province and the rest of the Anglican Communion."[30] The Commission was never established but the wording of this resolution was used to form the mandate for the Lambeth Commission on Communion, which produced TWR.

Constitutions and Canon Law

Since the formation of the ACC, the recognition of new Anglican provinces has taken place through agreed, Communion-wide procedures. These have undergone revision in the last twenty years and at ACC-10 (1996) Canon John Rees presented new guidelines for the membership of new provinces.[31] Five years later, the 2001 Primates' Meeting received a presentation from Norman Doe on a previously under-explored area—canon law in the Communion.[32] His paper made reference to a

27. LC 1998, Res. IV.3.b(iii).
28. LC 1998, Res., III.8(h).
29. LC 1998, Res., III.8(i).
30. LC 1998, Res., IV.13(b).
31. ACC-10, 105–12.
32. Doe, "Canon Law and Communion."

possible concordat between provinces (a precursor of the later covenant proposal). This led to a consultation in 2002 which identified forty-four shared principles of canon law across the Communion. The Primates subsequently "recognized that the unwritten law common to the Churches of the Communion and expressed as shared principles of canon law may be understood to constitute a fifth 'instrument of unity.'"[33] ACC-12 (2002) welcomed the establishment of a Network of Anglican Legal Advisors which would "produce a statement of principles of Canon Law common within the Communion," "examine shared legal problems and possible solutions," and "provide reports to the Joint Standing Committee of the Primates Meeting and the Anglican Consultative Council as the work progresses."[34] This work, referred to in TWR,[35] led to the production of *The Principles of Canon Law Common to the Churches of the Anglican Communion* for Lambeth 2008.

FORCES DRIVING EVOLUTION

The preceding sketch has demonstrated that the Covenant is part of the significant institutional evolution of the Anglican Communion over the last forty years. There have been four main driving forces behind these changes.

First there is the growth of the Communion, particularly in the number of provinces. This was clearly if variously related to the ending of colonial status as Britain moved from Empire to Commonwealth. The number of autonomous churches began growing significantly in the 1950s. At Lambeth 1958, the proportion of native African bishops at the Conference rose from 6 percent ten years earlier to 30 percent.[36] This was the beginning of a major shift in the Communion away from the predominance of Anglo-American provinces. By the late 1970s, more than 15 provinces were created in what is now referred to as the "global south." Bishop Howe noted that at ACC-1 (1971), 21 provinces were present and "Representatives of western countries were in a minority at Limuru, and the balance between members of European and non-European extraction

33. Report of the Meeting of Primates, April 17, 2002, para 6.
34. ACC-12, Res. 13 (2002). See also http://www.acclawnet.co.uk/.
35. TWR, §§113 – 114.
36. Howe, *Highways and Hedges*, 14.

was about even."[37] At ACC-8 (1990) 32 provinces were in attendance, and when ACC-14 (2009) discussed the Covenant, 39 provinces had been invited.

A *second* factor is the Communion's diversity. In addition to the growing cultural diversity, there is theological diversity. Anglicanism in England has long been diverse and the differences between high and low church mission movements have shaped provinces in different ways. In recent years, differences over women's ordination and same-sex relationships have been the focus of tensions, leading to several of the institutional developments noted above.

Third, the last forty years have seen major ecumenical developments. This has also been a significant factor in the Communion's development and a major feature of the work of the ACC since its birth.[38] ACC-2 (1973) noted that some provinces, following the recommendation of Lambeth 1968, sought to enter into ecumenical 'covenant' with local, non-Anglican churches.[39] By ACC-4 (1979) the tension between autonomy and being a communion of churches in conversation with other churches was evident. The report asked,

> How should the Anglican Communion as a whole respond to these or any other Agreed Statements? There can be no question of the abrogation of the proper synodical responsibilities in each member Church, yet it is a reasonable presumption that the Roman Catholic Church would expect a co-ordinated response from one Communion as a whole because the dialogue is at the world-wide level. Agreed Statements of this sort are a new species of document and their handling requires careful consideration by both Communions. The problem is one of the larger question of universal authority which faces Anglicanism today. Now is the time for rigorous thinking.[40]

ACC-6 (1984) considered it a strength that "a procedure has been developed to enable the provinces of the Anglican Communion to reach a consensus in responding to Agreed Statements."[41] The Secretary General noted that in relation to ecumenical conversations "we need to ensure

37. Preface, ACC-1, vii.

38. For a survey, see *The Vision before Us*.

39. ACC-2, 4; LC 1968, Res. 47.

40. ACC-4, 7.

41. ACC-6, 26.

that as far as is possible responses of different provinces are not contradictory" and that "the search for unity means that we need a clearer understanding of what consultation means and how we express *koinonia* at
the world level."[42] The report of ACC-7 (1987) stated that "The ACC has
a special responsibility for the theological and doctrinal discussions between Anglicans and other Christian families at the international level."[43]

Fourth, the success of earlier Commissions has led to their continued use and some developments can simply be seen as the natural outworking of one initiative leading to another. For example, the creation
of the IATDC established a structure which was then replicated in relation to ecumenical matters, and the two Commissions were recently
merged into the Inter-Anglican Standing Commission on Unity, Faith
and Order (IASCUFO). Similarly, the success of the Eames Commission,
established in 1988 by the Archbishop of Canterbury in response to tensions over women's ordination, set a precedent for a similar response
with the Lambeth Commission on Communion when tensions rose over
homosexuality.

Although institutional developments have been subject to theological reflection and evaluation—most notably in the work of the *Virginia*
and *Windsor* reports—they are not the outworking of a general theological blueprint but are instead responses to different challenges faced by the
Anglican Communion. This is not, however, to say that their evolution
has been unprincipled. As the next section shows, even before the more
detailed work of these two reports, a number of fundamental beliefs
about Anglican ecclesiology were frequently reiterated and shaped the
structures that subsequently developed.

PRINCIPLES GUIDING DEVELOPMENTS

Two principles have been at the heart of the identity of the Anglican
Communion and shaped the evolution described: autonomy and interdependence. The latter has led to extra-provincial bodies such as the
Instruments and other structures, while the former has led to clear limits
on their power and authority.

42. Ibid., 11–12.

43. ACC-7, 85.

Provincial autonomy has long been central to Anglican identity.[44] As noted earlier, the first Lambeth Conference made clear that it was not a Synod and the Lambeth Conference 1930, in Resolution 48, affirmed that "the true constitution of the Catholic Church involves the principle of the autonomy of particular Churches based upon a common faith and order." When the LCB was reformed in 1958, it was made clear that it dealt with matters referred to it "subject to any limitations upon such references which may be imposed by the regulations of local and regional Churches." The LCB was only authorised "to take such action in the discharge of the above duties as may be appropriate, subject to the condition that with regard to Churches, provinces and dioceses of the Anglican Communion its functions are advisory only and without executive or administrative power."[45] Ten years later, the new instrument established was the Anglican *Consultative* Council and in his Preface to the report of the first meeting Bishop Howe was clear that the members "came together not to legislate but to consult."[46] His preface to the report of ACC-5 (1981) points to a key principle correlated with that of provincial autonomy—the dispersed nature of authority within Anglicanism: "In a fashion typical of Anglicanism, it came into being because the Churches were aware there was a need for it: there was no pre-ordained plan on paper. And, typically of Anglicanism, it is not a central power, but a little organization of the whole family whereby the dispersed authority and universal allegiance to Christ and the Gospel is—to some extent—co-ordinated by consultation and conference."[47] The language of co-ordination, consultation and conference points to the fact that, alongside autonomy, communion depends on mutual recognition and the nurturing of interdependence through common counsel. This too has long been part of the Communion's self-understanding, famously captured in the resolution of the 1930 Lambeth Conference which states the churches of the Communion "are bound together not by a central legislative and executive authority, but by mutual loyalty sustained through the common counsel of the bishops in conference."[48]

44. For a discussion of the meaning of autonomy see Doe, "Communion and Autonomy in Anglicanism."

45. LC 1958, Res. 61.

46. ACC-1, vii.

47. ACC-5, 7.

48. LC 1930, Res. 49.

The balance between the whole and the parts is one of the issues which until recently the Communion still had not fully addressed despite the evolution of the Instruments, and one to which the Covenant offers a response. The nature of the unanswered questions is explored in the following section before the Covenant's proposed answer is noted and evaluated.

UNRESOLVED TENSIONS

As far back as 1930 it was acknowledged that the nature of the Communion as a fellowship of autonomous churches could lead to a crisis. [49] As the number of autonomous provinces grew and structures for consultation developed, this danger was again recognised. In his 1985 study, former Secretary General John Howe wrote of two watersheds that the Communion had been approaching since the 1960s. He judged it to have crossed the first by establishing new provinces so it was not a matter of missionary outreach but "existence everywhere as part of the universal catholic Church: the transition from what we have described as head office and branch offices to being a world-wide family."[50] However, he noted that the second watershed had not yet been crossed: "The indigenous sharing of a faith requires an adequate universal agreement on the acceptable limits of faith and practice in the Anglican Communion. The need is not for acceptance of a universal, total, and therefore imposed, canon law. In peoples and situations so different, there will always be diversity, and a measure of diversity is welcome . . . The emphasis here is on the need to agree the limits of interpretation, and consequently of practice."[51] Howe noted that "the need concerns not only the member Provinces in a world-wide Church, which holds together by common faith and affection, but also the need of other Churches to know more clearly where the Anglican Communion stands."[52] He concluded, "There is a case for more universal appreciation of the limits. That is a watershed that has not been crossed. One may doubt whether it has been attempted very energetically."[53]

49. *Lambeth Conference 1930*, Report on the Anglican Communion, 154–55.

50. Howe, *Highways and Hedges*, 17.

51. Ibid.

52. Ibid., 18.

53. Ibid.

Related to this is the question of Anglican identity. Howe acknowledged, as did his predecessor Stephen Bayne, that Anglicanism is not "confessional" but seeks to be diverse and comprehensive. However, "there are dangers that comprehensiveness . . . can produce excessive diversity which within the one Communion is a hindrance to witness to the gospel; and also hinders acceptance by other Christians that Anglicanism as a whole can be taken seriously."[54] Howe even expressed the concern that "the lack of an obvious and appreciated expression of the shared and universal faith has been an Anglican weakness for too long."[55]

An attempt to address these challenges, which proved unsuccessful and was quickly forgotten, occurred in 1990 and has some significant similarities to the Covenant. ACC-8 (1990) received a paper entitled "Provincial Constitutions: Autonomy and Interdependence" commissioned by the Secretary General and written by David Chaplin, the first secretary of the Church of England's Partnership for World Mission. It proposed a Draft Common Declaration to be included in provincial constitutions along with a suggested article "on the relation of the Province to other Provinces of the Anglican Communion."[56] It also proposed that, without establishing a higher court of appeal, a provincial constitution "could at least ensure that inter-Anglican consultation takes place by permitting reference or appeal outside the Province when matters of doctrine and discipline are in dispute" and suggested the Primates' Meeting as "the appropriate body to become the Committee of Reference for the Communion to which disputed doctrinal, moral and pastoral matters might be referred."[57] The vision of the proposal is summed up in the conclusion:

> The intention of the form of Fundamental Declarations suggested, and of the proposal that reference or appeal to the Primates' Meeting should be allowed in the case of disputes involving faith and order, is, while upholding Provincial autonomy, to balance it with a clear statement of a Provinces' obligations and interdependence as a member church of the Anglican Communion. The Churches of the Anglican Communion 'are indeed independent, but independent with the Christian freedom which recognises the

54. Ibid., 37.

55. Ibid., 39.

56. Chaplin, "Provincial Constitutions," para. 15

57. Ibid., paras. 17–18.

restraints of truth and love. They are not free to deny the truth. They are not free to ignore the fellowship' (Lambeth Conference 1920 Encyclical).[58]

The document is only mentioned in passing in the report of ACC-8; it is noted that "there was no high level of enthusiasm in any Section for the Common Declaration."[59] ACC-8 Resolution 21 then stated that the Council regarded "the document 'Provincial constitutions: autonomy and interdependence,' circulated to the Council, as premature."

Similar ideas, independently and unaware of this earlier proposal, came from Norman Doe in his 2001 paper to the Primates concerning canon law. He proposed a study which could recommend "ways for each church to develop its own communion law to increase the profile of communion, to define inter-Anglican relations, and treat inter-Anglican conflict." He suggested that "the Primates could draft a statement of the ius commune, in a draft concordat, for each church to implement." Following consultation this could lead to "A Declaration of Common Anglican Canon Law and Polity" issued by the Primates' Meeting "in the form of a concordat" and then "individual churches, perhaps in groups by means of covenants" could "begin work on incorporation of the Declaration into their legal systems. Each church would have a body of distinctly Communion Law."[60] Three years later, the Lambeth Commission developed some of these ideas in relation to canon law and proposed an Anglican Covenant which, after three rounds of consultation, is now being considered for adoption by the provinces. In the light of this historical survey, what evaluation can be made of the proposed Covenant?

EVALUATING THE PROPOSED COVENANT

Although the Covenant is often perceived to have been born in the context of divisions over same-sex relationships, it does not address this subject directly, and can only be understood in the light of the wider history discussed in the previous sections of this chapter. Although the Covenant is a significant development in the life of the Communion we have seen that it arises out of a long history of similar developments, particularly

58. Ibid., para. 20
59. ACC-8, 142.
60. Doe, "Canon Law and Communion."

over the last forty years, which have seen extra-provincial structures created to nurture interdependence. The various forces described above that led to those other innovations have also shaped the Covenant.

At the heart of the Covenant is its articulation of a shared faith, mission and structures of common life (sections 1 to 3), and its proposed means for resolving disputes (section 4). These address what Bishop Howe identified as the next "watershed" in Communion life over a quarter of a century ago: articulating Anglican identity and recognising the need to define and discern limits to Anglican diversity. This was also the concern of the proposal made over twenty years ago at ACC-9 (1990) but then rejected as "premature." It is, therefore, difficult to defend the view that the Covenant is simply a hurried, *ad hoc* response to try and hold the Communion together in the face of differences over homosexuality. The key question is instead whether the Covenant is consonant with the principles that have guided the Communion's evolution.

The most common critique of the Covenant is that it represents at best the diminution and at worst the destruction of provincial autonomy. The history sketched earlier has highlighted previous developments, both of the Instruments and of other bodies such as the various Commissions of the Communion, which strengthened and deepened the processes that enabled interdependence. These too could be seen as challenging autonomy, but in contrast, the Covenant creates no new body but seeks to use existing structures—particularly the Standing Committee—in order to oversee the Covenant's implementation in the Communion. While giving this body new powers could undermine the principles of dispersed authority or provincial autonomy, the Covenant has been carefully designed to prevent this and is therefore consistent with the principles that have shaped the Communion's evolution. Five points should be noted.

First, it is clearly stated that "Each Church, with its bishops in synod, orders and regulates its own affairs and its local responsibility for mission through its own system of government and law and is therefore described as living "in communion with autonomy and accountability."[61] Each church further commits to "respect the constitutional autonomy of all of the Churches of the Anglican Communion."[62]

---

61. Covenant, 3.1.2.
62. Ibid., 3.2.2.

Second, the first three sections of the Covenant do not go beyond the Communion's traditional faith and order and so each covenanting province "recognises in the preceding sections a statement of faith, mission and interdependence of life which is consistent with its own life and with the doctrine and practice of the Christian faith as it has received them. It recognises these elements as foundational for the life of the Anglican Communion and therefore for the relationships among the covenanting Churches."[63]

Third, it is clearly stated that the mutual commitment expressed in the Covenant "does not represent submission to any external ecclesiastical jurisdiction. Nothing in this Covenant of itself shall be deemed to alter any provision of the Constitution and Canons of any Church of the Communion, or to limit its autonomy of governance. The Covenant does not grant to any one Church or any agency of the Communion control or direction over any Church of the Anglican Communion."[64]

Fourth, the Standing Committee does not act on its own but rather, "The Standing Committee of the Anglican Communion, *responsible to the Anglican Consultative Council and the Primates' Meeting*, shall monitor the functioning of the Covenant in the life of the Anglican Communion *on behalf of the Instruments*."[65]

Fifth, although the Standing Committee can "determine a view" and "make a declaration," any action by the Standing Committee has only the force of a "request" or "recommendations."[66] These are to be made to the Instruments and/or to the autonomous provinces and "Each Church or each Instrument shall determine whether or not to accept such recommendations."[67]

How this will work out remains to be seen, but the Covenant is clearly in continuity with the Communion's evolution over recent decades, and is faithful to the principles of interdependent autonomy-in-communion. It upholds the vision of Lambeth 1908 by enabling a proper regard to "the just freedom of its several parts, and to the just claims of the whole

63. Ibid., 4.1.2.

64. Ibid., 4.1.3.

65. Ibid., 4.2.2, italics added.

66. Ibid., 4.2.4—4.2.7.

67. Ibid., 4.2.7.

Communion upon its every part."[68] It nurtures a Communion where member churches recognise they are "independent with the Christian freedom which recognises the restraints of truth and love" and thus acknowledges, in the words of the Lambeth 1920 encyclical, that "They are not free to deny the truth. They are not free to ignore the fellowship."[69]

BIBLIOGRAPHY

Anglican Communion Reports

IASCER. *The Vision Before Us.* London: Anglican Communion Office, 2008. Online: www.anglicancommunion.org/ministry/ecumenical/commissions/iascer/docs/the_vision_before_us.pdf.

IATDC. *For the Sake of the Kingdom.* London: Anglican Communion Office, 1986. Online: http://www.anglicancommunion.org/ministry/theological/iatdc/docs/for_the_sake_of_the_kingdom_1986.pdf

IATDC. *Communion, Conflict and Hope.* London: Anglican Communion Office, 2008. Online: http://www.anglicancommunion.org/ministry/theological/iatdc/docs/communion_conflict_&_hope.pdf.

The Principles of Canon Law Common to the Churches of the Anglican Communion. London: Anglican Communion Office and Anglican Communion Legal Advisers Network, 2008. Online: http://www.acclawnet.co.uk/docs/principles.pdf.

Anglican Consultative Council Reports

ACC-1 (1971). *The Time is Now.* London: SPCK, 1971.
ACC-2 (1973). *Partners in Mission.* London: SPCK, 1973.
ACC-3 (1976). *Report of the Third Meeting.* London: Anglican Consultative Council, 1976.
ACC-4 (1979). *Report of the Fourth Meeting.* London: Anglican Consultative Council, 1979.
ACC-5 (1981). *Report of the Fifth Meeting.* London: Anglican Consultative Council, 1981.
ACC-6 (1984). *Bonds of Affection.* London: Anglican Consultative Council, 1984.
ACC-7 (1987). *Many Gifts, One Spirit.* London: Church Publishing, 1987.
ACC-8 (1990). *Mission in a Broken World.* London: Church Publishing, 1990.
ACC-10 (1996). *Being Anglican in the Third Millennium.* London: Morehouse, 1997.
ACC-13 (2005). *Living Communion.* London: Church Publishing, 2006.

Lambeth Conference Reports

Conference of Bishops of the Anglican Communion: Encyclical Letter from the Bishops with the Resolutions and Reports. London: SPCK, 1908.
Conference of Bishops of the Anglican Communion: Encyclical Letter from the Bishops with the Resolutions and Reports. London: SPCK, 1920.

68. LC 1908 Encyclical Letter, *Conference of Bishops* (1908), 41.
69. LC 1920 Encyclical Letter, *Conference of Bishops* (1920), 14.

Lambeth Conference 1930: Encyclical Letter from the Bishops with the Resolutions and Reports. London: SPCK, 1930.

The Report of the Lambeth Conference 1978. London: CIO Publishing, 1978.

Report of the Meeting of Primates, April 17, 2002. Online: http://www.anglicancommunion.org/acns/news.cfm/2002/4/17/ACNS2959.

General

Anglican Congress 1963. *Report of Proceedings*, edited by E. R. Fairweather. London: SPCK, 1963.

Chadwick, Owen. "Introduction." In *Resolutions of the Twelve Lambeth Conferences 1867–1988*, edited by R. Coleman. Toronto: Anglican Book Centre, 1992.

Chaplin, David. "Provincial Constitutions: Autonomy and Interdependence." Unpublished paper commissioned for ACC-8 (1990).

Doe, Norman. "Canon Law and Communion." No pages. Prepared for the Primates' Meeting, 2001. Online: www.anglicancommunion.org/acns/news.cfm/2001/3/8/ACNS2406.

———. "Communion and Autonomy in Anglicanism: Nature and Maintenance." Prepared for the Eames/Lambeth Commission, 2004. Online: http://www.anglicancommunion.org/commission/process/lc_commission/docs/autonomy.pdf.

Groves, Phil. "A Model for Partnership." PhD diss., University of Birmingham, 2009.

Howe, John. *Highways & Hedges: Anglicanism and the Universal Church*. Toronto: Anglican Book Centre, 1985.

Kaye, Bruce. "Why the Covenant Is a Bad Idea for Anglicans." No pages. Online: http://www.brucekaye.net/AOJ.

No Anglican Covenant Coalition. "Ten Reasons Why the Proposed Anglican Covenant Is a Bad Idea." No pages. Online: http://noanglicancovenant.org/docs/10reasons-a4-c.pdf.

Second Anglican Encounter in the South. *Second Trumpet*. No pages. Online: http://www.globalsouthanglican.org/index.php/blog/comments/second_trumpet_from_2nd_anglican_encounter_in_the_south_kuala_lumpur_10_15.

Stephenson, Alan M. G. *The First Lambeth Conference: 1867*. London: SPCK, 1967.

2

The Covenant and the *Via Media*

Compatible or Contradictory Notions of Anglicanism?

EDMUND NEWEY

A POLITICALLY-MOTIVATED COMPROMISE LEADING TO exclusion rather than embrace; a process that has arrived at the lowest common denominator, far removed from the Gospel, neither inspiring nor offending anyone; "a human attempt at managing unity,"[1] rather than something of God. These, variously, are criticisms that have been levelled at the Anglican Covenant during the period of painstaking consultation and editing since the appearance of the Nassau draft in April 2007. Their thrust is, first, that the Covenant goes too far, secondly, that it does not go far enough, and thirdly, that it introduces a novel and alien model into the Anglican pattern of theology and inter-relationship.

Diverse and partially contradictory though they are, each of these criticisms has at least a *prima facie* plausibility. They are also united by a common conviction that there was a time when things were better. For many of my colleagues in the parish ministry of the Church of England the Anglican Covenant is, at best, a necessary evil: necessary for the survival

---

1. A phrase from the Southern African response to NDC, cited in Doe, *Covenant*, 17 n.30.

of the Communion,[2] but evil (or at least less than good) because its affirmations, however carefully worded, enshrine the fall from grace that we have collectively undergone. Yet the prelapsarian state looks different according to one's perspective: was it a time of tolerant doctrinal latitude, held together, perhaps, by common prayer and sacramental practice; was it an era of solid adherence to scriptural foundations and catholic tradition; or was it a period when the relationship between churches and theological parties was characterised by appreciative respect rather than anathema, recrimination and schism?

Faced with these questions, in this chapter I revisit the question of the Covenant's compatibility with the methods, sources and norms of Anglican theology. Specifically I examine the much-criticised notion of the Anglican *via media*. Rightly reacting against triumphalistic portrayals of the middle way as a path of effortless irenic superiority, recent historiography has tended to dismiss the *via media* altogether.[3] It is instructive, though, that the complaints made against the *via media* closely resemble my three categories of criticism of the Anglican Covenant. For some scholars of the seventeenth-century Church of England, the *via media* was merely an instrument of royal propaganda, designed to discipline the state into religious conformity: a political wolf in theological disguise. By the turn of the eighteenth century, some have argued, this piece of power politics had evolved into something tamer, but theologically just as dangerous: a myth of "moderation," by which ever greater doctrinal diversity could be justified.[4] Equally significantly, in the sixteenth and seventeenth centuries the incipient *via media* was attacked as an innovation in theological method. The insistence that "Holy Scripture containeth all things necessary to salvation" is a case in point.[5] From the Roman Catholic perspective this seemed to derogate from the need for Church tradition to supplement and clarify the apparent deficiencies and inconsistencies of scripture, whilst from the Reformed point of view, by deviating from the strict interpretation of *scriptura sola*, it allowed excessive latitude.[6]

---

2. Chapman, "Catholicity and the Future of Anglicanism," 124.

3. One recent instance is Milward, "A *Via Media* in the Elizabethan Church?"

4. Quantin, *The Church of England and Christian Antiquity*, esp. 16 n.79. For the eighteenth century see Walsh and Taylor, "The Church and Anglicanism in the 'long' eighteenth century," 56–57.

5. 39 Art., Art. 6: "Of the Sufficiency of the Holy Scriptures for Salvation."

6. Chadwick, "Epilogue: Reflections on Tradition in Fact and Belief," 293. Of course,

Taking as its starting point these similarities between critiques of the Covenant and the *via media*, this chapter falls into three sections. In the first I draw together some of the more fruitful presentations of the Church of England's *via media* as they emerged from theologians of the sixteenth and seventeenth centuries, before offering a tentative working definition of the *via media* as it may be held to have characterised Anglican thought and practice at that period. I am well aware of the selective and controversial nature of my interpretation, but offer it with the conscious aim of rehabilitating the middle way as a *theologically* respectable *method*. *Theological* because it is arrived at not by a compromised process of triangulation from opposing doctrinal positions, but by a determined search for evangelical substance and catholic breadth; a *method* because, although its unfolding has often had an improvised quality, the *via media* has, at its best, embodied tradition as *paradosis*, the living interpretative quest of a Church attentive to the promptings of the Spirit in each successive age. In the second section I briefly consider the ways in which some recent theologians have sought to assess, employ and develop such insights. Here we shall see how the image of "the three-legged stool" of scripture, tradition, and reason, so often proclaimed to be the hallmark of Anglican method, is in fact a distortion of the *via media* at its best. In conclusion I explore the bearing such insights may have both on the text of Anglican Covenant and on the ways in which the churches of the Communion seek to respond to it. At this stage it is impossible properly to assess the spirit as well as the letter of the Covenant text, but if, in patient acceptance of the necessary labour of communion, our response to it is one of trust as well as interrogation, then the blessings of a truly sacramental covenant may at length be realised.[7]

|

Paul Elmer More's influential essay, "The Spirit of Anglicanism" concisely expresses an older view of the *via media*. He argues that, underlying the

---

from the perspective of a writer like Richard Hooker the middle position of the Church of England was not an innovation at all, but the elucidation of a principle that had once seemed self-evident: that we cannot know scripture to be the word of God except by the authority of the Church and by reason. See Hooker, *Lawes* III.8.14 (FLE I, 231–32).

7. On "trustful interrogation," see Williams, *On Christian Theology*, 144.

compromised origins of the Anglican middle way, there is, "a profounder impulse, pointing in a positive direction, and aiming to introduce into religion, and to base upon the "light of reason," that love of balance, restraint, moderation, measure, which from sources beyond our reckoning appears to be innate in the English temper."[8] More's essay, opening the valuable compendium, *Anglicanism*, still contains many useful judgements, but its appeal to a putative national temperament, peculiarly favourable to the way of moderation, is not sustainable. Yet More's perspective was far from unique. It continues a line of argument found as early as Archbishop Matthew Parker and most famously expressed by Simon Patrick, who commended "that virtuous mediocrity which our church observes between the meretricious gaudiness of the Church of Rome and the squalid sluttery of fanatic conventicles."[9] The complacent and at times triumphalist tone of statements such as these, according to which the Church of England claims to be "the only well ordered vineyard" in Christendom, presents us with the unacceptable face of the *via media*.[10]

Yet alongside this self-congratulatory apologetic tradition, in which the Church of England is uniquely able to discern the narrow path of truth leading between equal and opposite heresies, there stands an alternative picture of the *via media* that is both intellectually more sustainable and theologically more creative. In this understanding, the *via media* is a way of pursuing the Christian faith that seeks comprehension, not in the sense of the toleration of divergences from doctrinal orthodoxy often associated with the Latitudinarians,[11] but in the sense of catholicity or wholeness.

This is perhaps best seen in the thought of Lancelot Andrewes. Towards the end of his sermon for Easter 1609 he is speaking about the mediating office of Christ, with particular reference to the gifts of justice and peace:

8. More and Cross, *Anglicanism*, xxii.

9. As Peter White observes, "the French ambassador, visiting Archbishop Parker in 1564, 'noted much and delighted in our mediocrity, charging the Genevans and Scottish of going too far in extremities.' Parker himself took considerable pride in that moderation, claiming that it resulted from a primitive orthodoxy and purity." White, "The via media in the early Stuart Church," 213. Simon Patrick, *An Account of the New Sect of Latitude-men*, cited in More and Cross, *Anglicanism*, 12.

10. Patrick, *Latitude-Men,* 8, cited in More and Cross, *Anglicanism*, 13.

11. This characterisation of the Latitudinarian school may in itself be inaccurate. See Donald Greene, "The Via Media in an Age of Revolution," 312–13.

> [Christ's] office being to be "a Mediator"; *Medius* "between God
> and man," where should a Mediator stand but *in Medio?*
>
> Besides, the two qualities of good, being to be *diffusivum* and
> *unitivum*, that is the fittest place for both. To distribute, best done
> from the centre. To unite likewise, soonest meet there. The place
> itself has a virtue specially to unite, which is never done but by
> some middle thing. If we will conclude, we must have a *medius
> terminus*; else we shall never get *majus* and *minus extremum* to
> come together. Nor in things natural either combine two elements
> disagreeing in both qualities, without a middle symbolizing with
> both; nor flesh and bone, without a cartilage between both. As for
> things moral, there the middle is all in all. No virtue without it. In
> justice, incline the balance one way or other, the even pose is lost,
> *et opus justitiæ pax*, "peace is the very work of justice." And the
> way to peace is the mid-way; neither to the right hand too much,
> nor to the left hand too little. In a word, all analogy, symmetry,
> harmony, in the world goeth by it.[12]

In this passage Andrewes offers a vision of the whole pattern of the
Christian faith both in its historical and theological grounding and in its
ethical outworking. As so often in his work, the vision is centred on the
mediating person and work of Christ, not merely as an example to follow,
but as a living reality in which to participate. Andrew Louth's dictum that
"it is participation, not moral imitation, that stands at the centre in the
New Testament," applies perfectly to a thinker such as Andrewes.[13] Just as
in classical Platonic philosophy the middle is conceived of as the centre
from which all is distributed and in which all is united—most notably in
the case of justice and its chief fruit, peace—so, in Andrewes's theology,
Christ is the centre from whom all receive and in whom all are one. In this
sense the *via media* is, at root, the way of Christ: both a path of discipleship, as in the gospel descriptions of those who follow Jesus *en hodoi*,
but more fundamentally a participation in the mediating work of the one
who names himself as "the way, the Truth and the Life."

Andrewes is not simply advancing a general theological principle
here. He is laying the theological groundwork for his understanding of
the Church of England's middle way. Christ, in his person and work,
is a mediator not by compromise, but by comprehension, and the conception of the Church here is of a body, formed in Christ's image, that

---

12. Andrewes, *Ninety-Six Sermons*, Volume Two, 250.
13. Louth, *The Origins of the Christian Mystical Tradition*, 199.

shares and continues the mediating embrace of his ministry. The Church, thus understood, is not just a particular historical reality taking shape in Jacobean England, though it is of course that. It is also, in a phrase of Richard Hooker, whose thought I shall explore further below, the "Church of Christ which was from the beginning is and continueth until the end"[14] and its middle way is not one of compromise or compulsion, but one that constantly renews the calling to enlargement of vision, until it has the scope of Christ himself. As Nicholas Lossky has written: "Nothing is more foreign to [Andrewes's] preaching than doctrinal relativism or disciplinary laxity . . . [His] purpose remains essentially positive in that it is an appeal to conversion, or reconversion, to the living Tradition of the Church . . . the breath of the Holy Spirit."[15]

Admittedly Andrewes does not always adhere entirely to this large conception of the *via media*. In his work of controversy, *Tortura Torti*, he adopts a negative conception of the *via media*: "we follow neither Calvin nor the Pope, where either has forsaken the footsteps of the fathers."[16] Yet it is the deeper, comprehensive sense of the middle that remains most characteristic. Andrewes's thought is most fruitful when it rejects the static model of the middle way, defined negatively over and against Geneva and Rome, and affirms the dynamic sense of the *via media* metaphor. In the midst of heated controversy, the middle way is seen by Andrewes as the only sure *path* both to peace on earth and to heavenly salvation:

> He came, *to guide our feet into the way of peace*. A way of *peace* then, there shall be, whereof all parts shall agree, even in the midst of a world of *controversies*. That, there need not such a do in complaining, if men did not delight, rather, to be treading *mazes*, then to walke in the *waies of peace*. For, even still, such a way there is, which lyeth faire enough, and would lead us sure enough to *Salvation*; if, leaving those other rough *labyrinthes*, we would but be *shod with the preparation of the Gospell of peace.*[17]

This path, "which lyeth fair . . . and would lead us sure" is, for Andrewes, the *via media* of the Church of England. His assertion is, of course, far from self-evident and recent research has sought to draw attention to the

---

14. Hooker, *Lawes* III.1.10 (FLE I, 201).

15. Lossky, *Lancelot Andrewes the Preacher (1555–1626)*, 276.

16. Andrewes, *Tortura Torti*, 96.

17. Andrewes, *Ninety-Six Sermons*, Volume One, 36.

highly politicized ways in which such rhetoric was deployed, in Andrewes's lifetime and subsequently.[18] Yet, while it is clear that Andrewes was closely involved with the anti-Calvinist movement at the court of James I, we should not allow the conflicted ideological context to let us lose sight of his compelling theological case. Gregory Dodds has illuminated the continuities between Erasmus and Andrewes here: "Andrewes's *via media* rhetoric was not simply referring to a moderate middle space. Like Erasmus, Andrewes defined moderation and the *via media* as a "middle" trajectory between God and man, earth and heaven. This vertical *via media* helped shape his conception of the horizontal *via media* found on this earth. For Erasmus and Andrewes, the middle way was a middle pathway on which human beings made progress from earthly issues to heavenly salvation."[19] With the scrupulosity of a historian, Dodds does not let us forget those who were being excluded by such strategies, but as he does so he perhaps misses the theological value of Andrewes's method, which in a situation of conflict over specific issues, looks to a broader and deeper conception of God's work in Christ to reframe the debate in terms that are theological, rather than simply pragmatic and political.

Dodds's research has shed light on the influence of Erasmian thought on Andrewes, but more significant still is the inheritance of Richard Hooker, who taught Andrewes and whose works he edited. Andrewes's theology is deeply imbued with the spirit of Hooker's *Lawes of Ecclesiasticall Politie* and, like that work, whilst undoubtedly arising from a context of heated controversy, is remarkably resistant to the lure of polemic or definition by the negative terms of controversy. One of the chief characteristics of Hooker's thought is his constant desire to mediate between opposing positions by seeking common ground. The celebrated chapter "Of the Sacrament of the Body and Blood of Christ" in the Fifth Book of the *Lawes* exemplifies this method. In this chapter Hooker carefully examines the theological positions of those who might be considered his opponents and affirms what they have in common. It is instructive that the chapter's peroration cites *De coena domini*, a work of the mediaeval Cistercian theologian, Arnold of Bonneval, taken by Hooker to be written by the patristic author Cyprian of Carthage, and cited from an annotated

18. Tyacke, "Lancelot Andrewes and the Myth of Anglicanism"; McCullough, "Making Dead Men Speak."

19. Dodds, *Exploiting Erasmus*, 189.

edition of 1593 by the Calvinist writer, Simon Goulart.[20] This conjunction of times, schools and contexts is entirely typical of Hooker and indicates the "harmonious dissimilitude" in which he so often rejoices: "A more dutifull and religious way were for us to admire the wisedom of God which shineth in the bewtifull varietie of all things, but most in the manifold and yet harmonious dissimilitude of those wayes, whereby his church of earth is guided from age to age, throughout all generations of men."[21]

The examples cited in this section tend to indicate that the *via media*, as both a term and a method, was not a systematically implemented strategy, either politically or theologically. The middle way of the early post-Reformation Church of England is best seen not as an imposed compromise, but as a quest for theological catholicity in response to a remarkably broad spectrum of doctrinal positions.[22] It is undoubtedly true, as Peter Lake has argued, that "moderation," often seen as a hallmark of the *via media*, was "an ideologically charged category and one, moreover, subject to almost incessant polemical construction and reconstruction."[23] Yet the ongoing process of redefinition that Lake draws attention to indicates that the *via media* was a pathway negotiated step by step, the organic product of a particularly diverse theological and political climate: *ad hoc*, not top-down. As Peter White has written: "the *via media* was exactly that, implying movement as well as moderation."[24] Or, more fully, in John Donne's extended deployment of the dynamic sense of the metaphor:

> From extream to extream, from east to west, the Angels themselves cannot come, but by passing the middle way between; from that extream impurity, in which Antichrist had damped the Church of God, to that intemerate purity, in which Christ had constituted his Church, the most Angelicall reformers cannot come, but by touching, yea, and stepping upon some things, in the way. He that is

20. Hooker, *Lawes* V.67.11–13 (FLE II, 338–43). Though Hooker's position on the Lord's Supper is often described as receptionist, his very strong doctrine of participation qualifies this: "the bread and the cup are his body and blood because they are causes instrumental upon the receipt whereof the participation of his body and blood ensueth" (*Lawes* V.67.5; FLE II, 334).

21. Hooker, *Lawes* III.11.8 (FLE I, 253).

22. I borrow the term "spectrum" from Peter White, who sees it as preferably to the more common model of a polarity. White, "The *via media*," 212.

23. Lake, "Joseph Hall, Robert Skinner and the Rhetoric of Moderation at the Early Stuart Court," 181.

24. White, "The *via media*," 217.

come to any end, remembers when he was not at the middle way; he was not there as soon as he set out. It is the posture reserved for heaven, to sit down, at the right hand of God; here our consolation is, that God reaches out his hand to the receiving of those who come towards him; and nearer to him, and to the institutions of his Christ, can no Church, no not of the Reformation, be said to have come, than our does.[25]

This passage, from a sermon preached before Charles I, offers us a later articulation of the perspectives found in Hooker and Andrewes: the *via media* as a path to be walked in both humility and confidence, not immune from stumbling and error, but always seeking and sharing in Christ.

II

Completely sifting the theological grain from the polemical chaff is an unending task that the previous section has scarcely begun. Nonetheless my intention has been to show that, for all that the precise lens of modern historical study has undoubtedly seen through some of the mists of wishful thinking, its focus on the realities of political context has tended to overlook any genuine theological value in the *via media*. The historiographical determination to unearth political motives has risked creating an ahistorical category of "royal propaganda" that excludes the possibility of theology's virtuous influence on practical policy. In recent years, however, a handful of theological scholars have acknowledged that grounds remain for a positive assessment of the *via media* as an Anglican vocation: hard-won, by no means unique, but still an inspired means of learning to hold together insights and gifts that might well appear incompatible. Olivier Loyer, for instance, has described Richard Hooker's thought, widely held to be paradigmatic of the *via media*, as a "conjoining theology,"[26] working out the insight that grace does not destroy but perfects nature.[27] The particular gift of Hooker and many of his seventeenth century successors is to trace the scriptural lineage of this Thomistic

---

25. Donne, *Fifty Sermons*, 236 37, cited in Grierson. *Criticism and Creation*, 64–65.

26. Loyer, *L'Anglicanisme de Richard Hooker*, 383. More recently, William Harrison has shed further light on Hooker's middle way and its continuities with the doctrine of *theosis* as found in the Fathers and Thomas Aquinas. Harrison, "The Church."

27. Aquinas, ST 1a 1.8.

perspective. By demonstrating its thoroughly evangelical nature, Hooker advocated a form of theology that is at once rigorous and comprehensive. This is not the idealised picture of George Herbert's "The British Church" with its "perfect lineaments and hue / Both sweet and bright,"[28] so much as a continually-renewed determination to be faithful to the scriptures— and above all the gospel testimony of Jesus's person and work.

A common illustration of the theoretical approach characteristic of the *via media* is the image of the three-legged stool of scripture, tradition, and reason, in which each leg is held to exercise an equal load-bearing function. In fact this image seriously misrepresents the theological method of the sixteenth- and seventeenth-century Church of England in general, and of Richard Hooker in particular. The passage in which Hooker most clearly elucidates his method reads as follows: "what *Scripture* doth plainly deliver, to that the first place both of credit and obedience is due; the next whereunto is whatsoever any man can necessarily conclude by force of *reason*; after these the *voice of the Church* succeedeth. That which the Church by her ecclesiastical authority shall probably think and define to be true or good, must in congruity of reason overrule all other inferior judgments whatsoever."[29] Here the encounter with scripture is clearly primary, but that encounter is served by the tools of reason and the Church's living tradition of interpretation.[30] One can in fact go further and say that such a method is unavoidable because there can be no encounter with the authority of scripture that does not pass through the mediation of reason and tradition. Scripture is the centre, but it cannot be properly encountered except by employing the *interpretative lens* of reason within the *interpreting community* that is the Church. Thus, for Hooker, reason and the Church's teaching are not independent entities at the disposition of the inquiring individual's encounter with scripture, but divinely instituted gifts. Reason is the means and the Church is the context, without which scripture would remain inaccessible.[31]

28. Herbert, "The British Church," in *The Complete English Poems*, 101–2.

29. Hooker, *Lawes* V.8.2 (FLE II, 39); emphasis added.

30. Developing the research of W. David Neelands, Nigel Voak carefully illustrates the overlaps and distinctions in Hooker's use of the terms 'church,' 'tradition,' 'custom' and 'use,' arguing that "the religious authority of the Church is not based only on the authority of reasoning for Hooker, but also on the authority of tradition." Voak, *Richard Hooker and Reformed Theology*, 259–60.

31. "Reason; not meaning thereby myne owne reason . . . but true, sound, divyne

Rather than being uncomfortably poised on a three-legged stool, seeking to distribute equal weight to each of its legs, the Church of England is better envisaged as following an unceasing path of discovery and rediscovery, on which the scriptures continually unfold for us anew the living mystery of Christ. As Nicholas Lossky has written, focussing chiefly on Lancelot Andrewes, if seen as a compromise between Rome and Geneva, the *via media* of the early modern Church of England would tend "to confine any theological procedure to the terms of the strictly historical situation of conflict between Reform and Counter-reform. It would be some sort of *via tertia* uniquely defined by relation to the two antagonists, and therefore in some way negative."[32] Yet, rejecting such an interpretation, Lossky argues that Andrewes's thought is comprehensive, not in the sense of a Latitudinarian doctrinal pluralism, but in that it breathes the air of catholicity. Catholicity, as Lossky puts it, "not so much in the sense of 'universal' as . . . of fullness (according to the whole). Fullness, plenitude, *par excellence* is union with God."[33]

III

The text of the Anglican Communion Covenant wisely makes no mention of the *via media*, given its current chequered scholarly reputation.[34] Yet a good case can be made for the Covenant as promoting just those aims of fuller and deeper understanding espoused by the seventeenth century thinkers I have examined. It may be that the Covenant will prove to be a barrier to understanding and a means of foreclosing dialogue. The rather forced legalistic register and the scriptural and theological aridity of (the repeatedly debated and revised) "Section Four: Our Covenanted Life Together" seem to some to give the game away: are bonds of affection to become less affectionate and more binding, embracing the like-minded

---

reason, reson whereby those conclusions mighte be out of Ste Paule demonstrated and not probably discoursed of onely, reson proper to that science whereby the thinges of god are known; theologicall reason," Hooker, *Answer to the Supplication*, 24 (FLE V, 255); "the Church of Christ which was from the beginning is and continueth until the end," Hooker, *Lawes* III.1.10 (FLE I, 201).

32. Lossky, *Lancelot Andrewes the Preacher (1555–1626)*, 350.

33. Ibid., 351.

34. In addition to works cited above, Diarmaid MacCulloch's research should be mentioned, notably *The Later Reformation in England 1547-1603*.

and excluding those who demur? Yet the text and its accompanying introduction are grounded in a solid scriptural understanding of God's calling
and mission for the Church; they are well-informed theologically and historically literate; their tone is resolutely positive and outward-orientated.
If this dimension of the Covenant wins through, it could become not only
a way of sustaining an enriching conversation across the diverse contexts
in which Anglicans live,[35] but also in consequence a means of sharing in
God's healing and reconciling mission for "our blessed but broken, hurt-
ing and fallen world."[36]

Clearly the effortless superiority of a wrongly conceived *via media*
is no way to engage such diversity or reach out to such a world: it would
paper over divisions and preach peace where there is no peace. Yet, in the
deeper and humbler form that I have sought to trace in this chapter, the
via media may be the road on which Christ is met. In an article of 1982,
"Authority and the Bishop in the Church," Rowan Williams describes the
bishop's authority as "An authority to unify: not an authority to abolish
or minimize conflict within the community, but the task of referring all
sides of a debate to the unifying symbol over whose ritual recollection he
presides, in such a way as to show the face of strangers or opponents in
the Church as Christ's face for each other."[37] This vision of the episcopal
task may seem idealistic in the light of recent experience, yet its summons to find in Christ *both truth and unity* remains crucial and must be
the central task of the Anglican Covenant and the Anglican *via media*
alike. It asks us as a Church to raise the quality of our disagreements,
so that they are capable of moving beyond caricature, or even tolerance,
to charitably appreciative mutual insight. We see here something of the
toil that is a necessary part of the Church's communion, as indeed of any
properly committed relationship. As Nicholas Sagovsky has argued, "it is
not the presence of conflict that is unhealthy for communal life, but the
premature suppression of conflict in the interests of inauthentic unity."[38]

The world of sixteenth- and seventeenth-century England was a
place of extreme conflict, where divergent political and theological positions were held with a passionate conviction that could lead to exile and

35. Charlotte Methuen, "'In which the pure word of God is preached and the
Sacraments be duly administered,'" 24.

36. Covenant, 2.2.1.

37. Williams, "Authority and the Bishop in the Church," 99.

38. Sagovsky, *Ecumenism, Christian Origins and the Practice of Communion*, 8.

bloodshed. Yet it was in this context that the *via media* slowly evolved. When Hooker, in the first book of the *Lawes*, commends the "good of mutuall participation" and the human desire "to have a kind of societie and fellowship even with al mankind,"[39] we must read his words against the backdrop of the powerful political and religious forces that threatened such fellowship. The *via media* of the Church of England that he advocated was a means of establishing just the kind of "civill societie" that promotes these goods, and his excursus in this passage on the delight that human beings take in difference, far from being rhetorical fancy, is a potent piece of advocacy for "the wonderful delight [of] an universall fellowship with all men."[40]

The degree to which Hooker and the Church of England of his day succeeded in realising the comprehensive purpose of the *via media* is of course open to question and, as we have seen, scholars continue to debate the details of its motivation and implementation. Yet the theological moves instigated by Hooker, Andrewes and other contemporary advocates of the middle way were designed to resituate the debate on the common ground—or, better, *pathway*—of discipleship of, and participation in, Christ. The same motivation underlies the Anglican Communion Covenant. Its introductory preamble invokes the Church's "participation in the communion which is the divine life itself, the life of the Trinity," as not only the source and goal of our common life, but also its witness "to the hostile and divisive power of the world."[41] It is this participatory grounding that informs the bold claim made in Section Three of the Covenant itself: "Trusting in the Holy Spirit, who calls and enables us to dwell in a shared life of common worship and prayer for one another, in mutual affection, commitment and service, we seek to affirm our common life through those Instruments of Communion by which our Churches are enabled to be conformed to the mind of Christ."[42] This sentence may seem to make too big a claim for the Instruments of Communion. Can these four fallible human institutions—the Archbishop of Canterbury, the Lambeth Conference, the Anglican Consultative Council and the Primates' Meeting—plausibly lay claim to *enabling* conformity to the

---

39. Hooker, *Lawes* I.10.12 (FLE I, 107).
40. Ibid.
41. Covenant, Introduction, paras. 1 and 3.
42. Covenant, 3.1.2.

mind of Christ? Yet, if we read the sentence's claim in a sacramental sense, perhaps we should expect nothing less. Clearly it would be extraordinary to claim that the Instruments *alone* conform us to Christ, but as means of integrating our private and collective prayer, worship, study and sacramental life, they may yet be effectual catalysts of grace.

Arguing in favour of the proposals of *The Windsor Report* as a forum for promoting constructive disagreement, Bishop Thomas Breidenthal believes that:

> we [should] welcome genuine disagreements that arise out of the matrix of Christian faith, on the grounds that they provide an opportunity for a deeper communion and a more powerful witness to our commitment to Jesus Christ. There can be no more powerful witness to Christ than our willingness to stay at the table, in humility, with those who disagree most with us. It is not the temptation to disagree, but to exclude that weakens our witness. May the "instruments of unity" which enable our communion—however they end up being construed—render us more able to disagree, not less.[43]

One might add that the "table" at which Breidenthal calls us to stay is, essentially, the holy table of the Eucharist, in proximity to which none can claim to be more powerful or more excluded or holier than anyone else, because all are equally sinful, undeserving and yet welcome.

For all the frustrations of the Covenant process, and cumbersome and lethargic though the Instruments of Communion may be, in our current context they may well be the best means we have to continue to walk and work together. On the path to truth and unity in the Church haste, fear and self-pity are unhelpful properties. Fleeing Jerusalem for Emmaus, Cleopas and his fellow disciple exhibited all three of those qualities, yet in their eucharistic encounter with the Stranger their hearts were enlarged and their eyes opened. In a sermon commenting on this famous passage, Lancleot Andrewes sees the village of Emmaus as a figure for despair, signifying "a people forlorn":

> It was their case this day that went to Emmaus: say they, supposing Christ to be dead, *nos autem sperabamus,* 'we were once in good hope' by Him, that is, while He lived; as much to say as 'Now He is in His grave, our hope is gone, we are even going to Emmaus.' But then after, as soon as they saw He was alive again, their hope

43. Breidenthal, "Communion as Disagreement," 198.

revived, and with their hope their labour; and presently back again to Jerusalem to the Lord's work, and bade Emmaus farewell. So He leads us to labour; labour, to hope; hope, to our restoring; our restoring to Christ's, Who, as He hath restored Himself, will restore us also to life. And this keeps us from going to Emmaus. It is used proverbially. Emmaus signifieth 'a people forlorn:' all that are at *sperabamus*, have lost their hopes, are said to go thither; and thither we should all go, even to Emmaus, but for the hope that breathes from this verse, without which it were a cold occupation to be a Christian.[44]

It must be our hope that, for a global communion on the road to its own Emmaus, the Covenant can enable the converting encounter with one another *in Christ* necessary to send us on the road back to Jerusalem. Fostering that level of commitment to the labour necessary in the service of Christ and his Church was the highest aim of the *via media* in the sixteenth- and seventeenth-century Church of England and should be our highest hope and expectation for the Anglican Communion Covenant now.

BIBLIOGRAPHY

Andrewes, Lancelot. *Ninety-Six Sermons.* 5 vols. Oxford: Parker, 1841.
———. *Tortura Torti.* Oxford: Parker, 1851.
Breidenthal, Thomas. "Communion as Disagreement." In *Gays and the Future of Anglicanism: Responses to the Windsor Report,* edited by Andrew Linzey and Richard Kirker, 188–98. Hants, UK: O Books, 2005.
Chadwick, Henry. "Epilogue: Reflections on Tradition in Fact and Belief." In *Scripture, Tradition and Reason: A Study in the Criteria of Christian Doctrine,* edited by Richard Bauckham and Benjamin Drewery, 288–97. Edinburgh: T. & T. Clark, 1988.
Cassidy, Joseph. "Radical Anglicanism: A Vision for the Future." In *The Hope of Things to Come: Anglicanism and the Future,* edited by Mark Chapman, 88–101. Affirming Catholicism. London: Mowbray, 2010.
Chapman, Mark. "Catholicity and the Future of Anglicanism." In *The Hope of Things to Come: Anglicanism and the Future,* edited by Mark Chapman, 102–24. Affirming Catholicism. London: Mowbray, 2010.
Dodds, Gregory D. *Exploiting Erasmus: The Erasmian Legacy and Religious Change in Early Modern England.* Erasmus Studies. Toronto: Toronto University Press, 2009.
Greene, Donald. "The Via Media in an Age of Revolution: Anglicanism in the Eighteenth Century." In *The Varied Pattern: Studies in the 18th Century,* edited by Peter Hughes and David Williams, 297–320. Publications of the McMaster University Association for 18th-Century Studies 1. Toronto: Hakkert, 1971.
Grierson, Herbert. *Criticism and Creation: Essays and Addresses.* London: Chatto & Windus, 1949.

44. Andrewes, *Ninety-Six Sermons*, Volume Two, 207–8.

Harrison, William H. "The Church." In *A Companion to Richard Hooker*, edited by Torrance Kirby, 305–36. Brill's Companions to the Christian Tradition 8. Leiden: Brill, 2008.

Herbert, George. *The Complete English Poems*. Harmondsworth, UK: Penguin, 1991.

Lake, Peter. "Joseph Hall, Robert Skinner and the Rhetoric of Moderation at the Early Stuart Court." In *The English Sermon Revised: Religion, Literature and History 1600–1750*, edited by Lorrie Anne Ferrell and Peter McCullough, 167–87. Manchester: Manchester University Press, 2000.

Lossky, Nicholas. *Lancelot Andrewes the Preacher (1555–1626): The Origins of the Mystical theology of the Church of England*. Oxford: Oxford University Press, 1991.

Louth, Andrew. *The Origins of the Christian Mystical Tradition from Plato to Denys*. Oxford: Oxford University Press, 1981.

Loyer, Olivier. *L'Anglicanisme de Richard Hooker*. Lille: Atelier Reproduction des Thèses, Université de Lille III, 1979.

Mascall, E.L. *Via Media: An Essay in Theological Synthesis*. London: Longmans, Green and Co. 1956.

McCullough, Peter. "Making Dead Men Speak: Laudianism, Print, and the Works of Lancelot Andrewes, 1626–1642." *The Historical Journal* 41 (1998) 401–24.

Methuen, Charlotte, ""In which the pure word of God is preached and the Sacraments be duly administered": the Ecclesiology of the Church of England in the Context of the European Reformation." In *The Hope of Things to Come: Anglicanism and the Future*, edited by Mark Chapman, 1–25. Affirming Catholicism. London: Mowbray, 2010.

Milward, Peter. "A *Via Media* in the Elizabethan Church?" *Heythrop Journal* 52 (2011) 392–98.

More, Paul Elmer, and Frank Leslie Cross. *Anglicanism: The Thought and Practice of the Church of England Illustrated from the Religious Literature of the Seventeenth Century*. London: SPCK, 1935.

Quantin, Jean-Louis. *The Church of England and Christian Antiquity: The Construction of a Confessional Identity in the Seventeenth Century*. Oxford: Oxford University Press, 2010.

Sagovsky, Nicholas. *Ecumenism, Christian Origins and the Practice of Communion*. Cambridge: Cambridge University Press, 2000.

Tyacke, Nicholas. "Lancelot Andrewes and the Myth of Anglicanism." In *Conformity and Orthodoxy in the English Church, c. 1560–1660*, edited by Peter Lake and Michael Questier, 5–33. Studies in Modern British Religious History 2. Woodbridge, UK: Boydell, 2000.

Walsh, John and Stephen Taylor. "The Church and Anglicanism in the 'long' eighteenth century." In *The Church of England c. 1689–1833: From Toleration to Tractarianism*, edited by John Walsh, Colin Haydon, and Stephen Taylor, 1–64. Cambridge: Cambridge University Press, 1993.

White, Peter. "The via media in the early Stuart Church." In *The Early Stuart Church, 1603–1642*, edited by Kenneth Fincham, 211–30. London: Macmillan, 1993.

Williams, Rowan. "Authority and the Bishop in the Church." In *Their Lord and Ours: Approaches to Authority, Community and the Unity of the Church*, edited by Mark Santer, 90–112. London: SPCK, 1982.

———. *On Christian Theology*. Challenges to Contemporary Theology. Oxford: Blackwell, 2000.

3

The Litany of Law

Richard Hooker and the Anglican Covenant[1]

BENJAMIN M. GUYER

Yet all the Scriptures run
That God is great and one,
Or else there is no cause
Of nature or her laws;
To controul and comprehend
All beginning, course and end.

—Christopher Smart[2]

THE ANGLICAN COVENANT IS no small advance for the lived realities of Anglican ecclesiology. In the words of Norman Doe, adoption of the Covenant would be "a major historical development for worldwide Anglicanism."[3] It is not hard to see why. In the last decade, Anglicans have found themselves unable to deal in an efficient fashion with points of acute controversy, such as the nature and status of same-sex relationships, the practice of lay presidency at the Eucharist, cross-provincial episcopal

1. I thank Rev. Katharine L. Silcox for comments upon an earlier draft of this essay.

2. "Trinity Sunday," *Hymns and Spiritual Songs*, 64.

3. Doe, *Covenant*, 213.

action, and the subsequent creation of a new Anglican church in North America. Because the Anglican Communion lacks a formal way of handling contentious issues, its unity and coherence have been threatened and undermined by these developments. Although each Anglican province maintains its own canon law, and although these bodies of canon law reflect both a shared heritage and "common principles" of theology and order, there is no pan-provincial canon law which orients or shapes the relationships between provinces.[4] The Anglican Covenant aims to move the Communion beyond this impasse, not by altering provincial canon law but through a process of formal adoption by the provinces of the Anglican Communion.[5] When a province adopts the Covenant, it agrees to "common commitments and mutual accountability which hold each Church in the relationship of communion one with another."[6] As the Covenant text consistently reiterates, the end of this accountability is "interdependence."[7]

The present essay contends that the Anglican Covenant presents the Anglican Communion with an opportunity for a creative *ressourcement* of its own heritage, particularly the theology of Richard Hooker. His vision of law, set out in his *Of the Lawes of Ecclesiasticall Politie*, offers a singular hermeneutic for understanding the viability of the Anglican Covenant.[8] Hooker argues that law, which is inherently teleological, allows for participation in the divine life because law itself is part of the divine order. Beginning in God, law structures all other things and is present in creation, revelation, and society. The Church is unique among human societies because it alone operates at the nexus of grace and nature; even as it witnesses to the importance of law within every community, the Church also testifies that law is given to guide us to a "more divine perfection."[9] Law mediates between the eternal and the temporal because in defining societal order, law mirrors divine order in space and time.[10] It therefore

4. Doe, *Canon Law in the Anglican Communion*, 374.

5. Covenant, 4.1.3.

6. Covenant, 4.2.1.

7. Covenant, Introduction, para. 7; cf.Covenant, 2.1.4, 3.1.4, 3.2, 3.2.2, 4.1.1, 4.1.2.

8. Richard Hooker, *Of the Lawes of Ecclesiasticall Politie*. Citations appear as *Lawes* followed by book, chapter, and section number. I have preserved all original spelling. Unless otherwise noted, italicized emphases appear in the original text.

9. *Lawes* I.11.4 (FLE I, 115).

10. Charles W. Irish, "'Participation of God Himselfe;'" 171.

directs the Church away from any utopian hope of returning, within history, to a virginal time of pre-legal society. By placing ourselves under the divinely authored pedagogies of creation and revelation, human beings are directed and thus freed to create laws which will, in turn, better direct historical existence by patterning it after divine wisdom. The Anglican Covenant has an analogous function vis-à-vis the Anglican Communion. By offering interdependence as its *telos*, the Covenant may be understood as a law. It draws covenanting provinces into the present moment, and gives them the opportunity to more effectually signify, within space and time, the inspired peace which "surpasses all understanding."[11]

THE STRUCTURE OF LAW

In order to understand the grand scope of Hooker's design, we must set his work within its historical context. Written over the course of the 1590s and intended to comprise eight books, the *Lawes* is an unfinished polemic against Thomas Cartwright, a moderate Puritan who had clashed the previous decade with John Whitgift, the Archbishop of Canterbury, over the liturgy and polity of the Church of England.[12] Cartwright pleaded the soteriological necessity of ecclesiastical reform according to the Reformed model found in Geneva, but Whitgift denied that Cartwright's protest touched upon matters essential to salvation. The Archbishop defended the union of church and kingdom that Cartwright so detested, and pointedly underlined the authority of canon law and liturgical rubrics for all ministers in the Church of England, including those who desired further reformation. There was, however, more at stake. Puritans such as Cartwright argued that the Church has no right to author ecclesiastical law unless it is taken directly from Scripture. Theodore Bozeman describes Puritan thought as "primitivist" because it advocated returning to a purportedly lost, ancient age of pristine faith; historical development was to be not only avoided, but rejected.[13] In refusing Cartwright's call for reform, Whitgift and Hooker both rejected primitivist ideology. No form of polity has developed so perfectly that it no longer needs to consider its capacity for responding effectively to a changing historical context.

11. Phil 4:7.
12. Lake, *Moderate Puritans*, 6, 77–92.
13. Bozeman, *To Live Ancient Lives*, 15–19, 77–78.

Insofar as Hooker's *Lawes* is among the foundational works of Anglican theology, the rejection of primitivism is also foundational to the Anglican inheritance.[14]

The *Lawes* was intended as a late contribution to this debate. However, Hooker did not merely repeat earlier arguments, but offered a sustained consideration of how the Church works as a *society*. This is one of several important concepts in the *Lawes*, and in taking the time to define his terms Hooker was among those early Anglicans who preserved the methodological rigor of the scholastic inheritance for later generations.[15] In the first book of the *Lawes*, Hooker offers a bipartite definition of society: "Two foundations there are which beare up publique societies, the one, a naturall inclination, wherby all men desire sociable life and fellowship, the other an order expresly or secretly agreed upon, touching the manner of their union in living together."[16] Given this account, it is not surprising that Hooker is an important figure in the history of constitutionalism.[17] As is well known, constitutions are the hallmark of all modern societies, and if we read the *Lawes* from the vantage point of the present, we will see the importance of this definition for contemporary political thought.[18] But precisely because of our current political horizon, we must strive to apprehend that which would have been most immediately obvious to Hooker's own readers: in the first part of his definition, Hooker argued from natural law and set forth a thesis about *every* society in *every* age. He writes, "the Church is alwaies a visible *society*."[19]

14. The most easily accessible studies are Eccleshall, "Hooker and the Peculiarities of the English"; Brydon, *The Evolving Reputation of Richard Hooker*; and MacCulloch, "Richard Hooker's Reputation." However, recognition of Hooker's importance is neither a claim that his influence has been unvarying, nor an endorsement of a "great man" approach to history. Simply stated, Hooker did *not* invent Anglicanism *ex nihilo*. See Lake, "The 'Anglican Moment'?"

15. On Protestant Scholasticism, see especially Muller, *Post-Reformation Reformed Dogmatics*, vol. I, 27–84; Asselt and Dekker, *Reformation and Scholasticism*, and Trueman and Clark, *Protestant Scholasticism*, offer panoramic views upon both the modern period and historiographical issues.

16. *Lawes* I.10.1 (FLE I, 96).

17. Cromartie, *The Constitutionalist Revolution*, 141–46; Lloyd, "Constitutionalism," 279–83.

18. Thus Lloyd, "Constitutionalism," 255, defines "constitutionalist" as the belief that "power ought to be exercised within institutionally determined limits."

19. *Lawes* III.1.14 (FLE I, 205), emphasis mine; cf. *Lawes* I.15.2 and III.11.14 (FLE I, 131 and 261).

The Church is rooted in nature because it is rooted in the natural desire of human beings for social existence. Only when we grasp this fact can we understand the second part of Hooker's definition, which concerns determining an agreed-upon arrangement. This is just as important as his emphasis upon natural law. In the unfinished eighth and final book of the *Lawes*, Hooker offers the Pauline observation that "Without order there is no living in publique societie, because the want thereof is the mother of confusion, whereupon division of necessitie followeth, and out of division inevitable destruction."[20] Human decision-making has the capacity to preserve society, which is part of the natural order. What could be more unnatural and destructive than tearing apart that which nature itself impels?

As one might expect given the title of his work, Hooker grounds societal order in obedience to written law. He defines his central concept as follows: "That which doth assigne unto each thing the kinde, that which doth moderate the force and power, that which doth appoint the forme and measure of working, the same we tearme a *Lawe*."[21] This definition bears the marks of Thomas Aquinas's *Summa Theologiae*, for like Aquinas, Hooker believes that in and of itself law serves a positive purpose. This emphasis is key. Hooker explains, "A law therefore generally taken, is a directive rule unto *goodnes* of operation."[22] On the one hand, Hooker grants no place to those who claim that the exercise of authority *ipso facto* justifies any given law.[23] Voluntarism divorces law from its necessary moral content and opens the door to tyranny. Here again, we see Hooker's constitutionalism at work. In a justly celebrated *bon mot* later appropriated by John Locke, Hooker writes that societies were first founded because men and women "saw that to live by one mans will, became the cause of all mens misery."[24] Might does not make right. Law must be driven by reason and wisdom. Only then can it guide to a truly good end. On the other hand, yet wholly related to this, there is no place within Hooker's framework for division or antagonism between law and grace. God is the dispenser of grace and the author of law, and the

20. *Lawes* VIII.2.1 (FLE III, 331), referring to 1 Cor 14:40.

21. *Lawes* I.2.1 (FLE I, 58).

22. *Lawes* I.8.4 (FLE I, 84); emphasis mine.

23. *Lawes* I.3.1 (FLE I, 63).

24. *Lawes* I.10.5 (FLE I, 100); cited by John Locke, *Second Treatise of Government*, §94.

laws given by God through Scripture and nature are given for a particular reason. In God, nothing is arbitrary. "The being of God is a kinde of lawe to his working," Hooker explains, "for that perfection which God is, geveth perfection to that he doth." The gift of perfection comes through the operations of the Trinity, which are "eternally decreed" and thus "eternall lawe." Hooker does not elaborate on this but simply writes, "from the Father, by the Sonne, through the Spirit all things are."[25] Human existence and human law are, even if we are unaware of it, always already defined by a prior perfection.

Because of his scholastic commitment to conceptual clarity, Hooker's definition of law can be widely applied and further used to classify those laws which humans discern at work around them.[26] Hooker aids such an endeavor by offering a taxonomy of law borrowed directly from Aquinas, in which laws are classified according to what they orient. Hooker begins with *eternal law*, "*that order which God before all ages hath set down with himselfe, for himselfe to do all things by.*"[27] Following scholastic method, Hooker then draws a distinction within this definition, thereby proposing a first and second eternal law. W. J. Torrance Kirby helpfully summarizes the matter by writing that within Hooker's thought, the first eternal law concerns God's ability to create, whereas the second concerns God's governance of creation.[28] Hooker says little about the first eternal law; recognizing that it belongs to God alone, he advises his readers to not speculate upon it, for "our safest eloquence concerning him is our silence, when we confesse without confession that his glory is inexplicable, his greatnes above our capacitie and reach."[29] Law is the threshold of worship and the taxonomy of law is a contemplative ladder, the height of which is ineffable union with God.[30] In his discussion of the second eternal law, however, Hooker gives an important place to subjective human experience and our own capacity for speech. Human

---

25. *Lawes* I.2.2 (FLE I, 59).

26. I am indebted to Alister McGrath's considerations of discernment and natural theology in *The Open Secret*, 73–78.

27. *Lawes* I.2.6 (FLE I, 63); working out of Prov 8:23; 2 Tim 2:13; and Heb 6:17, among others.

28. Kirby, *Reformer and Platonist*, 47.

29. *Lawes* I.2.2 (FLE I, 59).

30. The language is intentionally Dionysian. See Kirby, *Reformer and Platonist*, 29–44; cf. Pseudo-Dionysius, *Mystical Theology*, esp. I.2.

beings perceive the second eternal law—the governance of creation—as a variegated harmony of laws which direct all created things. Amidst this diversity, we also perceive the benevolent intention of a master architect. If a Christian denies this, then he or she denies that which ancient pagan philosophers clearly understood: because the laws within creation are consistent, they must depend upon a law which is independent of them.[31] Stated more technically, in studying the second eternal law, we realize that the first eternal law is autonomous. In Aquinas's words, it is "not subordinate to an outside end."[32] Or, as Hooker elucidates, God alone is "that lawe which giveth life unto all the rest."[33] God is the author of creation, and his law is the source of all other laws.

The second eternal law, like law as such, is a taxonomic structure. It contains five divisions. The first is *natures law*, "which ordereth naturall agents" such as celestial bodies and other inanimate objects.[34] Next is *celestial law*, which applies to angelic beings. Angels are "lincked" in "societie" with human beings and, as Hooker expounds in the fifth book of the *Lawes*, are "intermingled as our associates" in liturgical worship.[35] The third law that Hooker discusses is the *law of reason*, "which bindeth creatures reasonable in this world, and with which by reason they may most plainly perceive themselves bound."[36] Penultimately, Hooker writes of *divine law*. This is the content of revelation and is intellectual no less than moral; it concerns "goodnesse" and "perfections," "knowledge of truth" and "the exercise of vertue."[37] The final category, *human* or *positive law*, is different from the others.[38] It concerns society and is authored directly by humans rather than God. As a society, the Church is located here, within the realm of positive law. We will explore this more fully in the next section. In sum, and when taken together, Hooker's fine distinctions indicate that his theology is ultimately one of providential order. Insofar as objects or beings are directed by the second eternal law, they

31. *Lawes* I.2.3 (FLE I, 60).

32. Aquinas, ST 1a2æ 91.1 ad 3.

33. *Lawes* I.1.3 (FLE I, 58).

34. *Lawes* I.3.1 (FLE I, 63).

35. *Lawes* I.4.2 (FLE I, 71), citing Ps 148:2, Luke 2:13; Matt 26:53; Heb 12:22; cf. *Lawes* V.25.2 (FLE II, 114).

36. *Lawes* I.3.1 (FLE I, 63).

37. *Lawes* I.5.1 and I.5.3 (FLE I, 73–74).

38. *Lawes* I.3.1 (FLE I, 63); cf. Aquinas, ST Ia2æ 91.3.

also conform to the first. Yet even if something is disordered by sin and refuses its appointed end, its very existence means that it is still directed in some way by the first eternal law. Nothing can subsist wholly against or outside of that law which is uniquely God's own.[39]

DIVINE PEDAGOGIES

Human beings are tasked with crafting positive laws which will direct both church and state to goodness. As noted immediately above, we experience the second eternal law in five diverse but interlocking ways, one of which is human society. Two things follow. First, because positive law is part of the second eternal law, our perception of the latter always already occurs within the specific historical context of the former. Greater or lesser degrees of harmony may be discerned when we compare positive laws and their effects with those other laws which together constitute the second eternal law. It is wholly conceivable that we will at some point recognize variance between the created world around us and our own political or ecclesiastical ecologies. Because church and state are both so-cieties, they are equally free to author laws which will better direct their existence. In drafting laws, each rejects primitivism. Second, positive law is located at the lowest point within the taxonomy of the second eternal law. By placing human laws at the furthest point from eternal law, Hooker claims that human law is the site at which human beings begin their re-turn to God, ascending ultimately to the sublime *apophasis* elicited by the first eternal law. We are not left alone in our task. Through nature and Scripture, God teaches us how to craft positive laws that emulate divine wisdom. Hooker explains, "Education and instruction are the meanes, the one by use, the other by precept to make our naturall faculty of reason, both the better and the sooner able to judge rightly betweene truth and error, good and evill."[40] Reason must be brought under divine pedagogy. This is not an inherently optimistic perspective but is instead realistic. Hooker well recognized that "The search of knowledg is a thing painful and the painfulnes of knowledge is that which maketh the will so hardly inclinable thereunto."[41] The capacity of reason is great, but capacity is not

39. *Lawes* I.3.1 (FLE I, 63).
40. *Lawes* I.6.5 (FLE I, 76).
41. *Lawes* I.7.7 (FLE I, 81).

necessarily coterminous with present reality. Rightly guided toil is the only means of genuine growth.

The first method of tutelage is "the schoole of nature," which teaches things that "profite manye waies for mens instruction."[42] The second method is "the schoole of Christ," which draws upon and surpasses the limits of human reason.[43] Nature is discussed as a form of pedagogy quite early in the *Lawes*. Writing of the orbit of planets, the light of the sun, the necessity of rain, and other elements of the natural order, Hooker asks, "See we not plainly that obedience of creatures unto the lawe of nature is the stay of the whole world?" Constancy is the *sine qua non* of creation, and because of this nature operates as a sure map and guide for society. Natural laws cannot be abrogated by created beings; to take a contemporary example, even the technological circumvention of the law of gravity in mechanical flight is merely temporary. So too "it commeth to passe in a kingdom rightly ordered, that after a law is once published, it presently takes effect far and wide, all states framing themselves thereunto."[44] Law is *discerned* as a stable, operative principle ever at work around us, and where a society is "rightly ordered" it functions precisely as nature does. All other things being equal, when natural reason is set within society it is capable of ascertaining a basic knowledge of ethics and morality.[45] However, because of sin, "so far hath the naturall understanding even of sundry whole nations bene darkned, that they have not discerned no not grosse iniquitie to bee sinne."[46] Relying upon natural reason alone, we apprehend nature and its laws dimly at best, and in the wrong social context our capacity for moral and ethical action is further hindered and undermined. In short, our natural propensity for society is threatened by our fallenness. And yet, even here creation teaches us. Hooker expects that just as "nature even in this life doth plainly claime and call for a more divine perfection," Christians will do the same.[47]

Perfection is given by Christ and mediated through Word and sacrament. In keeping with the general tenor of the *Lawes*, Hooker explains

---

42. *Lawes* I.12.1 (FLE I, 120).

43. *Lawes* III.8.16 (FLE I, 233).

44. *Lawes* I.3.2 (FLE I, 65–66).

45. *Lawes* I.8.9 (FLE I, 90).

46. *Lawes* I.12.2 (FLE I, 120–21).

47. *Lawes* I.11.4 (FLE I, 115).

that the sacraments have one end while the Scriptures have another. In baptism, "wee receive Christ Jesus and from him that saving grace which is proper unto baptisme."[48] In the Eucharist we are given "the *reall participation* of Christe."[49] Neither of these yields an articulate plan for society because both of these are wholly beyond natural reason.[50] Scripture is different; it is "fraught even with the lawes of nature" and consequently lends itself directly to the sort of pedagogy that is necessary for constructing and sustaining human society.[51] Hooker writes that "the principal intent of scripture is to deliver the lawes of duties supernaturall," and that in doing so "the same lawe that teacheth them, teacheth also with them such naturall duties as coulde not by light of nature easilie have bene knowne."[52] Grace reveals what sin prevents us from recognizing in creation. We do well to remember that Hooker lived and wrote in the wake of humanism and, like earlier figures such as Petrarch and Erasmus, he had an especially strong sense of the power of texts to preserve and communicate ideas across centuries. Oral cultures had their part to play in salvation history, but Hooker argues that the advent of writing was a "singular benefite" to later generations. An exclusively oral delivery has no record against which claims might be checked, and risks that its original message—or, in the case of Scripture, the original revelation—will become "maymed and deformed."[53] Through Scripture, the school of Christ offers an inspired and instructive text which communicates effectually across the ages, teaching us the way of salvation while also explicating the school of nature.

Laws must be made with the conscious recognition that these two schools offer instructions necessary for our wellbeing. We read, "lawes humane must be made according to the generall lawes of nature, and without contradiction unto any positive lawe in scripture. Otherwise they are ill made."[54] The laws of God do not change, just as the laws of nature are steadfast; the end of the latter is "the stay of the whole world" while

---

48. *Lawes* V.57.6 (FLE II, 248).
49. *Lawes* V.67.2 (FLE II, 331).
50. *Lawes* V.50.2 (FLE II, 207–8).
51. *Lawes* I.12.1 (FLE I, 119).
52. *Lawes* I.14.1 and I.12.3 (FLE I, 124 and 122).
53. *Lawes* I.13.1–2 (FLE I, 122–23).
54. *Lawes* III.9.2 (FLE I, 237).

the end of the former is resurrection unto everlasting life and the deifying vision of God. Between these two is the open and undefined space of new and changing historical contexts. The negative instruction here— "without contradiction unto any positive lawe in scripture"—means that although positive laws must, like the laws of nature, contribute to the wellbeing of creation, they also have no right to abrogate or weaken those laws which are given for our divine perfection. Laws are judged fit according to their ends and may be changed only when their stated end is no longer attainable.[55] This is a central difference between positive law, which is drafted by finite beings, and those laws which originate with God. Hooker emphasizes that the ends appointed by God, such as moral law and doctrine, do not change.[56] Ecclesiastical polity may change.[57] God has given the Church the right—Hooker claims that it is a "divine right"[58]—to author laws so that it might attain natural and divine ends.[59] Rooted in an inherent desire for social life, illuminated by the articulate grace of Scripture and thus capacitated to sound out the laws of nature, the Church is free to direct its common life according to what it discerns. Positive law is dynamic and may always be reformed. Primitivism has no place among the people of God.

"A MORE DIVINE PERFECTION"

We must now consider how the Anglican Covenant directs the Anglican Communion to "a more divine perfection." In order to better understand the congruity between the Covenant and Hooker's vision, we conclude by proposing and answering three simple questions. First, what does the Anglican Covenant say about God and Christian revelation? The over-riding theme in the Covenant is communion, which is understood as a

---

55. *Lawes* III.10.1 (FLE I, 239–40).

56. *Lawes* III.10.4 and III.10.7 (FLE I, 242–43 and 244–45).

57. Lest our point be misunderstood, we should emphasize that Hooker was a thoroughgoing episcopalian who believed that episcopacy was the form of ecclesiastical polity bequeathed by the apostles. The episcopate as such is non-negotiable, regardless as to whether or not it is *jure divino*.

58. *Lawes* VIII.6.2 (FLE III, 387).

59. *Lawes* III.10.2 (FLE I, 97–98).

call to participate in the Triune life of God.[60] The Covenant text instructs us that the *telos* of the Gospel is God's desire to "restore in us the divine image" through repentance, baptism, and evangelism. This is not anthropocentric; redemption touches upon "the whole of creation" and only because of this is it "extended to all humankind."[61] The salvific economy given through Christ is defined here as an ecology of redemption. Rooted in Trinitarian participation, the outlook of the Anglican Covenant is necessarily maximal in its discussion of Christian life and witness. If we trace this participatory theme throughout the rest of the Covenant text, we find that it structures four other things. It "shapes and displays itself through the very existence and ordering of the Church," it exhorts obedience to the Great Commission, it maintains sacramental initiation as the beginning of Christian life, and it envisions participation in the councils of the Anglican Communion.[62] Participation is no mere ideal, but manifests itself in ecclesial structures and relationships, liturgical and sacramental rites, and the evangelical articulation of our shared calling. Most simply stated, communion is a way of life. As a pedagogic aid for discussing God and Christian revelation, the Covenant is wholly faithful to the apostolic inheritance. The Church is "caught up in the mystery of divine communion," and called to "reveal to the hostile and divisive power of the world the 'manifold wisdom of God' (Eph. 3:9-10)."[63] Christians are called to a revelatory and iconic role. In Hooker's terminology, the Covenant text clearly evinces that "duties supernaturall" are given and expected of all the baptized.[64]

Second, what does the Anglican Covenant offer the Anglican Communion as a society? As a singular family of churches, the Covenant understands the Anglican Communion within the theological framework of participation sketched above. The Anglican Communion subsists "within the universal Church" and therefore subsists within the same calling that first brought the Church into being.[65] This recognition does not dissolve the Anglican tradition but instead

60. Covenant, Introduction, para. 1, citing 1 John 1:2–4 and 1 Cor 1:9.

61. Ibid., para. 2.

62. Ibid., para. 1; Introduction, para. 4 and 1.1.8; 3.1.1; 4.2.1, 4.2.5, 4.2.8.

63. Ibid., Introduction, para. 3.

64. *Lawes* I.14.1 (FLE I, 124).

65. Covenant, Introduction, para. 4.

paves the way for recognizing its unique "distinguishing marks."[66] The Covenant text describes a "particular charism" which is given to the Anglican Communion and signified by its history, liturgical traditions, and doctrinal and ecumenical statements.[67] The Covenant's explication of the Anglican inheritance and vocation outlines those "foundations" which bear upon "the manner of [our] union in living together."[68] The Archbishop of Canterbury has stated that the Anglican Covenant is not a constitution.[69] Insofar as a constitution is taken as a founding document, he is correct. However, because the Covenant defines provincial autonomy with respect to interdependence (rather than vice versa), it directs and thus limits the exercise of authority.[70] It is therefore, in the strict sense of the term, constitutional.[71] Through the Covenant, the Anglican Communion is now finally given one of the principle political gifts that the Church of England, through Richard Hooker, bequeathed to the modern world centuries ago. Without the Covenant, the Anglican Communion is bound merely by a set of quasi-feudal, ecclesiastical oaths—undefined "bonds of affection"—which are incapable of effectively witnessing to a wider world based upon the more developed and intellectually sophisticated foundation of political constitutionalism.

Third, and following this same line of thought, if the Covenant constitutes the Anglican Communion with a set of clearly defined, shared ends, does it restrict or prohibit Anglicans from further developing and ordering their common life? In other words, might the Covenant become a new form of primitivism? The Covenant was not conceived as a document which might bring Anglican polity to an irrevocable and final form of development. The Covenant is explicitly open to amendment through due process. This procedure is as follows. First, a province may submit an amendment to the Standing Committee of the Anglican Communion, which will forward it to the Anglican Consultative Council, the Primates'

---

66. This language of "distinguishing marks" comes from St. Basil the Great, *Against Eunomius*, 2.4; cf. Florovsky, *The Eastern Fathers of the Fourth Century*, 91–107.

67. Covenant, Introduction, para. 4 and 1.1.2.

68. *Lawes* I.10.1 (FLE I, 96).

69. See the video at http://anglicancommunion.org/commission/covenant/index. cfm.

70. Covenant, 3.2.2 and 4.1.1.

71. See n.18 above.

Meeting, and "any other body as it may consider appropriate for advice."[72] With advice given by each of these, the Standing Committee then makes a recommendation on the proposal and submits it, with or without revisions, to all other covenanted provinces. The amendment goes into effect "when ratified by three quarters of such Churches."[73] By setting the ratification percentage so high, the Covenant directs us away from the easily contestable terrain of amendment by simple majority. Through this process, corporate Anglican discernment will be clearly visible to its members, other churches and particularly ecumenical partners, and the wider world. The Covenant invites participation and strengthens interdependence by allowing for the amendment of its text. Importantly, the Covenant's Introduction, which sets out the divine and natural ends of the Church, is not part of the Covenant itself. Rather, "The Introduction to the Covenant Text, which shall always be annexed to the Covenant text . . . shall be accorded authority in understanding the purpose of the Covenant."[74] Positive law may be drafted, altered, or revoked. The Trinitarian life which initiates all participation and gives all perfection can never be abrogated.

In conclusion, we proposed in our introduction that positive law has an iconic role in human societies, particularly that of the Church, because when drafted under the pedagogies of nature and grace it signifies divine order. Through a close study of Richard Hooker's *Lawes*, we have discussed positive law within the taxonomic context of the first and second eternal laws. Still following Hooker, we then outlined the ways that God provides us with instruction, so that we may create positive laws that also direct us to what is good. Finally, we read the Covenant against the main lines of Hooker's theology, noting that it begins with the Trinity, outlines and thus constitutes the Anglican way of life, and defines the means for provincial participation in Communion history. This is indeed a *ressourcement* of Hooker's work. We conclude then by offering a final observation. In his study of early medieval English law, the late Patrick Wormald offered the brilliant insight that law is like literature: it reveals the ways of a people.[75] In patterning covenanted life after the Trinity, the *telos* of the Anglican

72. Covenant, 4.4.2.

73. Ibid.

74. Ibid., 4.4.1.

75. Wormald, *The Making of English Law*, 416–76.

Covenant—interdependence —is held forth as an icon which reveals the ways of God. Should the Anglican Communion embody the same, it too will become an icon, not by nature but by grace. We have merely sought to emphasize with Hooker that "When supernaturall duties are necessarily exacted, naturall are not rejected as needlesse."[76] Indeed, without nature and its duties, there is no ecclesiastical society to begin with.

BIBILIOGRAPHY

Asselt, Willem J. van, and Eef Dekker. *Reformation and Scholasticism: An Ecumenical Enterprise*. Texts and Studies in Reformation and Post-Reformation Thought. Grand Rapids: Baker Academic, 2001.

St. Basil the Great. *Against Eunomius*. Translated by Mark Delcogliano and Andrew Radde-Gallwitz. Washington, DC: Catholic University of America Press, 2011.

Bozeman, Theodore. *To Live Ancient Lives: The Primitivist Dimension in Puritanism*. Chapel Hill: University of North Carolina Press, 1988.

Brydon, Michael. *The Evolving Reputation of Richard Hooker: An Examination of Responses 1600-1714*. Oxford: Oxford University Press.

Cromartie, Alan. *The Constitutionalist Revolution: An Essay on the History of England, 1450-1642*. Cambridge: Cambridge University Press, 2009.

Doe, Norman. *Canon Law in the Anglican Communion: A Worldwide Perspective*. Oxford: Clarendon, 1998.

———. *An Anglican Covenant: Theological and Legal Considerations for a Global Debate*. Norwich, UK: Canterbury Press, 2008.

Eccleshall, Robert. "Hooker and the Peculiarities of the English: The Reception of the *Ecclesiastical Polity* in the Seventeenth and Eighteenth Centuries." *History of Political Thought* 2 (1981) 63-117.

Florovsky, Georges. *The Eastern Fathers of the Fourth Century*. Vaduz: Büchervertriebsanstalt, 1987.

Hooker, Richard. *Of the Lawes of Ecclesiasticall Politie*. In *The Folger Library Edition of the Works of Richard Hooker*, vols. I–III, edited by W. Speed Hill. Cambridge, MA: Belknap, 1977–1981.

Irish, Charles W. "'Participation of God Himselfe:' Law, the mediation of Christ, and sacramental participation in the thought of Richard Hooker." In *Richard Hooker and the English Reformation*, edited by W. J. Torrance Kirby, 165–84. Boston: Kluwer Academic, 2003.

Kirby, W. J. Torrance. *Richard Hooker, Reformer and Platonist*. Burlington, VT: Ashgate, 2005.

Lake, Peter. *Moderate Puritans and the Elizabethan Church*. Cambridge: Cambridge University Press, 1981.

———. "The 'Anglican Moment'? Richard Hooker and the Ideological Watershed of the 1590s." In *Anglicanism and the Western Christian Tradition: Continuity, Change*

---

76. *Lawes* I.12.1 (FLE I, 119).

and the Search for Communion, edited by Stephen Platten, 90–121. Norwich, UK: Canterbury Press, 2003.

Lloyd, Howell A. "Constitutionalism." In *The Cambridge History of Political Thought, 1450–1700*, edited by J. H. Burns with Mark Goldie, 254–97. Cambridge: Cambridge University Press, 1991.

Locke, John. *The Second Treatise of Government.* In *Locke: Two Treatises of Government*, edited by Peter Laslett, 265–428. Cambridge: Cambridge University Press, 1988.

MacCulloch, Diarmaid. "Richard Hooker's Reputation." *English Historical Review* 117 (473) (2002) 773–812.

McGrath, Alister. *The Open Secret: A New Vision for Natural Theology.* Malden, MA: Blackwell, 2008.

Muller, Richard A. *Post-Reformation Reformed Dogmatics: The Rise and Development of Reformed Orthodoxy, ca. 1520 to ca. 1725.* 4 vols. Grand Rapids: Baker Academic, 1987–2003.

Pseudo-Dionysius. *The Mystical Theology.* In *Pseudo-Dionysius: The Complete Works*, edited and translated by Colm Luibheid and Paul Rorem. Mahwah, NJ: Paulist, 1987.

Trueman, Carl R., and R. Scott Clark. *Protestant Scholasticism: Essays in Reassessment.* Studies in Christian History and Thought. 1999. Reprinted, Eugene, OR: Wipf & Stock, 2007.

Smart, Christopher. *Hymns and Spiritual Songs for the Fasts and Festivals of the Church of England.* In *The Poetical Works of Christopher Smart*, Vol. II: *Religious Poetry 1763–1771*, edited by Marcus Walsh and Karina Williamson. Oxford: Clarendon, 1983

Wormald, Patrick. *The Making of English Law: King Alfred to the Twelfth Century.* Oxford: Blackwell, 1999.

4

Creation, Kenosis, and Ecclesia

Comparing Lionel S. Thornton and Bruce Kaye

JEFF BOLDT

T HIS CHAPTER RELATES LIONEL Thornton's doctrine of organic church order to Bruce Kaye's ecclesiological concerns about coercive authority in the Anglican Communion. Kaye has recently claimed that *The Windsor Report* is a "means of control" that constrains personal responsiveness to the Gospel, stifles change, and undercuts diversity in the Anglican Communion. Its recommendation of a Covenant is only a suspicious form of "contract" that "could be the beginning of the development of some kind of power."[1] Kaye is worried that a global, top-down structure is in the works that, through the Covenant, will necessarily inhibit each local church's ability to enculturate the Gospel in their respective contexts. Using insights from Thornton, I will argue that there is no reason to oppose the Covenant's requests for "gracious restraint"[2]

---

1. Kaye, *Conflict and the Practice of Christian Faith*, 120.

2. "Gracious Restraint" has usually referred to the three moratoria requested by TWR and received by the Instruments of Communion. The Covenant also upholds them since it not only requires the recognition of "the importance of instruments in the Anglican Communion to assist in the discernment, articulation and exercise of our shared faith and common life and mission" (Covenant, 3.1.4), but "to receive their work with a readiness to undertake reflection upon their counsels, and to endeavour to accommodate their recommendations" (Covenant, 3.2.1). If commonly expressed "commitments" are broken (Covenant, 4.2.1) The Standing Committee recommends "relational consequenc-

in principle, for they are essential to an organic, non-coercive polity. On the contrary, opposition to such restraints and limits stem from a form of social atomism that tends towards coercion itself, for by ignoring the intrinsic order of the Church an external order must be imposed to relate ecclesial parts to the whole. The point I want to make is that there are only two ways to think about ecclesial order: bodily or non-bodily; organic or non-organic.[3] The former has an intrinsic order to its parts, while the latter must be ordered extrinsically, by force as it were. My claim is that the Anglican Covenant falls into the organic category because it encourages each member to give themselves on behalf of the others through a common discernment and recognition of the inner order of Christ's Body, a common consent to this redeemed order, and a willingness to be reordered in accord with it, which could involve listening to requests for gracious restraint to that end, even requests that outline relational consequences. Thornton's organic ecclesiology, because it depends on the Pauline image of the body, can show why this polity preserves diversity, facilitates change, and is not coercive.

CHRISTOLOGY: THE UNIVERSAL PARTICULAR?

Kaye begins quite traditionally, with Christology as the starting point for his ecclesiology. According to Kaye, Jesus reinterpreted and re-contextualized Israel's cultural symbols of national identity (land, law, nation, and temple) by connecting them to himself and to his rule.[4] In this way he made it possible for the early Christians to "break out" of the "national and local framework of Israel to embrace a gospel to be preached universally to all people."[5] This definition of the local falls along cultural lines; although the universal Gospel of Christ took up aspects of local Jewish culture, (thereby simultaneously offering a paradigm for contextualization) it had to "break out" of its original context. What is left unclear is whether local Jewish culture is de-particularized as it is universalized

---

es" to the Instruments that might include suspension of participation in an Instrument (Covenant, 4.2.5).

3. For a discussion of this point in terms of homogenous and heterogeneous unity see Gilson, *From Aristotle to Darwin and Back Again.*

4. Kaye, *Conflict and the Practice of Christian Faith,* 14.

5. Ibid., 11.

in Christ and the early Church, since Kaye regularly puts the weight of particularity, and thus diversity, at the local level. If this is not the case, (and one hopes it is not since the risk of supercessionism is great) how do local cultures gain universal, "global" theological significance? This question is important, for it touches on the process whereby local theological particularities become globally normative.

PERSUASION AND COERCION, I: BRUCE KAYE'S PROBLEMATIC

Coercion is a concern of Kaye's, for he relates that because Christ's lordship is the universal message of the Gospel, it comes up against the coercive opposition practiced by the lords of each local culture. Two kingdoms clash and their strategies are utterly different: Jesus rules from the Cross with a non-coercive power that is subversive of the worldly "powers" who rule by force.[6] The main purpose of his Gospel message is that it be personally accepted. The problem is that worldly powers often get in the way of that acceptance by hindering an individual's ability to respond. This is especially damaging when the church wrongly absorbs the coercive expedients of the world rather than seeking to persuade it. At that point the church actually becomes its own worst enemy, since it coerces what can only be freely chosen.

Opposition between coercive power and the peaceful approach of Christ's Cross is an opposition between impersonal and personal ways of persuasion, which Kaye explains using ideas drawn from Rousseau. These ideas tend toward a Romantic dualism that severs human culture and institutions from natural, personal relationships, for Rousseau taught that the sympathetic imagination was the basis of human community since it allowed a stranger to enter into another's sufferings.[7] In time, however, culture and institutions stepped into human history with cold, unresponsive mechanisms, and alienated us from our sympathetic nature by imposing a static order upon individuals. Rousseau claimed that religious institutions are the worst in this regard because they claim divine legitimacy. This makes them hard to change even though change is essential for personal responsiveness. To be fair, Kaye does at times try to develop a more positive approach to institutional order. He admits that

6. Kaye, *Conflict and the Practice of Christian Faith*, 14–15.

7. Ibid., 52–53; Kaye, *Reinventing Anglicanism*, 246.

we are an institution-making species, and says that our institutions are not naturally alienating and mechanical.[8] Still, Kaye does not go very far in recognizing the goodness of this inescapable aspect of creation. Thus he ultimately recommends that Anglican churches ought to have a "radical non-commitment" to institutions.[9]

Having rejected rigid institutional order, Kaye argues that the Anglican Communion is held together by two moral virtues: persuasion and listening. Here the Cross is meant to do some hard work. Listening is a Christ-like virtue that helps us endure the sometimes-painful conflict involved in relating across the span of cultural differences.[10] But what kind of outcome does Kaye expect from this process? If persuasion has indeed occurred after prolonged listening, why should this not issue in commitments of common belief and action? Or is it that listening is the end itself, while actual agreement is only an incidental side-benefit (that is, that the Cross might be tied to listening though it has nothing to do with persuasion)? Kaye labels those who withdraw from the listening process as sectarians who can no longer cope with "strangers,"[11] but what if victims of coercion in the Church, be they conservative or liberal, believing that their Christ-like virtue is unpersuasive to their opponents, stop listening to their "victimizers"? Christ-like virtues, though not guaranteed mechanisms of persuasion, are intrinsically worthwhile, but can they be completely disconnected from consent and agreement? Of course not; the Cross is persuasive because it is freely undertaken out of love, not because it automatically affects an end. Yet it is clearly meant to persuade its listener to consent and submit to the boundaries of Christ's kingdom, the boundaries of his Body. Without these limits, virtues such as persuasion and listening risk being detached from the Cross altogether.

KOINONIA, CHANGE, AND DIVERSITY

The Cross sits uneasily in Kaye's system because of his disembodied understanding of *koinonia* (communion, participation, fellowship) in the Church. Let us look at his interpretation of 1 Corinthians 12 in which St

8. Kaye, *Reinventing Anglicanism*, 146.

9. Ibid., 248–49.

10. Kaye, *Conflict and the Practice of Christian Faith*, 135.

11. Kaye, *Reinventing Anglicanism*, 95.

Paul likens the Church to a Body of many interrelated parts. This image is an alright first attempt at describing the Church, says Kaye, but it is primarily a *static* snapshot opposed to the more *dynamic* ideal of love in chapter 13. Paul, we are told, explains this "more excellent way" as the active presence of God's love in the community, which continually reorders the Church:

> Paul does not settle a question of disorder or division with a form of order or an organizational structure. Rather he underlines the diversity of contribution by naming it as a gift from the risen Christ. He leaves open the full effect of that variety according to the core principle of love. Love is more abiding even than faith and hope, and it is certainly more fundamental than arrangements of order. This is extraordinarily high risk in group dynamic terms. In theological terms, it is a stunning assertion of confidence in the creative ordering of divine presence.[12]

Order, organic as it may be, is at odds with change and variety in Kaye's thought, and this despite the fact that organic order is normally seen to contain its own principle of motion and development. It is anything but static. For Kaye, on the other hand, the divine presence "creatively orders," but this is clearly not an organically developing order.

Kaye's notion of ecclesial unity relies on abstract moral qualities that reflect the ordered relations of the Trinity without any Christological, bodily mediation—a strange move since the virtues acquired by suffering are only gained in the body. Thus despite noting that the Trinity can be used "as a talisman for an ecclesiology already formed,"[13] Trinitarian *koinonia* and *perichoresis* (mutual indwelling) end up modeling the abstract liberal democratic virtues of "peace-making, pluralizing and persuading."[14] Without any explicit exegesis of scripture or the theological tradition Kaye boils down the doctrine of the Trinity in this way:

> Thus the doctrine of the Trinity speaks of wholeness and diversity, of faith as walking in trust, because there is yet openness. The doctrine speaks of an order of authority as gently persuasive, never complete and always yielding a contingent result. It speaks of argument as grounded in resonance, not shaped by logical rigidity. It is this character of this God that provides the confidence for

---

12. Kaye, *Conflict and the Practice of Christian Faith,* 16–17.

13. Kaye, *Reinventing Anglicanism,* 178.

14. Ibid., 126–27.

> Anglicans to believe, to act and to speak. For Anglicans this part of
> the theological tradition draws attention to the diverse and differ-
> ent ways in which God is present. In doing so it also draws atten-
> tion to the multifaceted character of the divine persuasion which
> draws people to God, and thus also to the nature of the confidence
> we have in believing and with which we persuade.[15]

This is a rather careless summary of Trinitarian theology, for the Trinity cannot be understood outside of the economy of Jesus' divine-human response to the Father. For, what in particular makes the three persons "diverse" but their unique way of interrelating as revealed in scripture? Simply making the Trinity a cipher for diversity does not tell us what diversity consists in. We will see with Thornton that the human body, specifically Jesus', will give us a better model of diversity.

In sum, Bruce Kaye's main worry with the Covenant is that it is over-ly rigid, impersonal, and, therefore, coercive. His alternative is problem-atic because its neglect of the created order (be it biological or cultural/institutional) cuts him off from a more productive way to approach the ecclesial problem of change, diversity, persuasion, and coercion.

REVELATION AND THE MODERN WORLD

The theology of Lionel Thornton is an alternative preferable to Kaye's for thinking about issues of change, diversity, persuasion, and coercion in the Church. Here I focus on Thornton's *Revelation and the Modern World,* in which he argues that the created order, inasmuch as it is taken up into the body of Jesus, is the basis for ecclesial order.

His main concern in this book is to deal with three related problems: the unity of revelation's form and content, a doctrine of creation in rela-tion to modern science, and a hermeneutic that unites critical science to traditional exegesis. Having earlier written well received books on the Incarnation, the Atonement, and on ecclesiology, this book, along with its two successors,[16] was not well understood in its time. However, renewed focus on the doctrine of nature and grace, the biblical hermeneutics

15. Ibid., 128.

16. The earlier works are *The Incarnate Lord, The Doctrine of the Atonement,* and *The Common Life in the Body of Christ.* The second and third volumes of *The Form of the Servant* are *The Dominion of Christ* and *Christ and the Church.*

coming from the *ressourcement* theologians, Russian émigré theology, and the theological interpretation movement make Thornton more understandable and relevant to our own time than, unfortunately, to his. Being under the influence of Greek and Latin patristic sources, these diverse contemporary theologies have reappropriated a concept of nature in which creation is seen to be most uniquely itself only in relation to a divinely intended supernatural end. In this way nature stands in an analogical relation to freely given grace such that the "things" that scriptural "words" refer to can also fittingly refer to Christ, their efficient and final cause.[17] This makes pre-modern figural exegesis with its multiple meanings look less ridiculous than it did to scholars of Thornton's day.

Thornton's approach is to say that revelation's divine content cannot be separated from the human form to and through which it comes.[18] Revelation comes to Israel and the Church, and in turn their response to revelation becomes a further medium through which it passes. Modern ways of dealing with the problem of revelation, says Thornton, have either reduced it to its human environment, which means human response overshadows revelation altogether, or dualistically separated it from its human context, as if revelation would sully itself by mixture with finite humanity. The former tendency is represented by philosophical materialists, while the latter includes the old Liberal biblical critics who wanted to "peel the onion" of scripture to isolate an ideal core of Christianity from all cultural forms. For Thornton, however, there can be no absolute division between revelation and the human response to it because Jesus is paradigmatically both the revelation of, and the response to, the Father. To treat revelation in a reductionist or dualistic way is to decide *a priori* that God is not triune. For, in Jesus' "Servant-Form," a phrase Thornton draws from the kenotic pattern of Philippians 2, the "lower" human nature is exalted and transfigured into revelation because of the divine's condescension to its organic limit.[19] This is possible because in the immanent Trinity the Son eternally responds to the Father before all worlds, which is the metaphysical basis for created forms, institutional orders, and persons to be taken up into Jesus' economic response. With Kaye, the three Persons of the Trinity are defined by an abstract relational principle

17. For example see Aquinas, ST 1a 1.10.

18. See Thornton, *Revelation and the Modern World*, I, v (19–23) for what follows. References are to chapter and section number, with page numbers in parentheses.

19. Ibid., p. x, and I, ii (6).

(diversity) that does not distinguish between them in any important way; in Thornton's work the Son's relationship to the Father gives a structure in which the Church's own response to God can be included.

Another dualism/reductionism related to the problem of revelation is that of modern society's attitude to nature. It begins, argues Thornton, with our modern notion of freedom, which, in rightly trying to escape coercion, becomes simply "freedom from control"—including God's control through the intrinsic order of his creation.[20] Free from that order humans either elevate themselves over nature as its masters, or, to the exclusion of any transcendent principle, reduce one another to mere *bits* of nature. The former option dominates creation, and the latter option leads to the idea that if people are just nature, and if nature is exploitable to humanity's interests, people can be exploited through the medium of nature, which is ironic given the original definition of freedom. Thus dualism and reductionism are reinforcing extremes.

CHRISTOLOGY: MICROCOSM AND MEDIATOR

Christianity offers two insights that challenge these tendencies and solves the problem of the relationship between revelation and creation. Firstly, it places humanity as the middle term between God and creation. We are neither reduced to, nor dominators of, creation, since we are supposed to be priestly mediators who, as microcosms of creation in humble identity with its order and elements (its "dust") bring it into a relation with God that elevates it beyond nature into the realm of grace. Secondly, Thornton shows how created order is a template for the kind of mutually dependent order found in scripture and the Church, all of which he together calls the three "organs" of revelation. This is because in humanity there is an "interpenetration" of creation and revelation by virtue of our priestly position in the cosmos.[21] The human *body* is central to this mediation, since it is through the body that creation's order is mediated back to God. The body is not just a part of creation, but a microcosm of the whole, which is simply to say that both the body and the cosmos share the same kind of organic rather than inorganic order, an order characterized by a mutual dependence of parts. In fulfilling Adam's vacant mediatorial role,

20. Ibid., IV, I (97).
21. Ibid., VI, ii (163–65).

the whole cosmos, its order and elements, were made to respond to the Father in Christ's body. And in responding, organic order as such became a medium of revelation. Jesus' reordered, unfallen body is, therefore, rightly called the "New Creation."[22] Further, the kind of order the cosmos and the body share became a sanctified template for the other organs of revelation, namely the Old and New Testament people of God, and the Bible, that written record of their response to God.

Kaye is also concerned to find the pattern of God's presence in creation's different cultural contexts in order to respond to the voice of God in them.[23] Yet in his work the voice and pattern are only vaguely described in terms of the Trinity. He is concerned that the Church respond to created individuals in different contexts, but for Thornton, responding to individuals must be a way of responding to the Father through the interdependent body of the Son. If the Holy Spirit has formed a pattern of mutual dependence in a culture that is analogically related to the New Creation of grace, that too can be taken into the Church. Otherwise creation must be called back to that pattern.

PERSONHOOD IN THE CHURCH

According to Thornton, because the Church is the Body of Christ it is also the New Creation. The kind of created order assumed and redeemed in Christ's body becomes the kind of order found in the redeemed community of persons. They too are one with creation through physical identity with it such that its order is taken up into the higher realm of personhood. Here an analogy to the "Form of the Servant" is instanced in the relationship of higher to lower in human anthropology, which is to say that the "person" elevates the body by submission to its limits.[24] The body is, then, the condition for personhood's manifestation, while personhood unifies and carries the body beyond itself. Having elevated created order, human persons carry that same order into relationships such that the order of persons in the social organism reflect the order of parts in creation generally, and in the body in particular. Yet because each part of the body has its own unique limits, without which it would be useless to

22. Ibid., VI, v (182–88).

23. Kaye, *Reinventing Anglicanism*, 131, 250.

24. Thornton, *Revelation and the Modern World*, X, iv (310–11).

the whole, so does the Body of the Church. The Covenant represents such an ecclesiology since each member must graciously restrain itself for the sake of the Communion.[25]

Reminiscent of Kaye's concern with listening, Thornton also explains that an "educational discipline"[26] is necessary among Christ's members because knowledge of other persons demands that we rightly dispose ourselves toward them in order to see their relation to the Body. Although personhood is apprehensible as a simple whole ("by faith" as it were), it has an element of inscrutability—the "Image of God"[27]—that can only be seen as a character unfolds over time. If not, the risk is "atomism."[28] On analogy to physics, which used to hold that atoms were exhaustively knowable in isolation from their relational frame, or to Liberal biblical science, which would collect "original facts" only to impose on them an external order supplied by the mind of the investigator, Thornton says that atomism occurs when persons are abstracted from the natural web of relations that give them depth.

This does not mean, as Kaye claims, that the natural, dynamic order found in a local culture's web of relations can simply be taken over by the Church through a process of enculturation. According to Thornton, the powers[29] that oppose Christ arise from disordered relations in the world, not from static order as such. Jesus' body is the pattern and goal to which all rearrangements are made, and rearrangement is always toward a greater discipline on behalf of the whole. Disordered cultures, then, must be called back to this order.

DIVERSITY AND CHANGE

This "discipline" might seem to squash diversity, but Thornton draws a metaphysical illustration from Leibniz to show how unity is the basis for diversity in Christ. For Leibniz creation is a unity not through any cross-connection of one part, or "monad," to another, but in relation to God's preordered harmony. In themselves, monads are shut up like "houses

---

25. See n.2.

26. Thornton, *Revelation and the Modern World*, V, iv (31–32).

27. Ibid., X, ii (301*f*), vi (323–25).

28. Ibid., II, vi (53).

29. "The spirit of the age," Ibid., III, iii (66).

with no windows," yet they microcosmically "reflect" the whole ordered web of relations ("the pre-ordained harmony") from their own unique position.[30] Outside of this order they have no particularity. Further, each unit in this organic order only affects the others indirectly through God's pre-ordained harmony. The analogy to our theological point is clear. Inasmuch as each member—and for Thornton this can refer to diverse cultures, national churches, or individuals—fulfills its function in Christ's Body and maintains its given "measure" and "proportion,"[31] it reflects him who is the preordained harmony, Jesus. Unity is not through cross-connections of human fellowship but directly to Christ, the "Whole."[32] Thus each part of the Body maintains an incommunicable aspect that is "inscrutable"[33] to other parts, their soul being perfectly knowable to God alone. This inscrutability, though a result of their self-limitation and *relational distance* from every other member, is precisely what allows them to image both God's inscrutability and his lowly self-communicating love, each in its own unique way. In other words, a foot cannot fully understand what it is like to be a hand, although it can benefit from the hand's service. Leibniz has the further insight that representation does not only go on at every different structural "level" of an organism, but at every "stage"[34] of its development as well, which should put to rest the worry that organic order is static. All this can be put in terms of "response:"[35] insofar as every (temporal or structural) member of the Body is capable of fulfilling its diverse kenotic function, that part can respond to God's will. But note that the equal ability to respond rests on diversity, and that diversity depends on unity.

PERSUASION AND COERCION, II: LIONEL THORNTON'S RESOLUTION

By ignoring the pre-ordained harmony, however, monads not only turn into atoms without particularity; they become entirely knowable and

---

30. Ibid., X, ii (299-300).
31. Ibid., VII, ii (231–33).
32. Ibid., IX, iii (270f).
33. Ibid., X, ii (300f), vi (325).
34. Ibid., X, iii (304f).
35. Ibid., X, iii (304).

controllable, which opens the door to coercion. The example Thornton uses is drawn from early modern physics, which proceeded as if it could control nature by imposing an external order on it so that the spheres of knowledge could become more and more specialized in search of an illusory, anthropocentric power: "For if the smaller the sphere of knowledge the narrower the corresponding range of knowledge becomes, then the greater the mastery in such a compass the less significant that mastery might actually be, and yet the more delusive in its apparent perfection!"[36] The greater the appearance of control over fully "scrutable" atoms,[37] the more obscured nature's own intrinsic order became because nature was reduced to the sum of its parts.

This can easily be applied to ecclesiology when spheres of denominational or provincial authority become smaller and smaller in an attempt to effectively respond to local cultures. Kaye thinks that relational distance caused by institutions is reduced the more locally dispersed and personal a church becomes, which, to return to an earlier point, suggests that there is a goal to the listening process: mutual understanding. Yet according to Thornton, relational distance can never be abolished even at the local level, since it is the basis for Christ-like mutual submission. Christians submit to one another out of an apophatic regard for the inscrutability of the other. For, "[t]he soul is known perfectly to God himself" because "human inscrutability corresponds to the divine image in man, the image which is common to all, yet unique to each individual."[38] Uniqueness is due to each person's internal perspective on the preordained harmony, though it is paradoxically manifest in an external mode to others by kenotically submitting to them. Because inscrutability cannot be abolished at the most proximate level, gracious restraint of the will must form the basis for interpersonal understanding, not vice-versa. So, if gracious restraint is necessary at the most proximate level, why not at the provincial level, too?

To sharpen the contrast, Kaye seems to advocate an approach that withholds consent of the will until mutual understanding is achieved. On Thornton's terms it is unsurprising that Kaye subtly subordinates persuasion to listening in an endlessly deferred search for understanding,

36. Ibid., III, viii (86).

37. See n.33.

38. Thornton, *Revelation and the Modern World*, X, ii (301).

because inscrutability cannot be abolished. Yet this does not prevent Thornton from advocating consent, for if understanding, persuasion, and listening are to happen at all, they must rest on prior volitional restraints. In short, consenting to discerned limits is how each member "responds" to the Father for the sake of Jesus' whole Body.[39] This is the simple ecclesiology represented by the Covenant. Its listening process is neither purposeless nor predetermined, for it is meant to facilitate each church's personal responsiveness to the Father given the limits particular to each provincial member. Kaye, however, has no clearly articulated goal for listening, yet his recommendation of personal responsiveness at the local level paradoxically presses toward a goal: scrutability. On his terms spatial and cultural distance make persons inscrutable such that global institutional orders become untenable, thus the quest for local scrutability. Here the risk of coercion arises through atomizing local churches away from the kenotically constraining frame of the whole Body, which opens the door to the imposition of external order and artificial agreements. Unconscious as it may be—and the more dangerous because unconscious—this is where Kaye's brand of congregationalism tends. For order and agreement must come from somewhere.

A GLOBAL ECCLESIOLOGY?

Thus we return to the question of how local theological particularities, on analogy to the Jewishness of Jesus, are received globally without coercion. Specifically, let us consider how there might be different local opinions on the local-global relation within the Anglican Communion. Chapter 3 of Kaye's *Conflict and the Practice of Christian Faith* outlines Australia's approach to Christian pluralism as one of Anglican disestablishment without, however, an absolute secularization of public space. Rather, state owned schools began to teach an inoffensive "non-dogmatic Christianity"[40] with particular denominations filling in the details on a different schedule. This seems to bear some resemblance to the departicularized global Anglicanism Kaye advocates. For him, the attempt to agree on provincial particulars would be futile, so the global must be generic. It may not be deliberate, but for the sake of argument suppose that Kaye

39. See n.35.
40. Kaye, *Conflict and the Practice of Christian Faith*, 60.

is proposing a normative ecclesiology based on a local Australian ideal. Why accept Australia's local tradition about how global relations must work? Are there other local proposals? How would we decide which locally proposed model ought to be received? This, after all, is one of the present arguments within Anglicanism, and it cannot be denied that what is at stake here is a conception of the local-global relation that will gain universal recognition. Yet if the Australian ideal goes global it compromises itself, for according to Kaye the only general claim that can tie the churches together is that of Christ's lordship rather than a universal concept defining the relationship of that lordship to the various localities. Such a concept would be too particular and it would demand too much from other particular localities. But then, the lordship signified by such concepts is not generic either.

The dilemma suggests that universal doctrinal ideals about ecclesial order are inescapable—something the Australian ideal is biased against. For neither doctrinal particularity nor the unique lordship of Christ signified by doctrine can stay at the local level. Rather, particularity must be deliberately embraced. Therefore just as Jesus the Jew became relevant to every local culture without sacrificing his own local culture—his Jewishness—there must be a way for local particularities to gain a global acceptance without being departicularized since that would be analogous to supercessionism.[41] But to escape a top-down imposition, these particularities would have to be discerned and received through common mechanisms of consent such as the Covenant recommends based on Anglican tradition. If, as with Kaye, the need for such mechanisms is not explicitly acknowledged, particular local doctrines could covertly replace the object of faith by obscuring the important distinction between doctrinal symbol and thing signified. But once the distinction between Christ and doctrine is recognized, doctrine can play a proper role. For the lordship of the living Jesus must be distinguished from any doctrine about the ordering of local cultures to that lordship, but the inseparability of the two must also be consciously admitted and dealt with through a common organic mechanism of consent. If not, the Australian ideal will edge out and replace Christ's lordship thus imposing uniformity on local

41. This would mean that having "broken out" of local culture, the general Gospel has also broken free of particularity and, therefore, diversity, for the diverse must be particular. But if the Gospel is not particular, then it is not diverse, that is, different, from any particular local culture.

diversity against Kaye's intention. The drive to smaller spheres of ecclesial control, therefore, risks enslaving the churches to an unconscious top-down ordering, which in this case is Kaye's local Australian ecclesiology or something like it.

CONCLUSIONS

Bruce Kaye's system suffers because he is not able to incorporate creation's order into the Church via the body of Christ, whose eternal response to the Father is the basis for the Church's own consenting response. According to Thornton, the Church's members participate in this response by disciplining themselves to submit to their particular limit in the Body for the good of the whole. The particularity of each member depends on unity, for personhood derives from the unique position occupied in the organic frame of relations. This frame is not static, but dynamically includes a temporal depth.

In keeping with this temporal aspect each member must also submit to an educational discipline to discern the Church's intrinsic order reflected in every other member, which is where the cruciform virtues of listening and persuasion enter. Unlike Kaye, however, who seems to eschew a goal for the listening process, Thornton has a clear end for listening: a common understanding that rests on a prior submission of will to a common order. Thornton takes seriously the inscrutability of the human person, and by extension the local church, for the inscrutability of the part is inseparable from its reflection of the whole. Kaye breaks these up, which is why he oscillates from an endless listening process to the atomization of local churches in an attempt to gain some scrutability. Unfortunately atomization abstracts from created order, inevitably "coercing" atoms into a new, external frame. For Kaye, this may be something like a local Australian doctrine of ecclesial order, which in anathematizing a global mechanism for discerning ecclesial order, can only be globalized by unconscious (or worse, conscious) imposition. This shows the necessity of having a global mechanism if coercion is to be avoided. For a local particularity to become universally relevant to the whole Church, a process of consent is necessary. Even when Christ "broke out" of his local Jewish context to become universal—and it must be stressed that this implies no departicularization—this was through a process of consent to the Father.

A further problem for Kaye is that a personal response to Christ does not adequately differentiate the parts of Christ's Body, since the response of one Christian to Christ says nothing of that person's response to other Christians; their relation to Christ does not distinguish them from one another. That could only be the case if Thornton is right about Christ being the Whole in which they are parts—parts that have kenotic limits and kenotic restraints. Because kenosis is the distinguishing mark of an organic ecclesiology, the non-coercive restrains and consequences in the Covenant will feel coercive only to "disembodied" persons and churches who do not want to be embodied in a kenotic and organic social order.

BIBLIOGRAPHY

Gilson, Etienne. *From Aristotle to Darwin and Back Again: A Journey in Final Causality, Species and Evolution.* London: Sheed & Ward, 1984.

Kaye, Bruce Norman. *Reinventing Anglicanism: A Vision of Confidence, Community, and Engagement in Anglican Christianity.* Adelaide: Openbook, 2003.

———. *Conflict and the Practice of Christian Faith: The Anglican Experiment.* Eugene, OR: Cascade Books, 2009.

Thornton, Lionel S. *The Common Life in the Body of Christ.* Westminster: Dacre, 1942.

———. *The Doctrine of the Atonement.* London: John Heritage, 1937.

———. *The Form of the Servant*, Vol. I, *Revelation and the Modern World.* Westminster: Dacre Press, 1950.

———. *The Form of the Servant*, Vol. II, *The Dominion of Christ.* Westminster: Dacre, 1952.

———. *The Form of the Servant*, Vol. III, *Christ and the Church.* Westminster: Dacre, 1956.

———. *The Incarnate Lord: An Essay Concerning the Doctrine of the Incarnation in Its Relation to Organic Conceptions.* London: Longmans, Green, 1928.

5

Rowan Williams, Fyodor Dostoevsky, and the Future of the Anglican Communion

Ecclesiological Reflections on
Dostoevsky: Language, Faith, and Fiction

N. J. A. HUMPHREY

INTRODUCTION:
WHAT HATH ST. PETERSBURG TO DO WITH CANTERBURY?

IN 2007, WHILE ROWAN Williams was on sabbatical from his duties as Archbishop of Canterbury, he was a guest of the Jesuit community of Georgetown University in Washington, D.C., with which he has had a longstanding connection. During this time, he wrote *Dostoevsky: Language, Faith, and Fiction*. In advance of the 2008 Lambeth Conference, a book about the works of a nineteenth century Russian novelist was viewed by some as a pleasant scholarly diversion from the burdens of ecclesiastical office. Indeed, in an article in *Time Magazine*, David van Biema and Catherine Mayer described Williams as "now engaged in a little light recreation, working on a book about Fyodor Dostoevsky at

98

Georgetown University in Washington."[1] Perhaps this was intended to be tongue-in-cheek, or perhaps not. Either way, the book Williams produced in his "light recreation" is profoundly relevant to the current crisis in the Anglican Communion, and illuminates why Rowan Williams has come out so strongly in favor of the proposed Anglican Covenant.

On one level, *Dostoevsky* is an incisive piece of literary criticism that can be read as just that: one careful scholar's well-researched thoughts on Dostoevsky and an important contribution to Russian Studies in general. Nevertheless, I suspect that the context which helped bring this book into being was bound up with Rowan Williams's role as an archbishop in a church in conflict. I believe that the questions raised by reading Dostoevsky intrigue Williams not only on their own terms, but because they are important questions to address within his own context as a church leader.

In this essay, I will read *Dostoevsky* as an extended theological reflection on how one might imagine the life of faith within a fallen world and, more specifically, within a church—or communion of churches—that does not live up to one's hopes and dreams. I believe that examining how the archbishop reads Dostoevsky helps us understand his steadfast support for the Anglican Covenant. Thus, in this essay, I will use Williams's book on Dostoevsky as a heuristic, while also drawing on some of the archbishop's other writings and public statements to exegete both Williams's reading of Dostoevsky and how that reading explains his support for the Anglican Covenant. I hope thereby to illuminate what Williams thinks the Covenant is, what he thinks it is good for, and why he thinks the Anglican Communion would do well to adopt it.

The general argument of this essay may be summed up in six points: First, Williams sees in Dostoevsky a certain notion of language. Second, this notion of language is bound to a particular ethic of engagement with the other. Third, this ethic is best understood in terms of *kenosis*, that is, Christ-like self-emptying, through which each participant becomes comprehensible as a gift to the other. Fourth, this ethic functions best when it is *mutually* kenotic, as this leads to mutual conversion to Christ. Fifth, the Covenant allows us to embody, as a communion of churches, the ethically-laden vision of kenotic engagement found in Williams's reading of Dostoevsky. And sixth, Williams's support for the Anglican

---

1. Van Biema and Mayer, "Saving Grace," no pages.

Covenant is not ultimately bound to whether or not outcomes follow-ing from the Covenant are "successful" by any human standards. Rather, embodying this ethic of kenotic engagement with the other is worthwhile and vocationally central to our identity as Christians, even if it is not mu-tually reciprocated. In Biblical terms, we are not only to do unto others as others do unto us, but we are to love others as Christ loves us, regard-less of whether others love us in return or not. The Anglican Covenant is worth supporting because it is our duty as Christians to speak, listen, and act kenotically, with God's help, in as Christ-like a manner as possible. This ethic is not simply ecclesiological, but missional, eschatological, and soteriological; its importance surpasses our various perspectives and con-texts, and impels us to look beyond the immediate, visible impact that our language or actions may have on any particular "other," whether that "other" is from "within" or "without."

DOSTOEVSKY, LANGUAGE, ECCLESIOLOGY

Williams provides the ecclesiologically-attuned reader with ample mate-rial from the very first page of *Dostoevsky* when he writes that Dostoevsky's "novels ask us, in effect, whether we can imagine a human community of language and feeling in which, even if we were incapable of fully real-izing it, we knew what was due to each other; whether we could imagine living in the consciousness of a solidity or depth in each other which no amount of failure, suffering, or desolation could eradicate."[2] Statements like this give the ecclesiological reader ample hope to find insights in this study that are pregnant with implications for the future of Anglicanism. I believe it fair to say that Williams values the Anglican Covenant because he sees it as an exercise in articulating what, as Christians in communion, we owe to each other. It is an experiment in imagining a community with "solidity" and "depth," one so grounded in communion that "no amount of failure, suffering, or desolation could eradicate" it. And, in the arch-bishop's view, such an enterprise must also be deeply cognizant of all the ways in which human beings *fail* to render what is "due to each other."

But what is it that we owe to each other? The answer that Williams gives, lavishly illustrated from Dostoevsky's works, is that human beings owe it to each other to remain in conversation. It is only through ongoing

2. Williams, *Dostoevsky*, 1.

conversation that authentic, committed, and meaningful community is made possible. However, while conversation creates the *possibility* of community, *communion* is only possible when people use language responsibly so that they recognize their essential, God-given interdependence. Williams writes that "Dostoevsky in effect argues that this necessity of saying what is recognizable is finally grounded in the order established by a creator: recognition is possible because we are all at the most basic level of our being made to resonate with the interdependent life of a universe that is addressed and sustained by a Word from God. Our problem—if we believe this—is how to live so as to allow that resonance to shape what we say and do."[3] Along the same lines, in his February 2010 General Synod Presidential Address, Williams stated, "I make no apology . . . for pleading that we try, through the Covenant, to discover an ecclesial fellowship in which we trust each other to act for our good—an essential feature of anything that might be called a theology of the Body of Christ."[4] The trust for which the *primus inter pares* of the Anglican Communion pleads can only be established and maintained if Anglicans remain engaged with one another through the use of a shared language, or as Williams himself put it in a significant address at the 1998 Lambeth Conference, a shared "grammar of obedience."[5]

Dostoevsky offers particular insight into the archbishop's understanding of language as a "grammar of obedience." Williams writes that Dostoevsky "sees language itself as the indisputable marker of freedom: confronted with what seeks to close down exchange or conflict, we discover we can always say more. This is emphatically and evidently a liberty that *depends* on otherness."[6] Likewise, the Anglican Covenant is important to the future of the Anglican Communion because it enshrines the sort of linguistic engagement that is dependent on otherness. Williams's challenge to those of us on either side of any conflict is to remain engaged, because it is only through such engagement that we learn what it means to love each other as Christ loves us, and are thereby better equipped to witness to that Love to a world that is truly "other" and in need of Christ's saving embrace. In other words, it is only through such engagement that

3. Ibid., 12.

4. Williams, "Presidential Address, General Synod February 2010," no pages.

5. Williams, "Making Moral Decisions," 11.

6. Williams, *Dostoevsky*, 11.

we are able to speak, listen, and act in a truly Christ-like way in the church and in the world. Our "grammar of obedience" thus frees us to be missional, *despite* and *in the midst of* our conflicts. In this view, the Anglican Covenant is not merely a tool for managing or resolving conflict—though it is clearly intended to function in such a manner wherever possible—but a vehicle for translating the language of engagement into the language of mission.

RESPONSIBLE TO AND FOR THE OTHER

At the end of 2009, shortly after the final text of the proposed Anglican Covenant was released to the provinces of the Anglican Communion, a video was posted on the Archbishop of Canterbury's website. Sitting in front of a fireplace, the archbishop explained that he supports the Covenant because it addresses a "need to build relationships," and more specifically, the Communion's "need to have a sense that we are responsible to one another and responsible for each other. In other words, what we need is something that will help us know where we stand together, and help us also intensify our fellowship and our trust."[7] The phrase that Williams uses, "responsible to one another and responsible for each other" is distinctly reminiscent of Father Zosima's famous dictum in *The Brothers Karamozov* that we are "responsible for all."[8] In commending the proposed Anglican Covenant to the provinces of the Communion, does Williams mean the same thing by "responsibility" as he understands Dostoevsky to mean by it? This question requires us to take a closer look at what Williams writes about Dostoevsky's understanding of responsibility.

Chapter 4 of *Dostoevsky* is entitled "Exchanging Crosses: Responsibility for All," and in it Williams traces the theme of responsibility through Dostoevsky's writings, particularly *Crime and Punishment* and *The Brothers Karamozov*. In his treatment of this theme as it is displayed in the character of Zosima and others, Williams notes, "There are several meanings given to 'taking responsibility for all.'"[9] From an ecclesiological standpoint, one meaning in particular is key: Williams maintains that

7. Williams, "A message from the Archbishop of Canterbury on the Anglican Communion Covenant," no pages.

8. Dostoevsky, *The Brothers Karamozov*, Book IV, Chapter 1, 320.

9. Williams, *Dostoevsky*, 164.

Dostoevsky's use of the "language of responsibility" leads to "the conviction that there is no circumstance in which it is either impossible or useless to seek whatever action or involvement one can that will give space or time to the other for his, her, or its flourishing before God."[10] Likewise, the commitments entailed by the Anglican Covenant would clearly be lived out over time, particularly in times of conflict. To commit to the Covenant is to recognize that it is never "impossible or useless" to take the "space or time" necessary in order to seek another's "flourishing before God." Such an undertaking does not guarantee any reconciliation or resolution to the conflicts in which we embroil ourselves, but it is a commitment nonetheless to engage with each other despite the possibility, and indeed, the likelihood, of failure—or at least of failure as we would judge it.

But if the Covenant does not provide a guaranteed mechanism for conflict resolution or for "success" as we would measure it, what good is it? From the archbishop's point of view, the Covenant is simply one more means available to the churches of the Anglican Communion to engage in what he has elsewhere termed "commitment without evasion."[11] It is commitment, and the dialogue that flows from such commitment, that interests the archbishop.

Commitment is foundational to responsibility, and according to Williams, responsibility is essentially dialogical—or, to use a Hegelian term Williams also deploys, "dialectical."[12] Williams asserts that in Dostoevsky's understanding, the "point" of "dialectical negation is the *recognition* of self in the other . . . In the simplest terms, it means that the self remains a locus of feeling and thought, and specifically of love."[13] Dostoevsky's conception of dialectic is fundamentally dialogical because it gives itself up to love of the other. Those who engage in true Dostoevskian dialogue, as opposed to pure Hegelian dialectic, need not fear being swallowed up in any irresistible, impersonal machinations. Without love, *true* dialogue cannot even begin. Williams writes, "Responsibility is a bracketing and

10. Ibid., 169.

11. This phrase is taken from Williams, "Trinity and Ontology," 87.

12. Many authors have undertaken assessments and critiques of the influence of Hegel on Rowan Williams. Of these, a sampling may be found in the following: Hobson, "Rowan Williams as Anglican Hegelian"; Russell, "Dispossession and negotiation: Rowan Williams on Hegel and political theology"; and Raven, *Shadow Gospel*.

13. Williams, *Dostoevsky*, 174 and endnotes.

quieting of the self's agenda for the sake of another voice."[14] This "quieting . . . for the sake of another" is at the heart of Williams's ethic of kenotic love, as we shall see in greater detail below.

Further on in Chapter 4, Williams describes at length the relationship between responsibility and dialogue that is truly other-centered. Williams writes,

> Developing an identity in the processes of converse and exchange is not a different thing from taking responsibility for all. What happens in the apparently radical assault on the ego . . . is, it seems, inseparably bound up with the linguistic task of hearing and articulating, voicing, the other; it is about letting one's own voice be molded by that encounter, silenced in its own uncritical or pre-critical confidence so that the exchange is real—a matter neither of treating the other as the peg on which to hang preprepared ideas and ego-centered concerns, nor of abandoning one's own voice in abjection before the other, but of discovering what the other can say in one's own voice, and what one can say in the other's voice. In that mutual displacement, something new enters the moral situation, and both speakers are given more room to be who they are, to learn or grow by means of this discovery of "themselves outside themselves."[15]

In sum: Being responsible to each other requires a commitment to engage with one another, and engagement is the *modus operandi* of lived responsibility. Indeed, Williams pointedly notes that the Russian word for "engagement" may also be translated as "communion."[16] Similarly, in his February 2010 General Synod Presidential Address, Williams states, "The Covenant specifically encourages and envisages protracted engagement and scrutiny and listening in situations of tension, and that is one of the things that makes it, in my view, worth supporting."[17] The question for both Williams and Dostoevsky is not whether we *ought* to live responsibly, but *how* to live responsibly, that is, in a way that is accountable to God and to each other through Christ.

14. Ibid., 172.
15. Ibid., 174.
16. Ibid., 133.
17. Williams, "Presidential Address, General Synod February 2010," no pages.

KENOSIS, GIFT, AND RECOGNIZABILITY

Williams stresses that Dostoevsky's approach to living out responsible dialogue is not easy, noting that "although Dostoevsky does not directly quote the biblical injunction to 'carry each other's burdens' (Gal 6:2), his concept of responsibility is almost unimaginable without the theological underpinning of a model of corporate life in which the basic image was to do with the sharing and exchange of suffering."[18] Likewise, in Williams's view, the "model of corporate life" enshrined in the Anglican Covenant is precisely intended to allow for a greater sharing of "each other's burdens" in a responsible and loving manner, for most importantly, responsible dialogue is grounded in love.[19] Williams elucidates this point when he writes, "Love for the freedom of the neighbor is inevitably love that looks critically at its own definition of freedom. The neighbor's freedom cannot be loved if one's own is exalted over all other priorities; so to love freedom in others, actual or potential freedom, is to embark on a process of decentering the self (a better phrase than 'emptying' or 'denying' the self)."[20] From this perspective, to "love your neighbor as yourself" is to take seriously the impact and consequences, intended and unintended, of the exercise of one's own freedom on the ability of the other to exercise his or her freedom. This is a difficult consciousness to maintain, and should not be used as an excuse for inaction; the intent is not to paralyze but to clarify, insofar as possible, how freedom and mutuality, independence and interdependence, are inseparably related. Williams adds that "the

18. Williams, *Dostoevsky*, 181.

19. To cite but one recent instance of the archbishop's linking of the Covenant to the task of sharing each others' burdens in Christ-like love, the structure of the 2011 "Archbishop's Advent letter to Anglican Primates" frames his argument in support of the adoption of the Anglican Covenant within the context of a review of the ways the provinces of the Anglican Communion have attempted to support each other in their various sufferings, thus modeling the archbishop's approach to how Anglican corporate life is to be lived out, and implicitly linking that model to his support for the Covenant. In paragraph 7 of that letter, Williams writes, "In spite of many assurances, some Anglicans evidently still think that the Covenant changes the structure of our Communion or that it gives some sort of absolute power of 'excommunication' to some undemocratic or unrepresentative body. With all respect to those who have raised these concerns, I must repeat that I do not see the Covenant in this light at all. It sets out an understanding of our common life and common faith and in the light of that proposes making a mutual promise to consult and attend to each other, freely undertaken." (Williams, "Archbishop's Advent Letter," 3.)

20. Williams, *Dostoevsky*, 183.

conversion of the individual to self-renewal occurs when something of that divine decentering breaks through."[21]

If this sensitivity to, and genuine love for, the freedom of the other ultimately requires a "decentering of the self," what does this "decentering" entail? Despite Williams's stated preference above for the term "decentering" over "emptying," the latter term has greater resonance with the traditional language of Christology, drawn as it is from Philippians 2:5–11, in which Paul writes that Christ "emptied himself" in the Incarnation. The theme of decentering the self for the sake of the other that Williams finds in the novels of Dostoevsky has its roots in Orthodox monastic understandings of *kenosis*, or self-emptying.[22] But *Dostoevsky* is not the archbishop's first engagement with this Orthodox moral vision; years before his elevation to the See of Canterbury, Williams brought this understanding of *kenosis* to bear upon Anglican discourse.

At the Lambeth Conference of 1998, while still Bishop of Monmouth in the Anglican province of the Church in Wales, Williams delivered an address "on making moral decisions" to a plenary session of the assembled bishops.[23] This address in many ways outlines the themes that Williams was to explore in greater depth nine years later in *Dostoevsky* on the eve of the Lambeth Conference of 2008. Near the end of this address, Williams stated simply that "Christian unity is 'Christ-shaped' or it is empty."[24] While Williams does not specifically define "Christ-shaped" here, earlier in the address he gives some very definite indications of what this term might mean when he writes of "the God of self-emptying"[25] and "the self-emptying of God in Christ."[26] We imitate the self-emptying action of Christ when our actions manifest "the completely costly directedness to the other that is shown in God's act in Christ."[27] Thus, if the essence of a

21. Ibid.

22. For an in-depth examination of the influence of the Orthodox monastic tradition of *kenosis* from the eleventh through the nineteenth centuries on Dostoevsky's thought, see in particular Ziolkowski, "Dostoevsky and the Kenotic Tradition."

23. "Address at Lambeth Plenary on making moral decisions." This address was later re-published as "Making moral decisions" in the *Cambridge Companion to Christian Ethics*. Citations to page numbers in this essay are to the version published in the *Cambridge Companion*.

24. Williams, "Making Moral Decisions," 13.

25. Ibid., 7.

26. Ibid., 8.

27. Ibid., 7.

Christ-shaped life is self-emptying, one could re-state Williams's assertion as "Christian unity is self-emptying or it is simply empty." This interpretation is certainly consistent with Williams's view of the purpose of the Anglican Covenant as a way for the Anglican Communion to engage in "Christ-shaped" or "self-emptying" moral decision-making.

Williams argues, in essence, that *kenosis* is central to making room for the other so that engagement may be both possible and productive. As Williams writes in *Dostoevsky*, "when we have nothing with which to engage, we stop speaking and stop developing. It is in one sense true that we can say what we like; in another sense, manifestly not true, since we are performing linguistically within a world in which we have to make ourselves recognizable to other speakers, as they are to us."[28] We must be speaking the same language, or, as Williams writes elsewhere in *Dostoevsky*, "The absolute necessity for *recognition*" means that "speech may be free but it needs to be *hearable*—otherwise it fails finally to be language at all. And I as speaker need to acquire the skills to listen or my response will be no response."[29]

Likewise, in "Making moral decisions," Williams writes, "The model of action which actively promotes the good of the other . . . and which reflects the self-emptying of God in Christ, presupposes that every action of the believer is in some sense designed as a gift to the Body."[30] But in order for any action to be received as a gift, it must "be the sort of thing that can be received, the sort of thing it makes sense to receive; something recognisable within the symbolic economy of the community, that speaks the language of the community. In the Christian context, what this means is that an action offered as gift to the life of the Body must be recognisable as an action that in some way or another manifests the character of the God who has called the community."[31] In order to recognize something as a gift, we first have to recognize that we are speaking the same language of faith, and in order to recognize that we are speaking the same language of faith, we need to be able to recognize in that language the "character of the God who has called the community," which is manifested above all in the "self-emptying of God in Christ."

28. Williams, *Dostoevsky*, 11.

29. Ibid., 134.

30. Williams, "Making Moral Decisions," 8.

31. Ibid.

Further on, Williams states that "if I am serious about making a gift of what I do to the Body as a whole, I have to struggle to make sense of my decision in terms of the common language of the faith, to demonstrate why this might be a way of speaking the language of the historic schema of Christian belief. This involves the processes of self-criticism and self-questioning in the presence of scripture and tradition, as well as engagement with the wider community of believers."[32] There is here an implied *accountability* that the speaker has, not only to sources of authority such as scripture and tradition, but to the communities to which the speaker's words are addressed. At the end of this Address, Williams describes engagement with mutual accountability as a "staying alongside"[33] and explains that this engagement "implies that the most profound service we can do for each other is to point to Christ."[34]

It is clear from what Williams has said and written about the Anglican Covenant quoted elsewhere in this essay that he believes the Covenant makes it more likely (though by no means guaranteed) for all parties in a conflict to speak to each other in ways that the other parties can hear. The Covenant plays an important role in this process of recognizability through kenotic engagement because, as Williams writes in *Dostoevsky*, "What we cannot do is to think as though the terms of our moral commitment could be revised when things get difficult."[35] But as things stand now, without anything like the Anglican Covenant, there simply are no clearly defined, agreed-upon terms for *any* common moral commitment, and thus, when things get difficult, there aren't even any terms to be revised.[36] The Anglican Covenant provides a foundation of common commitment through which we are able to speak and listen to each other.

32. Ibid., 13.

33. Ibid., 14.

34. Ibid.

35. Williams, *Dostoevsky*, 242.

36. As Williams writes in paragraph 7 of his 2011 Advent Letter, "I continue to ask what alternatives [to the proposed Anglican Covenant] there are if we want to agree on ways of limiting damage, managing conflict and facing with honesty the actual effects of greater disunity. In the absence of such alternatives, I must continue to commend the Covenant as strongly as I can to all who are considering its future" (Williams, "Archbishop's Advent Letter," 3).

Of course, Williams is not naïve enough to think that the Anglican Covenant would *guarantee* that all parties listen and hear each other. As he writes in *Dostoevsky*,

> The fact that Christian faith regards a particular human narrative as basic allows us to think that the processes of choice and self-definition that impose themselves on human agents may be not just open in a general way to grace or hope, but effective enactments of divine purpose. Yet that divine purpose does not lend itself to being "narrated" in a way that would foreclose the possibilities of failure or cost. What the perspective of God's purpose contributes is the conviction that there is something that makes it worthwhile *continuing* the narration—and thus the processes of self-defining which narrative works with—because divine purpose cannot be extinguished even if it can be defeated in any one measurable time span.[37]

Applied to our current ecclesiological situation, these words amount to an argument on Williams's part that the Anglican Covenant is worthwhile even if it leads to failure "in any one measurable time span" because there is always the possibility for re-engagement, a possibility that remains open by God's eternal grace despite our temporal—and ultimately temporary—failures. For ultimately, "Christ is, within history, the possibility for us of a future without fear of the other, an assurance that within other and more conflicted dialogues there is still the potential for life."[38] The Anglican Covenant holds out the potential that through it and by God's grace, we can overcome our perpetual "fear of the other" and find abundant new life in Christ. But we can only do this if we use the Anglican Covenant to keep us "staying alongside" one another.

CONCLUSION: THE ANGLICAN COVENANT AS A CHALLENGE TO DEEPER DISCIPLESHIP IN COMMUNION

The archbishop's support for the Anglican Covenant is grounded in his conviction that the Covenant, when used correctly, will enable greater communication, engagement, and mutual accountability in the Anglican Communion. The challenge, of course, is learning how to use

37. Williams, *Dostoevsky*, 59.
38. Ibid., 139.

the Covenant well. All written texts are subject to misinterpretation and abuse, whether intentionally or unintentionally. And in times of conflict, the likelihood that a text such as the Anglican Covenant will be used with charity and mutual trust by all concerned is, admittedly, not very high. The Archbishop of Canterbury appears to understand that there are no guarantees, yet he supports adopting the Anglican Covenant nonetheless. I believe this is because his support is not grounded in any confidence in the Covenant's ultimate pragmatic utility—though he clearly hopes it has some—but because it embodies an ethic that is foundationally Christ-centered.

From this perspective, the Anglican Covenant is a challenge to deeper discipleship in Communion with each other. This challenge entails unwavering commitment to the other, regardless of the other's commitment to us, and a willingness to stay alongside the other, even when the other does not want (or is for any reason unable) to stay alongside us. In short, it is a challenge to be as faithful to the other as God in Christ is faithful to us.[39] Faithfulness is most obviously satisfying and functional when it is *mutual*, but faithfulness does not necessarily *begin* with mutuality. It is perfectly possible to be *unilaterally faithful* to an unfaithful other, simply for the love that one bears the other. Such faithfulness is fraught with tension and can easily lead to unhealthy, dysfunctional, and abusive responses from the other to whom one is faithful. Jesus Christ certainly found this to be true of those who betrayed and crucified him. But the mystery of the Christian faith invites us to embrace freely that same kenotic engagement with the other that Christ embraced when he was crucified, because through that embrace the chords of estrangement and death are by God's sovereign grace broken, and we are thereby made partakers of Christ's resurrection life, both in the here-and-now and in the world to come. The movement from estrangement to engagement, and from engagement to deeper discipleship in communion is, at least in part, what Rowan Williams means when he asks us, through the novels of Dostoevsky, "whether we can imagine a human community of language and feeling in which, even if we were incapable of fully realizing it, we knew what was due to each other; whether we can imagine living in the

---

39. Notice the standard is *not* that we are to be as faithful to the other as the *other* is to us, but as *Christ* is to us.

consciousness of a solidity or depth in each other which no amount of failure, suffering, or desolation could eradicate."[40]

This is not to say that the Anglican Covenant would help us *accomplish* such a human community or consciousness. I for one believe we are not only "incapable of fully realizing it" but that we are incapable of realizing this vision at all—at least, not on our own. We desperately stand in need of the grace of God, without which all the human covenants in the world are not even worth the paper on which they are printed, no matter how laden they are with piety or good theology. But the Anglican Covenant is worth adopting because it reflects the best aspirations of a people who recognize that they have been called by God into communion with God and each other through Christ, and it reflects a confidence—a "reasonable hope"—in the abundant willingness of God to pour out unceasing grace upon those who *do* desire to live in communion with each other in Christ.

One thing that blocks us from receiving—or even asking—for that grace of communion is our lack of trust in the other. Conflict has a toxic effect in that it erodes our trust in each other, and when people stop trusting each other, they more often than not stop trusting that God will provide healing and reconciling grace. Any talk of "kenosis" or "trust" or "accountability" in such a toxic situation is likely to be met with suspicion that one side is really trying to manipulate the other into making all the sacrifices while that side holds on to the power—if neither the kingdom nor the glory. While this suspicion may in fact turn out to be *true*, that one side or the other *is* being manipulated (or, worse, attempting itself to manipulate) through a false or insufficiently Christ-like engagement, the corrective is usually found in turning the challenge we present to the other back on ourselves. If we require "sacrifice" or "restraint" or "accountability" of the other, how much sacrifice or restraint or accountability are we willing and able to muster on our own part? The fact of the matter is that while Christ-like speech and acts are what we all aspire to, and by God's grace at the best of times are what we engage in, we remain fallen and broken, incomplete and finite creatures, whose motives, conscious and unconscious, will almost always be mixed, if not downright tainted, by ungodly desires for power and control.

40. Williams, *Dostoevsky*, 1.

Under such circumstances, one could justifiably ask what motivation anyone would have to risk the sort of difficult engagement with the other that Williams and Dostoevsky, in their own ways, advocate—particularly if one is convinced of the truth or justice of one's own favored position. Williams's answer is actually quite simple and straightforward: to engage with the other is to imitate Christ. This simple and straightforward answer, however, has no obvious theological or political trajectory. Imitating Christ is neither "traditionalist" nor "progressive," neither "liberal" nor "conservative." Imitating Christ is simply loving, even when there is no obvious reason to love, nor any realistic hope that one's love will make any difference. None of this is to say that one does not, in fact, hold correct, orthodox, or just views apart from one's engagement with the other; nor is this to concede that one's opponent in any given conflict is not in fact fundamentally or even dangerously wrong. Rather, from the perspective of this ethic of kenosis, the other person's wrongness actually constitutes an *obligation* to engage, not so that "they" can be converted by "us," but so that *we both* can be converted by *God*. More challenging is the question of whether, in our own brokenness, we will be able to *recognize* God's grace at work in the other, particularly if it does not occur according to our preconceived notions or along our preferred timelines. Without the humility born of kenosis, we will not see God's presence in the other, nor will we even think to look for it.

When the final text of the Anglican Covenant was released to the provinces, the archbishop recognized that the Anglican Communion would never be conflict-free. Williams specifically noted that the Covenant is "a practical, sensible and Christian way of dealing with our conflicts, recognising that they're always going to be there."[41] The archbishop does not regard the Covenant as a tool for conflict resolution so much as an invitation to responsible relationship, within which reconciliation might, by God's grace, be made possible, but is by no means guaranteed. Should the Covenant be used to accomplish conflict resolution, this will be well and good. But the point of having a Covenant in the first place is not for *what it does* (or prevents others from doing), but for *what it challenges us to be*. And what does it challenge us to be? Better Anglicans? One might hope. Loving Christians? Most definitely. In the end, if one claims to abide by the Anglican Covenant but is unrecognizable as one who speaks the

41. Williams, "A Message from the Archbishop of Canterbury on the Anglican Communion Covenant," no pages.

language of Christian love, one has failed the challenge—and the opportunity—that the Anglican Covenant presents. The challenge the Anglican Covenant presents is well worth taking up, wherever one stands on the issues of the day, because at the end of the day, the challenge is to become what we all claim to be motivated by: the call to be faithful to the radical demands of the Gospel in our words and in our deeds, in a way that draws the world into the loving arms of Jesus.

BIBLIOGRAPHY

Dostoevsky, Fyodor. *The Brothers Karamazov*. Translated by Richard Pevear and Larissa Volokhonsky. New York: Vintage, 1990.

Hobson, Theo. "Rowan Williams as Anglican Hegelian." *Reviews in Religion and Theology* 12 (April 2005) 290–97.

Raven, Charles. *Shadow Gospel: Rowan Williams and the Anglican Communion Crisis*. London: Latimer Trust, 2010.

Russell, Matheson. "Dispossession and negotiation: Rowan Williams on Hegel and political theology." In *On Rowan Williams: Critical Essays*, edited by Matheson Russell, 85–114. Eugene, OR: Cascade Books, 2008.

Van Biema, David and Catherine Mayer. "Saving Grace." *Time Magazine* (June 7, 2007). Online: http://www.time.com/time/magazine/article/0,9171,1630227-3,00.html. No pages.

Williams, Rowan. "Trinity and Ontology." In *Christ, Ethics and Tragedy: Essays in Honour of Donald MacKinnon*, edited by Kenneth Surin, 71–92. Cambridge: Cambridge University Press, 1989.

———. "Address at Lambeth Plenary on making moral decisions - July 22, 1998." Online: http://www.lambethconference.org/1998/news/lc035.cfm. No pages. 1998.

———. "Making Moral Decisions." In *The Cambridge Companion to Christian Ethics*, edited by Robin Gill, 3–15. Cambridge: Cambridge University Press, 2001.

———. *Dostoevsky: Language, Faith, and Fiction*. Baylor, TX: Baylor University Press, 2008.

———. "A message from the Archbishop of Canterbury on the Anglican Communion Covenant." Online: http://www.archbishopofcanterbury.org/articles.php/1504/a-message-from-the-archbishop-of-canterbury-on-the-anglican-communion-covenant. No pages. 2009.

———. "Presidential Address, General Synod February 2010." Online: http://www.archbishopofcanterbury.org/articles.php/590/the-archbishops-presidential-address-general-synod-february-2010. No pages. 2010.

———. "Archbishop's Advent Letter to Anglican Primates." Online: http://www.archbishopofcanterbury.org/canterbury//data/files/resources/2268/Advent-letter-Abp-Primates-291111.pdf, 1–4. 2011.

Ziolkowski, Margaret, "Dostoevsky and the kenotic tradition." In *Dostoevsky and the Christian Tradition*, edited by George Pattison and Diane Oenning Thompson, 31–40. Cambridge: Cambridge University Press, 2001.

6

"Continue in that Holy Fellowship"

Covenanted Communion as a
Post-Communion Prayer

NATHAN G. JENNINGS

> When all committees have fulfilled their task, all papers
> have been distributed and all practical goals achieved,
> there must come a perfect joy. About what?
>
> —Alexander Schmemann[1]

THE ANGLICAN COMMUNION COVENANT has gone through multiple
drafts through the work and responses of multiple committees.
Papers have been and are being written for it (including, for example, this
one here being read), about it, and against it. Is there a practical goal to
the Covenant? I will let other essays in this volume address that question.
But in the statement above Alexander Schmemann mentions a "perfect
joy." What is that? In the case of a Covenant for our Communion, a perfect joy about what?

Schmemann, the father of liturgical theology, makes his answer
to this question clear throughout his work: the joy is that of being lost

---

1. Schmemann, *For the Life of the World*, 13.

together in wonder, love, and praise of our triune God. But if that is the goal, ought not the means be, at least in large part, determined by that very goal? I propose approaching the Anglican Communion Covenant as a prayer after communion: that we may continue in that holy fellowship and do all such good works as God has prepared for us to walk in.

I was asked to write a "liturgical theological" reading of the current Anglican Communion Covenant draft. What is liturgical theology? In order to answer that question as briefly as possible I will first address the meaning of the word "liturgy," that becomes the adjective in the phrase "liturgical theology." I will then add that word before the word "theology" and define the phrase.

The straightforward use of the word liturgy primarily refers to the Christian divine service, or, the service of Holy Eucharist. Related to this meaning are those formal texts that direct such service. For us, as Anglicans, those texts are contained in our various prayer book traditions. It has been popular since liturgical renewal in the twentieth century to define liturgy etymologically[2] as "the work of the people." "Liturgy," however, does not so much mean "the work of the people," but the "public service" of a wealthy benefactor on behalf of the people.[3] Our wealthy benefactor is God in Christ. The liturgy, therefore, is the work of God for God's people.

Let us assume then that "theology" simply means talk about God. When we add the adjective "liturgy" to the word "theology," we mean that we are talking about whom God is and the nature of his mighty deeds if the Christian liturgy is truly God's act of "public service" on behalf of humanity. In doing so, liturgical theology studies not so much simply the words of a given concrete Christian rite as its shape and ritual logic. Therefore, placement, order, relationship of parts, and the dialogue between words and gestures all provide points of departure for theological reflection.

---

2. From the originating Greek word λειτουργια.

3. Michael B. Aune has provided an excellent summary of the recent debate and growing scholarly consensus on this issue in his article "The Current State of Liturgical Theology: A Plurality of Particulars," this itself being, in turn, a summary of two previous articles in which he expounded these themes more in depth: "Liturgy and theology: Rethinking the Relationship" Parts I and II.

THE COVENANT AND MISSION

The preamble to the Covenant claims that we are covenanting together in order "to proclaim" the Gospel, "to offer God's love," and to "maintain the unity of the Spirit in the bond of peace" so that we can "grow up together" in spiritual maturity.[4] All of these things are, of course, meet and right. The founding reason is mission, moving to neighbor-love and from neighbor-love to Christian fraternal fellowship-love, ending in Christian discipleship. Who could be against such things? Further into the document, the shared *vocation* of the Anglican Communion (which is to say, that which we have been called by God to do in this world) is named as mission, and rightly so.[5] But, again, the question: what is the goal or end of mission itself? What is the love of God that we are offering to all? Is it not the divine service of God for the life of the world?

Approaching the Covenant from the point of view of liturgical theology, upon first reading the final text I was afraid that it was too tied up in mission as the ultimate rather than penultimate goal of Christian faith. The ultimate goal, following the good Father Schmemann, is worship: that "perfect joy." But on further reading of the Covenant I do not believe that it subordinates or even ignores liturgy in the name of mission. I think that it is grounded in the *ground* of mission: the liturgical life of the church. The Covenant recognizes both the centrality of worship to the life of Christians and the commonality of the historic liturgy[6] shared among all Anglicans.[7]

Besides the theological priority of worship over mission, and in fact more than likely because of it, talk of mission alone can itself be divisive. The language of mission can itself be used as a dividing line drawn between North American mainline understandings of the word and Evangelical and Global understandings. For example, North American

---

4. Covenant, Preamble. The Covenant Design Group's Commentary on the Draft states clearly that they "sought to emphasize more obviously the missionary element constitutive to our valuing of unity" (p. 2); I of course wish that they had gone one step closer and focused more clearly and explicitly upon worship.

5. Covenant, 2.1.2. This mission is, of course, shared with churches and traditions outside of the Anglican tradition (Covenant, 2.1.3).

6. The work of Byron Stuhlman guides much of my historical reading of prayer book texts, e.g., *Eucharistic Celebration 1789–1979*.

7. The various Prayer Book traditions will be the main resource "that Anglicans have historically turned for guidance" engaged in this reading of the Covenant text.

mainline understandings of the word "mission" have been defined by Western urbanization and industrialization and the "social gospel" of the nineteenth century. Evangelicals, on the other hand, mean something different by "mission." And different Evangelicals mean different things by it.[8] Since missionaries of these various stripes converted the Anglican world, all these stripes are seen in Anglican contexts throughout the world. More importantly, however, are the vast arrays of "Global" under-standings of the word "mission."[9] Part of their postcolonial edge is one that rejects the mainline post-Enlightenment fear of the spiritual and of Biblical authority. My point is not to develop missiology here, my point is just this: we can say that we are united in mission. But as soon as we begin to discourse concerning the nature of that mission the lines of division show up quite distinctly.

CONFESSION OR AUTONOMY?

One proposal to resolve the divisions found in competing missiological motives and discourses is through recourse to confessional theological systems or documents that unify through an authoritative discursive theo-logical standard. And it is true that the "historic faith that we confess,"[10] may be and has been construed to mean something like a Reformation-style Confession. So there are those who would have us adhere to the Thirty-nine Articles as Lutherans and Presbyterians adhere to their own various confessional documents.[11]

Some would point to the Chicago-Lambeth Quadrilateral as just such a document. And there would be good reason as it has been the guide of our ecumenical dialogue concerning the nature of communion with those

---

8. Traditional English Evangelicals are going to share, with North American mainlin-ers, a critical postcolonial edge. E.g., some of the conclusions of an Evangelical biblical scholar like N. T. Wright. On the other hand, American Evangelicals usually want a fairly apolitical "personal relationship with Jesus Christ."

9. See, for example, Michael Nai-Chiu Poon, *Church Partnerships in Asia: A Singapore Conversation.*

10. Covenant, Introduction, para. 4. The document itself actually outlines five lay-ers of inheritance: 1. the ancient apostolic church, 2. the patristic era, 3. the ancient British and Irish churches, 4. the Reformation, and 5. Anglican missionary expansion (Covenant, 2.1.1).

11. This represents the opinion of many of those involved, for example, in GAFCON.

who are not historically Anglican. The Chicago-Lambeth Quadrilateral, however, is a mere minimum guide for communion with other churches that are not Anglican.[12] *Anglican* communion can and should be thicker than the kind of bare minimum communion that is sought after by much ecumenical dialogue exactly because our communion is Anglican, and not merely that between different confessing traditions.

The word "confession" is itself a word that points to an ascetical[13] and liturgical act. Confession before the rulers of the world results in martyrdom. Martyrdom names the chief act of Christian witness. Baptism, as baptism into Christ's death and resurrection, is our ritual share in that witness. As a liturgical act, confession names the act of submission as Baptism, acceptance of the rule of faith, and repentance for sin—all overlapping Christian realities: conversion to Christ means identification with his atoning sacrifice. The ultimate Christian identification with that sacrifice is the acceptance of our own martyrdom, the *confession* of the faith before the powers of the world. Such identification demands repentance, and therefore *confession* on our part (although derived, etymologically, from different sources, their overlapping meaning in a Christian context still holds). Our ritual entry into that *confession* is Baptism in the water of Christ's death and burial.

With the Quadrilateral, therefore, the Covenant promotes the significance of the due administration of the two central ritual mysteries: Baptism and Holy Communion. What strengthens Anglican communion beyond mere Ecumenical communion is our shared prayer book tradition of liturgical worship. The commonality of the historic liturgy shared among Anglicans gives depth to the communion we enjoy.

Confessing the "historic faith" from a liturgical theological perspective entails our shared focus on Holy Eucharist, Baptism, the recitation of the creed, and the confession of sins in such a way that conforms to general and ancient catholic practice and, in particular, according to the rites and rubrics of our own unique prayer book traditions. As a corrective to mission, sound teaching also finds its ground in worship.

Another frequent expression of the nature of Anglican Communion is that of unity in autonomy. Being autonomous-in-communion[14] is

12. The first section affirms, with slightly expanded language, the Chicago-Lambeth Quadrilateral (Covenant, 1.1).

13. The current draft links mission to witness (Covenant, 1.2.5).

14. Covenant, 3.1.2.

another way to say catholic in worship; that is to say, the way in which worship both unites while allowing for diversity. For example, for many centuries the East and the West of Christendom remained in communion. The East celebrated the divine service according to various traditions, the chief of which was probably the liturgy of St. Chrysostom. The West, on the other hand, developed its own rites; the Roman rite would come to be the chief. While East and West remained in communion, they never understood themselves to be celebrating something different but the same spiritual worship: the Christian liturgy.[15] A congregation (here on earth) cannot simultaneously pray St. Chrysostom's anaphora and the Roman Canon. This does not mean they are not both worshiping the same God and sharing in the same mystical feast.

One of the most basic and fundamental differences in our shared worship that shows our autonomy in communion is that of the two prayer book traditions of the Anglican Communion: the English-Commonwealth tradition and the Scottish-American. The key difference between these two traditions focuses around the very prayer that gives us communion: the Prayer of Consecration or what we would now call the Eucharistic Prayer. This difference is at the heart of there being an Anglican Communion at all, rather than merely a Church of England.

Scotland and the United States represent the first two independent Episcopal churches from the Church of England that still, nevertheless, share a common tradition and a desire for, if not assumption of, Communion with the Church of England. The fact that full communion existed from almost the very beginning between the Episcopal Church of the United States of America and the Church of England on the one hand and the Episcopal Church of Scotland on the other (and eventually to follow between England and Scotland), grounds our two prayer book traditions as mutual recognition across liturgical difference. It could be argued that the two prayer book traditions form a deeper theological difference than the seemingly huge but in some ways merely surface differences that drive the current controversy in the Anglican Communion. I propose, therefore, that this unity across our different liturgical traditions is not simply a helpful metaphor for our current crisis, but its living, performative resolution.

---

15. Even now the disputes between East and West are not over the validity of their disparate liturgical rites.

To sum up, there are two potential problems with assuming that "mission" is the way to unity; one is theological, and one is historical. First, theologically speaking, worship always precedes and gives itself as the goal for mission. Inverting this logic in our dialogue, therefore, generates more problems than it solves. Historically, even structurally, as Anglicans we have suffered under missiological motives and discourses, which create division and "party spirit" when separated from liturgical motives and discourses. Both theologically as Christians, and historically as Anglicans, worship and especially liturgical worship grounds mission and heals division. Theologically as Christians the liturgy serves as both the ritual enactment of healed division in the act of communion proper, and also as the ritual goal for, and sacramental empowerment towards, Christian mission. Our shared Anglican tradition is a history of theological debates resolved through common prayer. Anglican mission has brought prayer-book worship from a European island throughout the world. Could we then subscribe to an Anglican Communion Covenant as an act of common prayer? I propose that the Anglican Communion Covenant performs a prayer after communion: that we may continue in that holy fellowship and do all such good works as God has prepared for us to walk in.

PRAYER AFTER COMMUNION

The Covenant assumes a Communion of Anglican churches throughout the world that wish to go out *together* from the place of their shared fellowship into mission in God's world. The preamble to the Covenant declares that the Churches of the Anglican Communion "covenant together," "in order to proclaim more effectively . . . the gospel, to offer God's love in responding to the needs of the world."[16] The Covenant is situated as a kind of "post-communion prayer" between the Anglican Communion we have assumed and enjoyed for some two hundred years and the future of our mission together in God's world.

Our two-branched Anglican prayer book tradition shares a post-communion prayer that directly reflects the directional logic of liturgy and mission in our common life:

16. Covenant, Preamble.

Almighty and everliving God, we most heartily thank thee for
that thou dost feed us, in these holy mysteries, with the spiritual
food of the most precious Body and Blood of thy Son our Savior
Jesus Christ; and dost assure us thereby of thy favor and goodness
towards us; and that we are very members incorporate in the mystical body of thy Son, the blessed company of all faithful people;
and are also heirs, through hope, of thy everlasting kingdom. And
we humbly beseech thee, O heavenly Father, so to assist us with
thy grace, that we may continue in that holy fellowship, and do all
such good works as thou hast prepared for us to walk in; through
Jesus Christ our Lord, to whom, with thee and the Holy Ghost, be
all honor and glory, world without end. Amen.[17]

As described above, liturgical theology reflects upon the nature of God
and his deeds not simply by looking at the words themselves, but by looking at the placement of ritual acts with respect to one another and the
dialogue formed by the relationship between the words of a prayer and
the liturgical actions within which those prayers are used. First, then, let
us situate the ritual location of the post-communion prayer before we
go into its own inner logic. What happens before the post-communion
prayer? The communion proper itself. We commune with the God who is
communion and find therein communion with one another.

The first section of the Covenant[18] clearly indicates the correla-
tion of communion with worship. Our communion is our worship; our
Anglican Communion is our shared worship tradition. And we enact
this, of course, quite literally in Holy Communion. The Covenant opens
quoting 1 John 1.2–3,[19] implying the link of communion with the life of
our triune God, "St. John makes it clear that the communion of life in the
Church reflects the communion which is the divine life itself, the life of

17. This is the version found in the American Prayer Book tradition (and in our
current 1979 edition; BCP 1979, 339). Variations throughout the communion are not
significant enough to alter the basic liturgical theological point that I am arguing here.

18. Covenant, 1.1.

19. "This life is revealed, and we have seen it and testify to it, and declare to you the
eternal life that was with the Father and was revealed to us—we declare to you what we
have seen and heard so that you also may have communion with us; and truly our communion is with the Father and with his Son Jesus Christ."

the Trinity."[20] Furthermore, "in the communion of the Church we share in the divine life."[21]

What, then, immediately follows the post-communion prayer? We receive the blessing of God and are dismissed for mission in the world.[22] Fellowship with God is the greatest blessing of being human and such divine fellowship in turn grants true fellowship with fellow human beings. This "blest communion, fellowship divine,"[23] inspires and directs the goal of mission. As people transformed by fellowship with the living God, we give that fellowship as a beacon to the nations: the Light of God's people Israel.

After communion, then what? Mission. But we transition from communion to mission through thanksgiving for that very gift of communion and fellowship. We give thanks with a prayer that, after its ritual enactment (or, after its assumption in our shared life for over two centuries), our fellowship with one another would continue and empower us to engage together God's mission. On this reading, we can look at our mission together as following the boundaries of ritual enactment on the one hand, and the assumption of full communion on the part of the various Anglican churches scattered throughout the world on the other.

COVENANT AS POST-COMMUNION PRAYER

I will now focus on key aspects of the text of the post-communion prayer itself, reading the Covenant like a commentary upon it. In doing so, I

---

20. Covenant, Introduction 1.

21. Quoting *The Church of the Triune God*, paras. 1–2.

22. Here, again, I am following the current shape of the American Prayer Book rite. Differences among the various concluding rites throughout the communion are not significant enough to vastly alter the liturgical theology I am arguing here with one exception: the *Gloria*. Historically in the American tradition, and still the case for many provinces, the post-communion prayer immediately precedes the *Gloria*, which in turn is immediately followed by the blessing and dismissal (even if implicit and not formal). Communion itself causes us to return not only to thanksgiving but also to doxology. I felt a need to acknowledge this important historic shape of our Anglican rite. I do not believe it weakens but only strengthens my argument that mission finds ground in our worship of God.

23. How, "For All the Saints," 287. Apropos of our current situation, the prayer of the hymn continues, "we feebly struggle, they in glory shine; yet all are one in thee for all are thine. Alleluia."

also read the Covenant as if it were a liturgy, directing the Communion in its corporate worship no less than in its corporate mission. The prayer begins:

> Almighty and everliving God, we most heartily thank thee for that thou dost feed us, in these holy mysteries, with the spiritual food of the most precious Body and Blood of thy Son our Savior Jesus Christ; and dost assure us thereby of thy favor and goodness towards us . . .

Communion is a gift of God.[24] When we receive the elements at the Eucharist this mystery enacts the greatest gift of God that human beings may receive: full fellowship with the triune God. In our post-communion prayer we acknowledge this communion as a gift and sign of God's grace. And a Covenanted Anglican Communion is also one that accepts such communion as a gift and sign of God's excessive gift.

In the post-communion prayer, we recognize that the first act we must perform in the face of such sheer and unmerited grace is thankfulness. We give thanks for the gift of communion. Likewise the Covenant gives thanks for the Communion we have as Anglicans. In the liturgy, we give thanks,

> that we are very members incorporate in the mystical body of thy Son, the blessed company of all faithful people; and are also heirs, through hope, of thy everlasting kingdom.

The Covenant reads, "[I]n the communion of the Church we share in the divine life."[25] The gift that we receive in the Holy Communion is not simply that of a single devout communicant entering into union with a one-dimensional God. The gift of communion is the gift that gives us church, and church as communion with a triune God.

This insight concerning the inherent connection between the liturgical act of Eucharist and the being of the Church represents the singularly greatest retrieval of the Liturgical Renewal Movement.[26] It makes no

---

24. Covenant, 2.1.1.

25. Again, here the draft quotes *The Church of the Triune God*, paras. 1–2.

26. Henri de Lubac's recovery of the *corpus verum* in his seminal work *Corpus Mysticum: L'Eucharistie et l'Église au moyen âge*, 1944, grounds the retrieval of the unity of Church and Eucharist. Lubac argued that the medieval church developed a semantic shift where the *corpus verum*, or Christ's true body shifted from referring to the gathered church body to the elements on the table. Likewise then, the *corpus mysticum*, or, mystical

sense to study the importance of the shape and performance of the liturgy on the part of the church if it is merely an arbitrary human event that the church does. If, on the other hand, the Eucharist constitutes the church as such, then liturgical theology becomes central to ecclesiology, and thus to other Christian discourses, such as soteriology, Christology, and theology proper (which is to say, discussion of the Trinity).

The very existence and ordering of the Church displays the Triune God, like an icon. Richard Hooker, one of our tradition's founding theologians, states that the "being of God is a kinde of lawe to his working."[27] What is Hooker's chief legal concern in his great work *Of the Lawes of Ecclesiasticall Politie*? Hooker is chiefly concerned with the law that binds human worship, the law that is liturgy. The life of God, as a kind of law "to his working," is also therefore, and perhaps primarily, a kind of liturgy, a liturgy of communion,[28] of ordered, rational enjoyment of the other. To this we are invited in Holy Communion[29] and for this we give thanks in the post-communion prayer.

> And we humbly beseech thee, O heavenly Father, so to assist us
> with thy grace, that we may continue in that holy fellowship, and
> do all such good works as thou hast prepared for us to walk in;

What do we do after such a divine communion? We pray to continue in fellowship with God and one another. Our shared Christian "bonds of affection and the love of Christ compel us always to seek the highest possible degree of communion,"[30] as the Eucharist places us upon the Christian journey to the highest possible communion with our God. We pray to continue in that holy fellowship, outside of its formal ritual

---

body of Christ, traded meaning with *corpus verum*, at first referring to the elements and then to the church. Thus the emphasis upon the elements in medieval sacramental theology and the loss of the inherent connection between the liturgy and the church as a body that gathers to perform those mysteries. Without the recovery of the church as *corpus verum*, liturgical theology makes little sense.

27. *Lawes* I.2.2 (FLE I, 59).

28. Biblical covenants are themselves a share in the extension of divine communion in and as human society (Covenant, Introduction 2).

29. Communion and Eucharist, and therefore communion and worship, name the same thing (Covenant, 1.2.3). Again, the document clearly links Anglican Communion with ecumenical communion (Covenant, 1.2.1).

30. Covenant, 3.2.7.

enactment. Only from within the bonds of such fellowship do we move together in mission.

After we pray to continue in fellowship, we then focus our prayer upon the work of mission: God's work in God's world through us. This work demands the right stewardship of our resources.[31] Such stewardship is the work of a Eucharistic people shaped by the ritual action of oblation found in the offertory.[32] The common good of communion directs our stewardship.[33] Stewardship itself cycles through the offertory at the Eucharist. Christian stewardship finds its place and meaning when we bring our gifts to God at the Eucharist. Even our mission is a liturgical act: we draw the world back to the God who gave it being.

Fellowship empowers mission. The goal of mission is fellowship with God and therefore with the people of God. The Communion has informally enjoyed that up till now. A Covenant makes such fellowship formal. As Anglicans, we have never been prone to walk away from the formal. Subscription to a formal Covenant document is a post-communion prayer for continuing in that fellowship after so many years of assuming it, of taking that gift for granted. Such a prayer, then, ought be concluded,

> through Jesus Christ our Lord, to whom, with thee and the Holy Ghost, be all honor and glory, world without end. Amen.

The Covenant has each member church affirm that, "by our participation in Baptism and Eucharist, we are incorporated into the one body of the Church of Jesus Christ."[34] The chief ritual mysteries, Baptism and Eucharist, are not products or external tools of the church but the central acts of the church's worship. Our worship is our incorporation into Christ's body. Our shared worship across differing prayer book traditions[35] defines our particular tradition and is therefore the means of the special unity within the body of Christ that we call the Anglican Communion.

31. Covenant, 2.2.1.

32. The Covenant document supports a virtue-ethic approach to our common life in naming "the common good" (3.2.1) as the *telos* of our particular communion. The "common good" is another way of naming "divine fellowship."

33. Covenant, 3.2.1

34. Covenant, 3.1.1.

35. I mean this on the same analogy made above to those churches of the East that share the same anaphora of St. Chrysostom, with, nevertheless, local variations in text and practice, etc. We share prayer book spirituality and worship and that makes us Anglican—willy-nilly.

COVENANT AND LITURGY

The Covenant grounds this shared vocation in our shared sacramental life. I want to examine especially the following paragraph of the Covenant:

> We are a people who live, learn, and pray by and with the Scriptures as God's word. We seek to adore God in thanks and praise and to make intercession for the needs of people everywhere through a common voice, made one across cultures and languages. We are privileged to share in the mission of the apostles to bring the Gospel of Christ to all nations and peoples, not in word only but in deeds of compassion and justice that witness to God's character and the triumph of Christ over sin and death. We give ourselves as servants of a greater unity among the divided Christians of the world.[36]

The first sentences focus on our liturgical foundation as Anglicans. Prayer, although many other things, is, especially for us who are Anglican, liturgical. Adoring "God in thanks and praise" concretely refers to the Eucharist and its Great Thanksgiving. Intercession for all people names the Prayers of the People.[37] Our various yet related books of Common Prayer make our praying "through a common voice" possible.

It is from this liturgical foundation that the paragraph proceeds to the place of mission in our common life. Liturgy and mission together, as unifying practices that we share and that enable us to share a common life, provide, thereby, a launching place for ecumenical dialogue and, even more robustly, an icon of ecumenical relationships.[38] The "thickness" of our communion as Anglicans provides a model for the communion that more disparate churches may hope to enjoy. So the Covenant itself, just like our post-communion prayer, moves from communion to mission and back again.

Because the language of mission can be used as a dividing line between North American mainline, Evangelical, and Global understandings

---

36. Covenant, Introduction, para. 6.

37. So, for example, the commentary acknowledges the Anglican Cycle of Prayer as the first among the various things it lists as sustaining our life together (p. 5).

38. Again, reiterating an assumption from the introduction, this grounding in the communion of worship has ecumenical ramifications. The "apostolic mission" is "shared with other Churches and traditions beyond this Covenant" (Covenant, 1.1.6.), simultaneously relativizing and maximizing the importance of signing on to an Anglican Communion Covenant.

of the word, we must therefore look to something more foundational for our communion as Anglicans. This is not just a theological concern, but a structural concern rooted in our shared history as Anglicans. When our focus deviates from worship we loose that which binds us. Without communion or fellowship, there is no mission. Although the text deserves further work towards making the liturgical unity-in-autonomy of Anglicanism explicit and central, nevertheless, in subscribing to an Anglican Covenant, a member church sustains the Anglican ground of mission *in* communion, enacted liturgically.

How, then, one might ask, can a non-liturgical document such as the Covenant be a prayer? Signing on to something, subscribing to something, is not the production of an artifact, but a performance. As Anglicans, with our tradition of "laws of ecclesiastical polity," we must construe signing or subscribing to a document as a kind of *liturgical* performance. That said, the very process of drafting and coming to agreement upon the Covenant is, in some ways, as important as the text itself. It is the *performance* of communion, of discourse (discourse itself being a mode of communion). It is the "fellowship divine" for which the Covenant would serve as our post-communion prayer.

Even disagreement about whether or not we should have an official Covenant document performs the importance and value of such a document. Further, even if we end without a formal Covenant document, the process itself has contributed to an already existing covenant of convention through shared tradition. Our dialogue as Anglicans has performed and continues to perform a relationship of covenant, whether we have a written document or not. To those who object that we have never had something like this before within the Anglican tradition, I would like to offer the possibility that, as with most things in the development of human tradition, we are moving form tacit to explicit rather than from nothing to fiat.[39]

If the Covenant is a post-communion prayer, then the commitments outlined in 3.2 together with the procedures of section 4 allow a relationship between the whole Communion and its respective provinces that is analogous to the relationship between pastor and communicant at the parish level. These commitments are the "disciplinary rubrics"[40] of the

---

39. See Covenant, Introduction, para. 5.

40. "Disciplinary rubrics" are those rubrics in every prayer book that explain the rules governing communication and excommunication. In the current American prayer

Anglican Communion. Without disciplinary rubrics, the enactment of Eucharist degenerates into mere metaphor; fencing the table protects those in pastoral need from the dangers of so great a sacrament. If the sacrament is merely metaphor, then the table needs nothing more than a metaphorical fence. Subscribing to a formal covenant document fences our Anglican Communion, keeping it from degenerating into mere metaphor. Fellowship that is real is fellowship that is capable of changing those who participate.

CONCLUSION

Worship and especially liturgical worship grounds our mission and heals division. What do we do, as Anglicans, when our communion seems to be breaking apart? What do we do after Anglican communion? My answer has been to look at how we pray after communion through focusing on our shared post-communion prayer. In summary, we first simply give thanks for the sheer gift of communion that God grants us by no merit or work of our own. We then give thanks for the fellowship of our church, which is a part of that magnificent gift. From that place of thankfulness we pray that our fellowship will continue and then, and only then, we pray for our part in God's mission to the world.

I pray the various provinces of the Anglican Communion subscribe to the Covenant as an embodiment of communion, as an *enactment* of our commonly acknowledged ground and goal of mission in the worship of the living God. My own prayer, therefore, is that the various provinces of the Anglican Communion subscribe to the Covenant as an act of common prayer, a "post-communion" prayer: "that we may continue in that holy fellowship and do all such good works as" God has "prepared for us to walk in," in order that we may together enter into that "perfect joy" of giving to God the honor and glory due his Name, world without end.

book this is found on p. 409.

BIBLIOGRAPHY

Anglican Communion Reports

International Commission for Anglican-Orthodox Theological Dialogue (ICAOTD). *The Church of the Triune God: The Cyprus Agreed Statement*. 2006. Online: http://www.anglicancommunion.org/ministry/ecumenical/dialogues/orthodox/docs/pdf/The%20Church%20of%20the%20Triune%20God.pdf.

General

Aune, Michael B. "Liturgy and Theology: Rethinking the Relationship, Part I—Setting the Stage." *Worship* 81 (2007) 46–68.

———. "Liturgy and Theology: Rethinking the Relationship, Part II—A Different Starting Place." *Worship* 81 (2007) 141–69.

———. "The Current State of Liturgical Theology: A Plurality of Particulars." *St. Vladimir's Theological Quarterly* 53 (2009) 209–29.

How, William Walsham. "For All the Saints," *The Hymnal 1982*. New York: Church Pension Fund, 1985.

Lubac, Henri de. *Corpus Mysticum: L'Eucharistie et l'Église au moyen âge*. Paris: Bayard, 1944.

Poon, Michael. *Church Partnerships in Asia: A Singapore Conversation*. Singapore: Armour, 2010

Schmemann, Alexander. *For the Life of the World*. Crestwood, NY: St. Vladimir's Seminary Press, 1973.

Stuhlman, Byron. *Eucharistic Celebration 1789–1979*. New York: Church Hymnal Corp., 1988.

7

The Universal Church of the Covenant
Called and Conscripted

CHRISTOPHER WELLS

ECUMENICAL VOCATION?

PERHAPS THE MOST SIGNIFICANT decision of the Covenant Design Group, from the start of its work, was to set forth the proposed Anglican Covenant within a maximally wide ecclesial ambit: the one Church of Jesus Christ, in the service of which, it is claimed, the Anglican Communion finds its particular vocation. The introduction to the final text devotes the first three paragraphs to the "one universal Church" of all who are baptized in the name of God—a communion "extended to all humankind" "for the whole of creation," as described in Scripture.[1] The Anglican Communion is placed within this context, in perhaps the most intriguing, and certainly the most theologically compact, sentences: "In the providence of God, which holds sway even over our divisions caused by sin, various families of churches have grown up within the universal Church in the course of history. Among these families is the Anglican

---

1. Covenant, Introduction, paras. 1–3. Cf. similarly Covenant, 1.1.1, 1.1.2, 1.1.6, 1.1.8, 1.2.5, *et passim.*

Communion, which provides a particular charism and identity among the many followers and servants of Jesus."[2]

What, according to the Covenant, is this gift of Anglicans, which God has graciously permitted to take root within the Church, even in the teeth of Christian rebellion? The word *charism* is never used again in the text, though several references to the *Eucharist* pick up an important cognate. The text speaks several times, however, of God's gifts, including the gift of communion itself.[3] And the remainder of the introduction focuses on the Anglican communion of churches as something "received": a common faith and order, and consequent affection, reflecting "God's own faithfulness and promises towards us in Christ (2 Cor. 1:20–22)."[4] On this basis, Anglicans in turn "give ourselves as servants of a greater unity among the divided Christians of the world," even as we recognize that "our life together reflects the blessings of God" *and* "exposes our failures in faith, hope and love."[5]

Later in the text, section 2.1 effectively recaps the structure and substance of the introduction—first sketching the universal pattern of Christian ecclesiology as communion in the Trinity for the world; then moving to the development of a particularly Anglican life under the sign of divine providence, marked by an admission of Anglican incompleteness amid continual "refashioning by the Holy Spirit" and "summons into a more fully developed communion life," incorporating humble repentance for our failures and sin; aimed finally at a larger "imperative of God's mission" into which the Anglican Communion is called: a "vocation" that is particularly "ecumenical" in character, defined as "the full visible unity of the Church in accordance with Christ's prayer that 'all may be one.'"[6] And one notes again the emphasis, and pains taken, on the last point, as may be seen by noting that 2.1.5, the ecumenical *denouement*, is the longest paragraph of the sub-section.

In keeping with this focus on a singular mission of the whole Church, in which Anglicans are called more and more to share with other families of churches, the second half of section 2 presents a remarkable

2. Covenant, Introduction, para. 4.

3. Covenant, Introduction, para. 3; 2.1.1.

4. Covenant, Introduction, para. 5; cf. para. 4.1.1.

5. Covenant, Introduction, paras. 6–7.

6. Covenant, 2.1.2–2.1.5.

development of the heretofore *Anglican* five "marks of mission," via a series of enlargements and ecumenical cross-references at 2.2.2 with accompanying footnotes. The initial words appearing in quotation marks following letters *a* to *e* are the marks of mission, after which follow, in each case, language that places Anglican commitments in a larger, universal and theological context:

1) "to bring all to repentance and faith";

2) "making disciples of all nations (Mt. 28:19) . . . and drawing them into the one Body of Christ whose faith, calling and hope are one in the Lord (Eph. 4:4–6)": the two classic proof texts for a common baptism shared by all Christians, citing ARCIC in a footnote;

3) "disclosing God's reign";

4) "as the Church stands" facing "the nations of the world," with Christ in the Spirit, citing two more ecumenical texts in the notes;

5) "as essential aspects of our mission in communion," citing once more the Anglican-Roman Catholic dialogue.[7]

Here perhaps is the most decisive proof that "Anglican" mission is articulated and elaborated by the Covenant in sustainedly ecumenical terms, without exception or apology: a smoking gun of catholic ambition, appearing not as a superficial patina of unity-in-diversity (as one finds in much ecclesiological literature of a denominational sort), but rather worked out in detail, accountable to Scripture and *its* terms; offered, finally, in a spirit of "conversion in the face of our unfaithfulness and failures in witness," to "awaken and challenge the whole people of God," "thankful that in our eucharistic communion 'Christ is the source and goal of the unity of the Church and of the renewal of human community,'" quoting the landmark achievement of multilateral consensus, *Baptism, Eucharist and Ministry* (1982).[8]

Whence this sustainedly ecumenical ecclesiology? Other tacks might have been taken, as other ecclesiologies have been tendered, each with some precedent in one and another strand of Anglicanism. Two contemporary examples ready to hand may conveniently illustrate the point. From the "right," members of the Fellowship of Confessing

7. Covenant, 2.2.2.
8. Covenant, 2.2.3—2.2.5.

Anglicans, launched via the 2008 Global Anglican Future Conference and its accompanying *Jerusalem Declaration*, envisage a re-structured Anglican Communion centered on a more clearly articulated statement of "orthodox" truth, with newly developed "confessing Anglican jurisdictions, clergy and congregations" formed to defend and propagate the gospel.[9] Meanwhile, from the "left," prominent leaders of the Episcopal Church, calling themselves the Chicago Consultation, propose a purportedly missiological vision of Christian communion—in effect, a Life and Work agenda of common *praxis* for flourishing not so much despite but in and through difference.[10] In both cases, traditional Faith and Order concerns—one Church visibly reconciled—quickly recede and/or disappear altogether, apparently because they are thought to be unnecessary and/or potentially dangerous.[11] And in this way, both amount to a *de facto*, at least, "canonization of denominationalism," in Christopher Hill's apt phrase.[12]

To understand why neither of the foregoing self-nominated "evangelical" and "progressive" alternatives have carried the day in the fashioning of the Covenant, one only needs to look at the last century and a half of Anglican reflection on *communion*—a fertile time of theological development, when "the seeds of today's Anglican Communion structures were being sown," in step with an emerging consensus regarding the orientation and aims of Anglican ecumenical commitments.[13] It is these

9. GAFCON, *Being Faithful*, 8. See especially the ecclesiological framing of the text at 4–9.

10. See Chicago Consultation, *The Genius of Anglicanism: Perspectives on the Proposed Anglican Covenant* (2011). A standard strategy here is a proposed appropriation of the *Covenant for Communion in Mission* (2005) produced by the Inter-Anglican Standing Committee on Mission and Evangelism (IASCOME), which presented itself as "a focus for binding the Communion together in a way rather different from that envisaged by the Windsor Report" (Intro., para. 6). See the following note.

11. As Gay Clark Jennings concludes her contribution to the Chicago collection, "Covenant for Mission," with a polemical flourish: "Most importantly, the *Covenant for Communion in Mission* eschews uniformity, punitive action and centralized authority in favor of our love for one another as brothers and sisters in Christ and belief that we are all called to do God's work in the world" (50). For GAFCON's outworking of the call to Christian unity, see esp. 38–40 and 59–60 in *Being Faithful*.

12. Hill, "The Ecumenical Moulding of Anglicanism and the Future of the Communion," 163.

13. IASCER, *Vision before Us*, 29. Cf. Poon, "The Anglican Communion as Communion of Churches: On the historic significance of the Anglican Covenant," and

commitments that we have made, and their internal logic and rationale, that I am interested to unfold in the present essay, not as an exhaustive survey, but as an examination of two influential instances that effectively codified the terms of Anglican ecclesiology of the last fifteen years. Both appeared in 1997 as the fruit of inter-Anglican research in the run-up to Lambeth 1998. Both took a range of Anglican ecclesial commitments as given, and attempted to propose reasonable and practicable, if in some ways revisionary, developments. And both attempted to combine specifically Anglican characteristics with a sense of ecumenical call, the language for which is by definition theological, attributed to God. Whatever we make of the Anglican Covenant, it is crucial to understand the purpose and application of this ecclesiology, its grammar and lexicon.

ARCHAEOLOGY OF A CALL

The Agros Report: "Beyond Anglicanism"

An early draft of the Ecumenical Advisory Group's Agros Report (1997) was prepared for the 10th Meeting of the Anglican Consultative Council (Panama, 1996) and then revised for Lambeth 1998.[14] The report was framed by the suggestion that "Anglicanism, as its identity has developed through successive Lambeth Conferences, is well-placed to make a significant contribution to the ecumenical movement. It might be argued that Anglican ecclesiological and theological method is, in fact, inherently ecumenical."[15] The principal aim of the ecumenical movement is "the reconciliation and visible unity of the Church of God,"[16] a cause to which Lambeth 1998 would again pledge Anglican allegiance: "This conference reaffirms the Anglican commitment to the full, visible unity of the Church as the goal of the Ecumenical Movement."[17] It is vital to see,

---

Davie, "Anglican ecumenism: The Liberal Catholic consensus and the Conservative Evangelical challenge."

14. See Vision before Us, 16. The Inter-Anglican Standing Commission on Ecumenical Relations (IASCER) was formally commissioned for its work by ACC-10 and by Lambeth 1998 as the successor to the Ecumenical Advisory Group. In turn, at Lambeth 2008 IASCER was folded, along with IATDC, into the newly formed Inter-Anglican Standing Commission on Unity, Faith and Order (IASCUFO).

15. Agros Report, para. 4.

16. Ibid., para. 2; cf. para. 13.

17. LC 1998, Res. IV.1(a). See similarly Lambeth 2008, in an expansive elaboration:

however, that this movement is first of all God's mission, and secondarily our own, as a creative work to which we are called. As *Agros* puts it: "The kingdom and God's intention for the unity of all humanity and creation within it provides the framework in which the Church's vocation to unity is most creatively explored."[18]

In this context of a universal call to unity, the report ventures some standard reflections on "Anglican comprehensiveness"—holding "together many diversities" within our own communion[19]—before hinting at what may be specifically *ecumenical* about the method of Anglican ecclesiology and theology, namely, a willingness to raise new questions about our identity and structures in light of an ever-increasing web of relationships in communion with non-Anglican churches, such as the Mar Thoma Church, the Old Catholic Churches of the Union of Utrecht, the Philippine Independent Church, and a variety of Lutheran churches. "What structures in the future will serve to nurture this growing unity?" the report's authors asked.[20] And before hazarding a tentative answer, they proposed a posture for approaching one, a posture of provisionality: "Through our developing experience of other Christian traditions and the sharing of worship, life and mission in many places, we grow in understanding a unity which is 'beyond Anglicanism' and which would be a more faithful sign of and effective instrument in the service of the unity of God's Kingdom."[21] A courageous idea—not original to the Ecumenical Advisory Group, but little discussed of late by Anglicans beyond the confines of professional ecclesiological reflection.[22]

Indaba Reflections, para. 71.

18. *Agros Report*, para. 25.

19. Ibid., para. 41; cf. para. 40.

20. Ibid., para. 42.

21. Ibid., para. 43.

22. Poon, "Anglican Communion as Communion of Churches," paras. 17–19, records several historical precedents, including: LC1930, Res. 49, which anticipated an entry by Anglicans "into communion with other parts of the Catholic Church"; LC 1948, Res. 74, which explained that reunion "must make the resulting Church no longer simply Anglican, but something more comprehensive"; and Robert Runcie's opening address at Lambeth 1988 on "the nature of the unity we seek," which spoke of the "radically provisional character" of the Anglican Communion. IATDC, *Communion, Conflict and Hope*, rejoins this tradition at para. 48, under the heading "dynamic catholicity": "For Anglicans the experience of catholicity has . . . been an experience of incompleteness. Anglicanism has never sought to be a world-wide church sufficient in itself. It has sought from the first to find its place in the life of the universal church, from its beginning to its

Here, the suggestion sets up a fascinating frame for a detailed survey of the major multilateral and bilateral proposals for visible unity involving Anglicans from 1961–1995. The ecumenical movement managed in these years to set forth articulately and succinctly the basic, necessary constituents for the full, visible unity of the Church, often characterized as *organic* unity. Starting from the high tide of World Council of Churches assembling and teaching (New Delhi, 1961; Uppsala, 1968; Nairobi, 1975), gathered delegates quickly agreed that "fullness" of communion (*koinonia*) between the "local churches" of the one Church must include: a commonly articulated and agreed faith; common sacraments celebrated together; a commonly recognized (at least, if not yet fully integrated) ministry; a commitment to regular, common counsel among and between all, hence a willingness to consider appropriate "structures of mutual accountability, authority and decision making" to facilitate this, including potentially synodical and primatial structures in the service of unity; and common witness and service, incorporating mission.[23] Most of these rudiments were in place and agreed upon in principle by the time of New Delhi's classic description of visible unity, and several successive assemblies added details here and there. At the same time, inevitable thorny questions about order and inter-ecclesial diversity and its limits emerged (e.g. at Canberra in 1991), in view of the persistent awkwardness of many churches, not one, in most places.

Whither, therefore, the much-touted *local* church and visible unity, amid a complicated sea of overlapping structures, ranged against one another in competitive or mutually disinterested formations and sub-cultures? And if the local church cannot be found, how shall we not despair of laying our eyes on the *universal* Church, the ostensible object of the ecumenical movement's vision from the beginning? Only, according to *Agros*, as various communions of Christians learn to embrace together a provisionality of unity by stages, such as that developed by the Anglican-Lutheran dialogue in Canada, whereby "full communion" is simply a step

---

eschatological consummation." For proof of this claim, the authors simply cite a famous passage from Ramsey, *Gospel and the Catholic Church*, 220. See similarly IASCER, *Vision before Us*, 35–37 *et passim*. Cf. Hill, "Ecumenical Moulding of Anglicanism"; Podmore, *Aspects of Anglican Identity*, 37–41; and, of course, Hanson, *Beyond Anglicanism*.

23. *Agros Report*, para. 59.

"on the way to 'full visible unity' which is described as the final vision and goal of the ecumenical movement."[24]

This goal, codified in numerous Anglican Communion texts including resolutions of successive Lambeth conferences,[25] has not translated in a straightforward way to every bilateral dialogue. *Called to Common Mission* (1999), the full communion agreement between the Episcopal Church in the United States and the Evangelical Lutheran Church in America, explicitly took as its frame the definition of the Anglican-Lutheran *Cold Ash Report* (1983): "To be in full communion means that churches become interdependent while remaining autonomous,"[26] and declined to mention full visible unity as a further, hoped-for goal. This fit with the Episcopal Church's 1979 "Declaration on Unity," which stated that "the visible unity we seek will be one eucharistic fellowship . . . a communion of Communions, based upon acknowledgement of catholicity and apostolicity."[27] That is, as the Episcopal Diocesan Ecumenical Officers spelled out the year before: "The visible unity we can accept will not be organizational or governmental merger; we do not envisage joining in one church body."[28] Here, therefore, we see a disagreement among Anglicans regarding the proper end of unity at which we should aim. All agree that full communion marks a step forward by distinct churches into a more mature mutual responsibility—hence interdependence—that may, as it is accepted, disrupt unilateralist habits. If, however, ecclesial autonomy is erected as an ecumenical ceiling of sorts, does this not amount, in the observation of Stephen Sykes, to a blithe acceptance of "the indefinite perpetuation of denominational" difference, as if to suggest that the Christian Church "may have catholicity without the inconvenience of unity"?[29] If, in a traditionally visibilist view, *Called to Common Mission* embraces an over-realized eschatology, seeming to rest content with full communion as end rather than weigh station, one nonetheless notes an

24. Ibid., para. 78.

25. See above, n. 17, for LC 1998 and 2008, themselves building on earlier precedents.

26. *Agros Report*, para. 65; cf. paras. 67ff. and paras. 75ff. Cf. ELCA, *Called to Common Mission*, para. 1.

27. Root, "Consistency and Difference in Anglican-Lutheran Relations: *Porvoo, Waterloo,* and *Called to Common Mission*," 303.

28. *A Communion of Communions: One Eucharistic Fellowship*, ed. J. Robert Wright, 31; cited by Root, op. cit.

29. Sykes, "Catholicity and Authority in Anglican-Lutheran Relations," 273.

effort in the text to maintain a proper hopefulness for *God's* future leading and continued call of his Church.[30] The closing paragraphs of the
agreement walk a tightrope in this regard, without major blunders but
also without particular courage or creativity. But this seems to confirm
the worry that Anglicans and Lutherans have, in this instance, reduced
communion to "the elimination of conflict between two expressions of
ecclesiastical parochialism."[31]

On this count, *The Agros Report* directs our attention to the object
lesson of the landmark *Bonn Agreement* (1931) between the Church of
England and the Old Catholic churches of the Union of Utrecht, enacting "intercommunion" between the two, in the parlance of the day (later
ratified at Lambeth 1958 as a full communion agreement between the
Old Catholic Church and the Anglican Communion). As *Agros* recounts,
each communion agreed to recognize "the catholicity and independence
of the other and maintain its own" and to accept that the other holds
"all the essentials of the Christian Faith," while eschewing uniformity of
doctrine, devotion, and liturgy.[32] On this basis, shared episcopal conse-
crations and sacramental fellowship ensued. By every measure, Bonn was
"ahead of its time."[33] By 1993, however, the bilateral dialogue had to be
reinitiated, as the two communions admitted, to their credit, that "we
have no structures which enable our bishops to make decisions together.
. . . [W]e also have no common synods in which clergy and people, with
their bishops, can make decisions together communally. This underlines
the fact that we are still two Communions, not one, and it also prevents

30. *Called to Common Mission*, para. 29, concludes: "We do not know to what new,
recovered, or continuing tasks of mission this Concordat will lead our churches, but we
give thanks to God for leading us to this point. We entrust ourselves to that leading in the
future, confident that our full communion will be a witness to the gift and goal already
present in Christ, 'so that God may be all in all' (1 Corinthians 15:28)."

31. Sykes, "Catholicity and Authority," 274. According to this criticism, ARCIC's
direct wrestling with structures and exercise of authority, tied to collegiality, primacy,
and a rich understanding of the local church, is preferable: see ibid. For a gentle—and
influential—pressing of the same concern as Sykes in the interest of a "full visible unity"
approach (finally with appreciative reference to Lambeth 1998, Res. IV.1), see Tanner,
"The Goal of Visible Unity: Yet Again." Tanner served on the Ecumenical Advisory
Group that produced *The Agros Report* and (with Sykes) on the initial IATDC team that
produced TVR.

32. *Bonn Agreement*, quoted in *Agros Report*, para. 82.

33. *Agros Report*, para. 82.

us from bearing witness together in the guardianship, maintenance and proclamation of the faith."[34]

Reflecting on the lesson of Bonn, Archbishop of Canterbury Robert Runcie wrote that it teaches us "the dangers of seeking only a comfortable half-way house on the ecumenical pilgrimage." That is, he continued: "Unity by stages is one thing; acquiescence, even contentment, with less than the full mutual participation unity implies is another. . . . We have the paradoxical achievement of sacramental communion without that which it is intended to signify: ecclesial communion."[35] In this context, the only sensible path is to repair, as *Agros* concludes, to the original argument for why we should want, and why we need, a visible fullness of common life in the first place, and then cultivate the "attitudes of mind and heart"—"charity and continuous conversion, *metanoia*"—"necessary for the ecumenical task."[36]

The Virginia Report: "A Catholic Doctrine of the Church"

Published the same year as *The Agros Report* with the similar aim of equipping the bishops meeting at Lambeth in 1998, *The Virginia Report* of the newly-formed Inter-Anglican Theological and Doctrinal Commission (IATDC) tackled questions of both Anglican identity and structure in a way that neatly complemented the commitments of the Ecumenical Advisory Group. The introduction of TVR frames its discussion in terms of the Eames Commission's mandate from Lambeth 1988 (Resolution 1) to address continuing Anglican disagreement about the ordination of women, in response to which the commission "offered guidelines on how Anglicans might live together in the highest degree of communion possible." As was recognized at the time, such a methodology—acknowledging degrees of communion *within* Anglicanism—marked an admission that the Anglican Communion has itself become an ecumenical project, according to which a commonly articulated and accepted faith and order can no longer be taken for granted without qualification, unless and until we "come to a common mind on a matter which touches the fundamental unity of the Communion."[37] In this light, TVR's introduction continues, it

---

34. *The Maryvale Statement*, quoted in *Agros Report*, para. 84.

35. Quoted in *Agros Report*, para. 83.

36. *Agros Report*, para. 92.

37. TVR, Intro. Cf. Vatican II, *Unitatis redintegratio*, para. 3 for an analogously in-

made all the more sense that IATDC should take up as a matter of urgency a second resolution of Lambeth 1988, namely, to explore "the meaning and nature of communion with particular reference to the doctrine of the Trinity, the unity and order of the Church, and the unity and community of humanity."[38] Finally, we are told, Lambeth 1988's Resolution 8 provided further impetus for the nascent mandate of IATDC, which resolution encouraged ARCIC to continue to explore a universal primacy in relation to collegiality and conciliarity. On all counts, Anglican ecclesiality and larger questions of Christian unity are taken to be intertwined, hence treated together unapologetically, as if to confirm the suggestion of *The Agros Report* that Anglican method is inherently ecumenical.[39]

Chapter one of TVR sets forth a posture for Anglican life in communion within a concertedly ecumenical context. From the start, we see that Anglicans locate themselves relative to a larger whole, identified as "the Christian community" and "the Church," that is, "the whole people of God."[40] Accordingly, setting a precedent for *The Windsor Report* and the Covenant, TVR describes certain aspects of this community, called "to graceful interdependence and unity in faith and doctrine," before situating Anglicans, and Anglican disagreements, with respect to it.[41] And while TVR anticipates that Anglicans will have gifts to share with others, not least as they similarly "find themselves passionately engaged in the

novative suggestion of "some kind of communion, though imperfect" (*quadam communion, etsi non perfecta*), persisting between the Roman Catholic Church and various other churches and communities, notwithstanding our estrangement from one another. On Anglican recognition of the methodology, see Hill's comment in "Ecumenical Moulding of Anglicanism": "What is God saying to Anglicans by their disunity and controversy, their impaired, imperfect communion, but that they have to work at the *general* Christian task of communion in diversity with their ecumenical partners, for their communion and the ecumenical unity of all" (163).

38. LC 1988, Res. 18.

39. I am more sanguine than Philip Turner about TVR's theological and ecclesiological coherence and craft, especially in light of its re-orienting ecumenical ambition. So far from playing into the hands of this or that aspect of postmodern pluralism, or uncritically accepting a too-idealized picture of the Church *sans* corruption and judgment, as Turner fears, I read TVR as an artful catechesis in catholic ecclesiology, aimed at a gentle advancing of longstanding Anglican commitments by deploying a more robust grammar and lexicon of communion (thence orderly accountability), drawn from recent multilateral and bilateral achievements, especially *Baptism, Eucharist and Ministry* and ARCIC. See Turner, "The Virginia Report: How Firm a Foundation?"

40. TVR, paras. 1.2; 1.5; 1.11; 1.13.

41. Ibid., para. 1.1, citing Jn. 17:20–21; cf. paras. 1.5 and 1.7.

midst of complex and explosive situations," it is also clear that Anglican structures must be renewed "in line with the emerging ecumenical convergence" regarding "the nature of authority and its exercise in the Church."[42]

Chapters two and three unfold the ecumenical and the Anglican in a patient dialectic, to an increasingly constructive end. Chapter two presents a now ecumenically standard systematic ecclesiology of trinitarian communion, noteworthy in this context for its artful ascent to an appropriation of Scripture's "diversity" of gifts to the building up of the body of Christ, "until all of us come to the unity of the faith and of the knowledge of the Son of God, to maturity, to the measure of the full stature of Christ."[43] The discussion is free of denominational reference: were the discussion transposed to another setting, there would be no indication of its provenance, save two superficial citations of Anglican reports.[44] And this is significant because it carves out a safe space for inquiry, in which the authors are able, seemingly without concern for the politically possible, to develop an argument about—again—*the Church*, with far-reaching implications for Anglicans. "The mutuality and interdependence of each member and each part of the Church is essential for the fulfillment" of her mission, the report teaches in a Pauline idiom, which means that "life in communion" requires attentiveness to one another, "particularly when conflict arises, so that the centre may never be forgotten."[45]

Chapter three fills out this picture of communion in Anglican terms with reference to shared faith, sacraments and ministry, structures, and mission—"elements," the commission notes, that "belong to the universal Church and are not unique to Anglicans," though they are "lived out in a recognisable and characteristically Anglican way."[46] Here the pedagogy of catholic ecclesiality for Anglicans becomes more pronounced, as we might expect from a theological and doctrinal commission presenting a piece of constructive ecclesiology with a view to winning hearts and minds to unity for the sake of faithfulness. Thus, the commission notes, not incorrectly, that members of the Church of England in the sixteenth

---

42. Ibid., paras. 1.8; 1.15.

43. Ibid., para. 2.26, quoting Eph 4:12–13.

44. See ibid., paras. 2.9 and 2.13.

45. Ibid., paras. 2.24–2.25.

46. Ibid., para. 3.1.

century "continued to understand themselves as the local embodiment of the Catholic Church."[47] In this spirit, we should claim as our own an ecumenically supple comprehensiveness, a genuinely "Anglican way," that yields at its best not only "generosity and tolerance to those of different views" but also "a willingness to contain difference and live with tension, even conflict, as the Church seeks a common mind on controversial issues."[48] On the basis of these virtues, while there may be no "legislative authority above the Provincial level" in the Anglican Communion, and provinces have been keen to protect their autonomy, "in practice autonomy has never been the sole criterion for understanding the relation of Provinces to one another. There has generally been an implicit understanding of belonging together and interdependence."[49] And if that is the case, does it not make sense—shifting more directly to a mode of intervention and prescription—for Anglicans to consider "whether their bonds of interdependence are strong enough to hold them together embracing tension and conflict while answers are sought to seemingly intractable problems"? For IATDC, the answer to this question seemed clear enough; and, in a kind of proleptic imagining of something very much like the Covenant proposal, the commission gratefully noted that "the call for more effective structures of communion at a world level. . . for the strengthening of the Anglican Communion and its unity into the next millennium" was on the agenda for Lambeth 1998. Likewise, opening out to an ecumenically fulsome cooperativeness, TVR marked again the question of a universal primacy, "exercised collegially and respecting the role of the laity in decision-making within the Church." Lambeth 1988 had itself kept the question alive, following ARCIC's lead, and meanwhile the Bishop of Rome issued an invitation to non-Roman Catholics in 1995's *Ut Unum Sint* to engage him on the matter.[50]

47. Ibid., para. 3.2.

48. Ibid., paras. 3.3–3.4.

49. Ibid., para. 3.28.

50. Ibid., para. 3.54. Para. 5.20 rejoins these themes in a direct and transparent way: "there is a question as to whether effective communion, at all levels, does not require appropriate instruments, with due safeguards, not only for legislation, but also for oversight. Is not universal authority a necessary corollary of universal communion?" This is the text Lambeth 1998 especially seized upon in its request for a decade of study of the questions raised by TVR: see n. 55, below. For similar themes, cf. paras. 6.22, 6.36.

The remaining chapters of TVR imitate the same dialectical pattern: delving into a theology of the Church in order to generate a rich grammar of the local and the universal, which is applied to Anglican structures, yielding a forceful set of prescriptions. When, for instance, individual provinces of the Communion take decisions without consultation "on matters which touch the life of the whole Communion," they fall afoul of a process of discernment and reception in the Church "which cannot be hurried."[51] For the "proclamation of the gospel to all humanity must embody its universal coherence," by using "the experience of fellow Christians as a way of discerning truth within the ambiguities of local tradition and culture."[52] Accordingly, the still developing "structures of unity and communion" of global Anglicanism "need now to be inspired by a renewed understanding of the Church as koinonia; a recognition of God's gift to the whole people of God of a ministry of episcope, exercised in personal, collegial and communal ways within and by the whole company of the baptised; by principles of subsidiarity, accountability and interdependence; and by an understanding of the Spirit led processes of discernment and reception."[53] In this way, the reality of the Church's communion guards the properly "embodied" character of local ecclesial life, and so strikes to the heart of "a catholic doctrine of the Church, which attempts to express what is, or should be, true of the Church in all places."[54]

51. Ibid., para. 4.13.

52. Ibid., paras. 4.14 and 4.23. Cf. similarly paras. 4.18, 4.25, 5.24–25, 6.37.

53. Ibid., para. 5.2.

54. Ibid., para. 4.24. In a striking encomium to catholic ecclesiology, this text continues, in a paragraph unlike any other in TVR (and without peer in TWR): "Our trinitarian theology (chapter 2) provides the basis of such an ecclesiology. It is no accident that it is rooted not just in the doctrines and experiences of the churches of the Anglican Communion, but in the convictions of the vast preponderance of Christians who have ever lived and of the public witness of their churches. In no sense is this ecclesiology untried or flimsy. Like certain forms of highly sophisticated modern metals, it is thin and exceptionally tough, proved in vast numbers of stresses. It is a vital resource, and to draw upon it is to show a wholly appropriate respect for the Church catholic." One supposes that Bishop Stephen Sykes drafted these sentences, since several of them appear verbatim sans quotation in his essay "*Odi et amo*: Loving and Hating Anglicanism," 205, followed on the next page by a footnote which marks "this argument" as "deployed" in chap. 4 of TVR.

CALLED AND CONSCRIPTED

To re-read *The Virginia Report* alongside *The Agros Report* in 2012 is to mark a critical step in the formal development of Anglican ecclesiology. To be sure, neither report was especially original or authoritative in and of itself, and Lambeth 1998 unfortunately only superficially "welcomed" TVR, without studying or appropriating it in a focused way.[55] Thus, the Communion proved much less equipped than it might have been to navigate escalating problems of division in the coming years, including: the ecclesio-political watershed of Lambeth 1998 itself, marking a heightened recognition of problems of authority and structure in the Communion; the formation of the Anglican Mission in America in 2000 as an irregular missionary jurisdiction in North America under the oversight of Rwanda and Southeast Asia, censured by then-Archbishop of Canterbury George Carey; and the election and consecration of Gene Robinson as bishop of New Hampshire in 2003 and consequent Communion fallout. Even so, TVR proved conveniently ready to hand, pertinent, and authorized—useful and necessary—for the work of both the Lambeth Commission and the Covenant Design Group, each of which largely adopted TVR's ecclesiology and proposed it as normative. In this way, the aforementioned crises, far from inspiring the last-minute manufacture of proposals aimed either at stemming innovation or codifying institutionalism, provided an occasion for the mass dissemination and potential reception of a catholic ecclesiology, incorporating a divine call to full visible unity, long since simmering on the stove of Anglican study and discernment, at the highest levels.[56]

55. LC 1998, Res. III. 8, imitating the report's pattern of theological argument about the Church in nine sub-resolutions, the most striking of which, sub-resolution *h*, "requests the Primates to initiate and monitor a decade of study in each province on the report, and in particular on 'whether effective communion, at all levels, does not require appropriate instruments, with due safeguards, not only for legislation, but also for oversight' (para. 5.20) as well as on the issue of a universal ministry in the service of Christian unity (cf. *Agros Report*, para. 162, and the Encyclical Letter of Pope John Paul II, *Ut unum sint*, para. 96)." The requested study never took place—until these matters were engaged on a more urgent basis in the guise of the Lambeth Commission on Communion.

56. The key sentence at 2.1.5 in the Covenant regarding an "ecumenical vocation of Anglicanism to the full visible unity of the Church" was added with the third, Ridley-Cambridge draft, apparently at the encouragement of IASCER, which passed in December 2008 resolution 16.08, expressing "concern that any Covenant should take adequate account of the need for a stronger affirmation of Anglicanism's ecumenical vocation, and our commitment to the biblical and patristic vision of Church unity, in

The present agony of the Anglican Communion illustrates that a simple juxtaposition of *interdependence* and *autonomy* does little to parse the relation between the two. On examination, one must be given precedence over the other: either interdependence is the primary commitment and autonomy relativized with respect to it, or vice versa. *The Windsor Report* saw this problem clearly, and solved it in favor of interdependence, in the idiom of *communion*: "Communion is, in fact, the fundamental limit to autonomy."[57] And the proposed Covenant does the same, while explicitly offering itself as an ecumenical laboratory, in which the Anglican Communion serves as the chief experiment for the potential edification of others. Should the tests we are running prove not only to relieve the symptoms of chronic division, endless wrangling, waste of resources, and distraction from mission but also begin to address and remove the deeper, root causes of our seemingly intractable rebellion, the drug—"non-coercive scriptural catholicity in mutual subjection and mission"[58]—could be approved for manufacture and brought quickly to the global market as at least one antidote to our besetting, ecumenical paralysis. "Stand up, take your mat and walk"! And, of course: "Do not sin any more, so that nothing worse happens to you."[59] In this way, the standing invitation to ecclesial provisionality may in fact serve as a kind of pre-ecumenical *praeparatio evangelica* for "families of churches within the Church" to hear and obey God's larger call to fullness of visible communion.[60]

The ecclesiology inscribed in the Covenant seeks to provide for us the way of intensified communion: a script for unity of a demanding sort. To accept it will be to continue to venture out of our bunkers of ecclesiastical autonomy, according to the given scriptural and theological terms, by

---

response to Christ's prayer that 'all may be one'" (*Vision before Us*, 229). TWR, by contrast, never speaks of an Anglican call or commitment to "full visible unity"; the closest it comes is at §49, which fails to mention common counsel, including common structures for decision-making, as an essential part of the mutuality of communion. In this respect, TWR's vision of "visible unity" seems closer to that of the *Cold Ash Report* than that of *The Agros Report*.

57. TWR, §82.

58. Ephraim Radner, a member of the Covenant Design Group, in a memorable interview with David Virtue, well before the CDG began its work—indeed, prior to the publication of TWR later that year. See Virtue, "Interview," no pages.

59. John 5:8; 5:14.

60. Covenant, Introduction, para. 4.

which *God* speaks and invites and we answer rather than initiate, "called according to his purpose."[61] In this way, the Covenant would conscript the Anglican Communion, pressing it into the service of providence, than which nothing less easily evadable can be conceived.

"We give ourselves as servants of a greater unity among the divided Christians of the world. May the Lord help us to 'preach not ourselves, but Jesus Christ as Lord, and ourselves as your servants for Jesus' sake' (2 Cor. 4.5)."[62] What other word should we wish to preach?—a divine Word, placed in our mouths to utter faithfully for Christ's sake, in the service of whom is "perfect freedom"[63]; written in order to circumscribe "all" for the sake of the Gospel.[64]

BIBLIOGRAPHY

Anglican Communion Reports

Ecumenical Advisory Group of the Anglican Communion. *The Agros Report*. London: Anglican Consultative Council, 1997.

Inter-Anglican Standing Commission on Ecumenical Relations (IASCER). *The Vision before Us: The Kyoto Report of the Inter-Anglican Standing Commission on Ecumenical Relations 2000–2008*. Compiled and edited by Sarah Rowland Jones. London: Anglican Communion Office, 2009.

Inter-Anglican Standing Commission on Mission and Evangelism (IASCOME). *A Covenant for Communion in Mission* (2005). No pages. Online: http://www.aco.org/ministry/mission/commissions/iascome/covenant/covenant_english.cfm.

Inter-Anglican Theological and Doctrinal Commission (IATDC). *The Virginia Report*. London: Anglican Consultative Council, 1997

———. *Communion, Conflict and Hope*. London: Anglican Communion Office, 2008.

General

Davie, Martin. "Anglican Ecumenism: The Liberal Catholic Consensus and the Conservative Evangelical Challenge." In *Paths to Unity: Explorations in Ecumenical Method*, edited by Paul Avis, 29–51. London: Church House Publishing, 2004.

ELCA. *Called to Common Mission: A Lutheran Proposal for a Revision of the Concordat of Agreement*. No pages. Chicago: ELCA, 1999.

61. Rom. 8:28.

62. Covenant, Introduction, para. 6.

63. Collect for Peace, BCP 1979, 57 and 99; cf. John 8:31–36.

64. Eph. 1 *et passim*; Acts 2. Cf. the comparably universalizing Ephesians 3:20–21, codified in the 1979 BCP as a concluding sentence of Scripture for Morning Prayer.

GAFCON. *Being Faithful: The Shape of Historic Anglicanism Today.* London: The Latimer Trust, 2009.

Hanson, A. T. *Beyond Anglicanism.* London: Darton, Longman & Todd, 1965.

Hill, Christopher. "The Ecumenical Moulding of Anglicanism and the Future of the Communion." In *Communion et réunion: Mélanges Jean-Marie Roger Tillard,* edited by Gillian Rosemary Evans and Michel Gourgues, 157–63. Leuven: Leuven University Press, 1995.

Jennings, Gay Clark. "A Covenant for Mission." In *The Genius of Anglicanism: Perspectives on the Proposed Anglican Covenant,* edited by Jim Naughton, 47–52. Chicago: The Chicago Consultation, 2011.

John Paul II. *Ut unum sint* (1995). No pages. Online: http://www.vatican.va/holy_father/john_paul_ii/encyclicals/documents/hf_jp-ii_enc_25051995_ut-unum-sint_en.html.

Naughton, Jim, editor. *The Genius of Anglicanism: Perspectives on the Proposed Anglican Covenant.* Chicago: The Chicago Consultation, 2011.

Podmore, Colin. *Aspects of Anglican Identity.* London: Church House, 2005.

Poon, Michael. "The Anglican Communion as Communion of Churches: On the historic significance of the Anglican Covenant" (2010). No pages. Online: http://www.globalsouthanglican.org/index.php/blog/comments/the_anglican_communion_as_communion_of_churches-_michael_poon.

Ramsey, Michael. *The Gospel and the Catholic Church.* 2nd ed. London: Longmans, 1956.

Root, Michael. "Consistency and Difference in Anglican-Lutheran Relations: *Porvoo, Waterloo,* and *Called to Common Mission.*" In *One Lord, One Faith, One Baptism: Studies in Christian Ecclesiality and Ecumenism in Honor of J. Robert Wright,* edited by Marsha L. Dutton and Patrick Terrell Gray, 296–315. Grand Rapids: Eerdmans, 2006.

Sykes, Stephen W. "Catholicity and Authority in Anglican-Lutheran Relations." In *Authority in the Anglican Communion: Essays Presented to Bishop John Howe,* edited by Stephen W. Sykes, 264–83. Toronto: Anglican Book Centre, 1987.

———. "*Odi et amo*: Loving and Hating Anglicanism." In *One Lord, One Faith, One Baptism: Studies in Christian Ecclesiality and Ecumenism in Honor of J. Robert Wright,* edited by Marsha L. Dutton and Patrick Terrell Gray, 193–207. Grand Rapids: Eerdmans, 2006.

Tanner, Mary. "The Goal of Visible Unity: Yet Again." In *The Unity We Have and the Unity We Seek: Ecumenical Prospects for the Third Millennium,* edited by Jeremy Morris and Nicholas Sagovsky, 179–90. London: T & T Clark, 2003.

Turner, Philip. "The Virginia Report: How Firm a Foundation?" In Ephraim Radner and Philip Turner, *The Fate of Communion: The Agony of Anglicanism and the Future of a Global Church,* 165–97. Grand Rapids: Eerdmans, 2006.

Vatican II. *Unitatis redintegratio* (1964). No pages. Online: http://www.vatican.va/archive/hist_councils/ii_vatican_council/documents/vat-ii_decree_19641121_unitatis-redintegratio_en.html.

Virtue, David W. "An Interview with the Rev. Dr. Ephraim Radner (Part Two)." No pages. Online: http://listserv.virtueonline.org/pipermail/virtueonline_listserv.virtueonline.org/2004-February/006615.html. February 13, 2004.

Wright, J. Robert, editor. *A Communion of Communions: One Eucharistic Fellowship. The Detroit Report and Papers of the Triennial Ecumenical Study of the Episcopal Church, 1976–1979.* New York: Seabury, 1979.

8

Documented Ecumenism

Why the Anglican Covenant is the Hope for Anglicanism and its Ecumenical Calling

MATTHEW S. C. OLVER

"A sincere intention to seek unity is incompatible with an intention to remain permanently uncommitted to any particular form of unity."

—Lesslie Newbigin[1]

"The Anglican Communion . . . provides a particular charism and identity among the many followers and servants of Jesus."

—Anglican Communion Covenant[2]

"This is a true story. Yet truth, as we know, is a many-faceted thing.
    Of one thing I am sure: This is not the whole truth."

—John Kiser[3]

1. Newbigin, *All in Each Place*.
2. Covenant, Introduction , para. 4.
3. Introductory note to Kiser, *The Monks of Tibhirine*.

INTRODUCTION

From the moment that the idea of an Anglican Covenant became a possibility with the publication of *The Windsor Report* in October, 2004, the most substantive and serious critique is that it would change the nature and character of the Anglican Communion. No one disputes that the Communion has never been constituted by canon law, *a la* the expanse of Roman Canon Law.[4] Though it looks nothing like even a basic form of canon law, were it to be adopted, "there is no way in which the Anglican Communion can remain unchanged"[5] by a functioning Anglican Covenant.[6] The purpose of this essay is to demonstrate that the Anglican Covenant is necessarily dependent on (at least) one aspect of Anglicanism's identity, "a particular charism,"[7] which the Covenant defines as "the ecumenical vocation to the full visible unity of the Church."[8]

From an ecumenical vantage, the Covenant text makes two very bold claims:

1) The vocation and *telos* of the Anglican Communion is inexorably and uniquely linked to the ecumenical imperative of the full, visible unity of Christians; and

2) the Anglican Covenant, by which churches can consciously choose to "reaffirm" and "intensify"[9] the bonds of affection that must bear the weight of communion between Anglicans, is at the same time being proposed to *other* churches and ecclesial communities to enable a correlative visible unity.

---

4. E.g., see Doe, "Common Principles of Canon Law in Anglicanism."

5. Williams, "The Challenge and Hope of Being Anglican."

6. Whether all or the majority of the Communion considers it a legitimate ecclesiological development remains to be seen. As of May 2012, eight provinces have officially responded to the Covenant: The Anglican Church of Mexico; the Anglian Church in the West Indies; the Church of the Province of Myanmar; the Anglican Church of Southern Africa (must be ratified by the next meeting of the province's provincial synod in 2013); the Church of Ireland; the Province of Southeast Asia; the Anglican Church of Papua New Guinea; and the Iglesia Anglicana del Cono Sur de America. See Episcopal News Service, "Two provinces align with Anglican Covenant." Some dioceses in the Episcopal Church have also adopted the Covenant at their diocesan conventions.

7. Covenant, Introduction, para. 4.

8. Covenant, 2.1.5.

9. Covenant, Introduction, para. 5.

Simply put, if the Covenant's ecumenical substructure is removed, its very *raison d'être* disintegrates. As we will see, the history of the Church of England and the Anglican Communion bears out the Covenant's ecumenical claims. What is perhaps most remarkable in the most recent chapter of the Communion's history—namely the Windsor Report/ Covenant development—is the unusual way in which the two documents make use of the theory and specifics of this history and marshal them in a completely unique way. The claim of the Covenant is both simple and revolutionary: the only solution to schism's possibility is to gather around the very same center of catholic norms that one day will centrifugally unify the now-scattered Church Universal.

A HISTORICAL EXCURSUS

The "ecumenical charism" of Anglicanism is discernable even within the sequence of sixteenth-century reformations that led to the independence of the Church of England. In the long run, reformation in England yielded a unique and markedly different ecclesial structure and ethos than those, both Protestant and Catholic, found on the European continent.[10] The first and most obvious of these differences is that the Catholic Church in England was separated *in toto* from papal authority, as the political transformation of Henry VIII's 1534 Act of Supremacy largely pre-dated the substantive reformations in theology and praxis that followed.[11] This event, coupled with the following three factors, produced an utterly singular atmosphere that resulted in an ecclesial identity where, as other churches have noted, recognizable "Catholic traditions and institutions . . . continue to exist:"[12]

    1) the clear "entent" to continue and "reverenetlye use" and "esteme"

10. E.g. see Neill *Anglicanism*, 31–132; Chapman, *Anglicanism*, 13–32; and Podmore, *Aspects of Anglican Identity*, 1–5.

11. Chapman, *Anglicanism*, 14. The Act of Supremacy declared the king to be "the only supreme head on earth of the Church of England." Quoted in Podmore, *Aspects*, 2. Except for the charge of "tyranny of the bisshop of Rome and all his detestable enormyties" in the first English litany (and liturgy) of 1544, "little official doctrinal or liturgical changed occurred" in this first phase of reform (quoting Podmore, *Aspects*, 2). For the original, Litany (1544), no pages. Elizabeth I's Prayer Book of 1559 excised this phrase permanently from the Litany.

12. *Unitatis Reditegratio*, §13.3.

the three "orders of Ministers in Christes church, Bisshoppes, Priestes, and Deacons, which Offices were evermore had in suche reverent estimacion. . .from the Apostles tyme;"[13]

2) the liturgical reform was quite conservative: Cranmer's overriding principle in paring down the medieval liturgy (principally the Sarum rite) was that it be "plain and easy to understand" (a phrase that appears twice in the 1549 Preface to the Book of Common Prayer), "evidently grounded" in "the very pure worde of God, the holy scriptures," and "agreable to the mynde and purpose of the olde fathers."[14]

3) The continuity of canon law in the Church of England, even after the first revision in 1604.[15]

All later phases of reformation in England took place within this unique framework. In fact, rather than pointing to abstract "principles," these three historical facts provide a solid context for a continued usefulness of the often maligned and misapplied term *via media*, which Newman coined in 1834.[16]

The structure that these realities created made possible a form of Christianity that Anglicans soon perceived as ecumenically useful. The reign of James VI and I is a surprising example of this with, among other ecumenical forays, his call for an ecumenical council, his assistance with the convening of the Synod of Dort (1618–19), and under whom there began conversations with members of the Greek Orthodox Church.[17] The English reformers frequently sought out the advice of non-English reformers. After the turmoil of the Civil Wars and the restoration of church and king in 1660, the 1662 revision of the Book of Common Prayer fully secured the episcopal establishment and enabled ecumenical contacts

13. English Ordinal (1550), Preface, no pages.

14. BCP 1549, Preface, no pages.

15. The Church of England "did not repeal the medieval canon law in areas" which the new canons did not address (Podmore, *Aspects*, 4).

16. Newman uses the term for the first time in 1834 in Tract 38, "Via Media No. 1," no pages.

17. See Patterson, *King James VI and I and the Reunion of Christendom*.

between the Church of England and other ecclesial bodies, including the Gallican church and the Moravians in the eighteenth century.[18]

In the late nineteenth century, to borrow the American William Reed Huntington's assessment of Newman's Tract XC, "the meteorite known in ecclesiastical history" as the Chicago-Lambeth Quadrilateral[19] caused such a stir upon impact that a fair appraisal is only now possible.[20] Particularly noteworthy is that one of the inspirations for Huntington, the chief architect of the Quadrilateral's first iteration, was a conviction that the Thirty-Nine Articles should "not continue to be considered one of the essentials of the Anglican position,"[21] a proposal that gained ground during the century and finally blossomed in the revision of the Declaration of Assent in 1975.[22] Instead, as the American House of Bishops put it in 1886, the cornerstone of Anglican teaching is "the principles of unity exemplified by the undivided Catholic Church."[23] The Quadrilateral, whose history through the American House of Bishops in 1886 and later at the 1888 Lambeth Conference is well known and easily accessible,[24] is the first concrete instance of a growing inclination to de-emphasize Anglican distinctives in favor of catholic norms.[25] That in itself is noteworthy, but

18. See Schofield, *Philip Melanchthon and the English Reformation*, esp. 116, 160, 161, 163–65, and 196–99. Peter Martyr Vermigli's connection to Cranmer and the Church of England is seen in *The Oxford Treatise and Disputation on the Eucharist*; see his dedication to Cranmer, 5–21. For a recognition that the *Unitas Fratrum* (now the Moravian Church) is "an antient Protestant Episcopal Church," see Yates, *Eighteenth-Century Britain*, 78.

19. The four parts are a) the Scriptures, b) the Apostles' and Nicene Creeds, c) the two dominical Sacraments, and d) the historic episcopate. Cited in BCP 1979, 876–78.

20. Huntington, "Tract XCI: The Articles of Religion from an American Point of View," no pages.

21. Huntington, *The Church Idea*, 176, quoted in Wright, *Quadrilateral at One Hundred*. See also Huntington's "Tract XCI." LC 1948 Encyclical Letter says something similar: "We find the authoritative expression of that faith and order in the Book of Common Prayer, together with the Ordinal" (*Lambeth Conference 1948*, 23).

22. See Podmore, *Apsects*, 43–57, including a discussion of the report issued in July 1968 at the requests of the Archbishops of Canterbury and York, *Subscription and Assent to the Thirty-Nine Articles*, and the growing concern about requiring subscription by clergy at ordination.

23. See this argument developed in Huntington, "Tract XCI."

24. See Wright, *Quadrilateral at One Hundred*.

25. It might be said that such a move is itself an "Anglican" move, but the point is simply that the matters emphasized by Anglicans were not anything that were unique to Anglicanism (e.g. the re-introduction of married bishops, the Prayer Book tradition,

even more so because of how early this proposal came in the history of the modern ecumenical movement and how its principles would be marshaled later by both the Church of England and the Communion as a whole. Whatever its weaknesses, the Quadrilateral helped inaugurate the modern ecumenical movement and offered the first specific proposal anywhere for doctrinal and organizational unity by a world-wide church speaking with a unified voice.

The advent of the twentieth century saw the posthumous publication of "A Short Story of the Anti-Christ" by the Russian Orthodox mystic Vladimir Solovyov, in which he depicts the unity of Catholic, Orthodox and Protestant Christians in the twenty-first century during the reign of the antichrist.[26] He was not alone in the late nineteenth and early twentieth centuries, as Bryn Geffert lays out in his history of developing Anglican-Orthodox relations in the post-war period.[27] The influential Russian Orthodox theologian Sergius Bulgakov went so far as to say that "the Episcopal Church is, of all the Protestant world, the nearest to Orthodoxy. Among the many tendencies in Anglicanism the Anglo-Catholic movement becomes more and more important; it is persistently devoted to reestablishment of ancient tradition and thus flows into the stream of Orthodoxy."[28] In 1910, the pan-Protestant Edinburgh Missionary Conference was convened for the sake of mutual cooperation in evangelistic work. The first meeting of Faith and Order took place seventeen years later, which would lead to the formation of the World Council of Churches in 1937 and whose agenda was deeply influenced by the Quadrilateral.[29] After the condemnation of the ecumenical movement in Pope Pius XI's *Mortalium animos*, the Roman Catholic Church officially entered the modern ecumenical movement in 1964 at the Second Vatican Council with the Decree on Ecumenism, *Unitatis reditegratio*.

In the context of this mounting tide of ecumenical goodwill, the Anglican Communion repeatedly stated, throughout the first half of the twentieth century, that the visible unity of Christians was a central priority. The "Appeal to all Christian People" from the 1920 Lambeth Conference

---

etc.).

[26]. Solovyov, *War, Progress, and the End of History*.

[27]. Geffert, *Eastern Orthodox and Anglicans*.

[28]. Bulgakov, *The Orthodox Church*, 191.

[29]. See Tanner, "The Ecumenical Future."

is a perfect example. The resolution makes a focused and winsome plea, first to those in "other ancient episcopal Communions in East and West," to which the Lambeth fathers say Anglicans are "bound by many ties of common faith and tradition," and second to "the great non-episcopal Communions," to whom is made a fervent appeal for the adoption of the episcopate as the best option for a ministry "possessing not only the inward call of the Spirit, but also the commission of Christ and the authority of the whole body."[30] Hand in glove, the bishops exuded a deep sense of their own apostolic obligation as bishops within the catholicity of the Anglican Communion and an equally firm belief in that Communion's "ecumenical charism." One of the first signs of this came in 1932 when the "Bonn Agreement" was passed by Convocations of Canterbury and York, establishing "intercommunion" between the Church of England and the Old Catholic Churches of the Union of Utrecht.[31]

At perhaps the apex of the Lambeth Conference's embrace of both a conciliar and ecumenical identity, the 1948 Lambeth Conference continued in this vein and issued a lengthy Encyclical Letter to all the faithful, which names this vocation specifically: "As Anglicans we believe that God has entrusted to us in our Communion not only the Catholic faith, *but a special service to render to the whole Church*," with a vision of "a united Church, Catholic and Evangelical, but no longer in the limiting sense of the word Anglican."[32] The Conference's Committee on the Unity of the Church went even further, arguing that the Communion must be "able to reach out in different directions and so fulfil *its special vocation as one of God's instruments for the restoration of the visible unity of His whole Church. If at the present time one view were to prevail to the exclusion of all others, we should be delivered from our tensions, but only at the price of missing our opportunity and our vocation*."[33] By 1995, the Church of England (and most other provinces) had entered into five agreements of "communion"

30. LC 1920, Res. 9, "Reunion of Christendom."

31. Meyer and Vischer, *Growth in Agreement*, 36–38. See also LC 1948, Res. 67, which encourages all the provinces to adopt the Bonn Agreement and "notes with satisfaction and approval" the "full intercommuion" between the American Episcopal Church and the Polish National Catholic Church achieved in 1940. In addition, LC 1958, Res. 46–47.

32. LC 1948 Encyclical Letter, in *Lambeth 1948*, 22; emphasis added. The scope and nature of the 1948 Conference can be seen also as the pinnacle of the bishops' sense that they are gathered in "council" and that they are acting like the local synods of the patristic age.

33 In *Lambeth 1948*, 50–1; emphasis added.

with a total of fourteen other ecclesial communities.[34] Stephen Neill put it famously: "The Anglican Churches have been the first in the world to consider soberly and seriously the possibility of their own demise."[35]

One final development that is unlikely to be listed in an ecumenical history, but is nonetheless extremely significant, is the revision of the Declaration of Assent (Canon 15), along with its Preface, in the Church of England in 1975. What is noteworthy, as described by Colin Podmore, is that as a "statement of identity," "the Church of England is given no denominational or confessional description. The term 'Anglican' does not appear . . . and neither do the words 'protestant' or 'reformed' (whereas 'catholic' appears three times—of the Church and of the creeds). The only name given is a purely geographical one—'of England.'"[36] Instead of "assent" to the Articles that are "agreeable to the Word of God," there is a declared "belief in the faith which is revealed in the Holy Scriptures and set forth in the catholic creeds and to which the historic formularies of the Church of England bear witness."[37] The Declaration, Podmore explains, requires "belief in the faith *in general* (and not 'the doctrine of the Church of England') but at the same time demand affirmation of loyalty to the Church of England's inheritance of faith" in the formularies.[38] Here we can see the fruit of the Quadrilateral's de-emphasis of Anglican distinctives in favor of catholic norms, all in a way both recognizable to Anglicans and amenable to other ecclesial communities.

The Windsor Report *and the Call for a Covenant*

At present, the Communion faces as real a possibility of its own demise as it ever has, though not, as Neill conceived, because of what lies directly over the next ecumenical horizon. While a fading memory for

---

34. In addition to the Old Catholic Churches, the others churches are a) Philippine Independent Church, Spanish Reformed Episcopal Church, Lusitanian Church in 1963; b) Church of North India, Church of Pakistan in 1972; c) Mar Thoma Syrian Church of Malabar in 1974; and d) Evangelical Lutheran Church of Finland, Evangelical-Lutheran Church of Iceland, Church of Norway, Church of Sweden, Estonian Evangelical-Lutheran Church, Evangelical-Lutheran Church of Lithuania in 1995. See Podmore, *Aspects*, 88–89.

35. Neill, *Anglicanism*, 432.

36. Podmore, *Apsects*, 57.

37. Quoted in Podmore, *Apsects*, 44 and 42 respectively.

38. Podmore, *Apsects*, 56; emphasis added.

many, the ecumenical history sketched above undergirds TWR and its proposal of an Anglican Covenant. The best place to see this influence is at the end of Section III, "Our Future Life Together," where the phrase "ecumenical law" is introduced.[39] The significance of the absence of Communion-wide canon law cannot be overstated and is one of the principle reasons why our ecumenical partners, in particular the Roman Catholic and Orthodox Churches, have expressed concern and confusion about what it means to be in conversation and enter into agreements with the Anglican Communion.[40] The subject of the final part of Section III is the recent growth of interest in canon law throughout the Communion, including the possibility of identifying "principles of canon law common to the churches within the Anglican Communion."[41] *The Windsor Report* fashions the argument as follows:

1) There is no official canon law for the Anglican Communion.[42]

2) Even further, "no church [i.e. province of the Communion] has a systematic body of 'communion law' dealing with its relationships of communion with other member churches."[43]

3) "This may be contrasted with the increasing bodies of *ecumenical law* in Anglican churches facilitating communion relations between Anglicans and non-Anglicans."[44]

Thus TWR concludes: "To the extent that this is largely descriptive of existing principles, it is hoped that its [the Covenant's] adoption *might be regarded as uncontroversial*."[45] The irony is thick and bitter: the Communion that long ago discerned an ecumenical vocation for itself now has nothing strong enough to hold her together in the face of internal disagreements

---

39. Between the release of TVR and the 2003 General Convention of the Episcopal Church, the Anglican Communion Legal Advisers' Consultation was created. See http://www.acclawnet.co.uk.

40 E.g. see Kasper, "The Aim of Our Dialogue has Receded Further," no pages; and Russian Metropolitan Hilarion's address given at Lambeth Palace to the Nicean Club.

41. TWR, §113.

42. TWR, §114–7.

43. TWR, §§116. That paragraph goes on to say that "inter-Anglican relations are not a distinctive feature of provincial laws."

44. TWR, §116, emphasis added; see n. 37 above.

45. TWR, §118; emphasis added.

and must instead rely on the ecclesial foundations of her ecumenical work to restore internal unity.

ECUMENISM AS ORDERING PRINCIPLE IN THE COVENANT

Communion Ecclesiology

The Anglican Covenant begins with an eight-paragraph Introduction[46] which provides the full theological and ecclesiological context for the Covenant itself. Those familiar with the work of John Zizioulas[47] and "communion ecclesiology"[48] will find its major themes quickly and efficiently delineated in the Introduction. Briefly, this ecclesiological perspective states that communion among Christians has its basis in the life of the Blessed Trinity and is made possible by the sending of the Second Person, Jesus the Son of God, through whom "God has called us into communion";[49] Jesus established "one universal Church, which is Christ's Body,"[50] and through the sacrament of Holy Baptism we are made a part of the "covenant of death to sin and of new life in Christ" and thereby "empowered to share God's communion in Christ with all people."[51]

Communion ecclesiology has only grown in influence among Anglicans over the last half century. Its most sustained use has been in the Anglican-Roman Catholic International Commission (ARCIC),[52] whose work was summarized beautifully in the latest statement from the International Anglican Roman Catholic Commission for Unity and Mission (IARCCUM), *Growing Together in Unity and Mission*. While not widely known, the work of IARCCUM, particularly with regards to

46. Covenant, 4.4.1 states: "The Introduction to the Covenant Text, which shall always be annexed to the Covenant text, is not part of the Covenant, but shall be accorded authority in understanding the purpose of the Covenant."

47. See his *Being as Communion* and *Communion and Otherness*.

48. E.g. De Lubac, *Splendor of the Church*; Tillard, *Church of Churches* and *Flesh of the Church, Flesh of Christ*; Tavard, *The Church, Community of Salvation*; McPartlan, *The Eucharist Makes the Church*.

49. Covenant, Introduction, para. 1.

50. Covenant, Introduction, para. 3.

51. Covenant, Introduction, para. 2.

52. See *Authority in the Church I* (1976), *Authority in the Church II* (1981), *Salvation and the Church* (1986), *The Church as Communion* (1990), and *The Gift of Authority: Authority in the Church III* (1998).

TWR and the Covenant, has been hugely significant. As Cardinal Kasper reiterated in his address to the 2008 Lambeth Conference, "The questions and problems of our friends are also our questions and problems."[53] Paul McPartlan, a Roman Catholic member of IARCCUM, argues that "in a very far-sighted way, right from the outset," ARCIC "has taken communion, or *koinonia*, as the central theme of all its texts."[54] This theme was marshaled by the Covenant Design Group by way of TWR, which in its discussion of ecclesiology and the necessity of a Covenant, is indebted most to IARCCUM.[55] As the Communion considers the Covenant, it is imperative that we recognize that the very ecclesiology articulated therein is the direct fruit of our forty-year dialogue with the Roman Catholic Church, work that has been repeatedly affirmed and embraced by successive Lambeth Conferences, Anglican Consultative Councils, and Archbishops of Canterbury.[56]

Ecumenical Roots of the Covenant

The Covenant is literally held together by generations of ecumenical work and premised on the proposition that God wills for the Anglican Communion to remain together for the sake of the unity of Christ's Catholic Church. Perusing the footnotes in the Covenant text reveals that nearly half of the citations are from ecumenical texts and agreements.[57] Undergirded by communion ecclesiology, ecumenism structures the Introduction to the Covenant and frames its portrait of the Anglican

53. Kasper, "The Aim of Our Dialogue Has Receded Further," no pages.

54. McPartlan, "IARCCUM: Growing Together in Unity and Mission," no pages.

55. IARCCUM, "Ecclesiological Reflections on the Current Situation in the Anglican Communion in the Light of ARCIC." For the ecclesiological sections of TWR, see §§1–11 for a general discussion, and then §§45–53, §§63–96, and §§121–35 as applied to the Anglican Communion in particular. See Cardinal Kasper's mention of this in Kasper, "The Aim of Our Dialogue Has Receded Further."

56. E.g. see LC 1968, Res. 52–4; LC 1978, Res. 33; LC 1988, Res. 8; LC 1998, Section IV.23.

57. Ten of the twenty-two direct citations come from ecumenical documents: two from our dialogue with the Orthodox Churches, *The Church of the Triune God* (n. 1) and the *Moscow Agreed Statement* (n. 12); one from ARCIC, *Church as Communion* (n.10); one from IARCCUM, *Growing Together in Unity and Mission* (n.13); four quotations from the Chicago-Lambeth Quadrilateral (nn. 4–7); and two from World Council of Churches statements: *Christ the Hope of the World* (n.11) and *Baptism, Eucharist and Ministry* (n.14).

Communion. The first three paragraphs set communion ecclesiology within a rich panoply of Scriptural sources. The ecclesiology is affixed Scripturally to the principle theme of covenant, first "with Noah, Abraham, Israel and David" which always "looked forward to a new covenant," given in Jesus Christ and "established in his 'blood. . .poured out for many for the forgiveness of sins' (Mt 26:28)."[58] The first mention of Anglicanism in para. 4 makes clear that its very existence is premised on schism's sin, which the Covenant seeks to remedy both internally and externally: "In the providence of God, which holds sway even over our divisions caused by sin, various families of churches have grown up within the universal Church in the course of history. Among these families is the Anglican Communion, which provides a particular charism and identity among the many followers and servants of Jesus."[59] The threat to the evangelical witness of the Church is threatened no less by the schism in the Anglican Communion than by its separation from other Christian bodies.

The Covenant's Ecumenical Viability

The first section of the Covenant, "Our Inheritance of Faith," contin-ues this theme in a slightly different, albeit more practical, way. It lists eight affirmations that every church makes by adopting the Covenant.[60] In this comprehensive summary—the catholic and apostolic faith, Scripture, Creed, dominical sacraments, historic episcopate, shared pat-terns of worship and apostolic mission—there is only one affirmation that is in any way distinctive to Anglicanism: "The historic formular-ies of the Church of England,[61] forged in the context of the European Reformation and acknowledged and appropriated in various ways in the Anglican Communion, bear authentic witness to this faith."[62] Note the restraint of this affirmation. The historic formularies are not a "con-fession." Instead, the signing church affirms that the historic formular-ies are a *witness* (echoing the Declaration of Assent[63]) to "the catholic and apostolic faith,"[64] something non-Anglicans could conceivably do

58. Covenant, Introduction, para. 2.

59. Covenant, Introduction, para. 4.

60. Covenant, 1.1.1–1.1.8.

61. 39 Art., BCP 1662, and the Ordering of Bishops, Priests and Deacons.

62. Covenant, 1.1.2.

63. See Podmore, *Aspects*, 56–57.

64. Covenant, 1.1.1.

(if allowed to interpret them in their historical context). Similarly, the final affirmation, "its participation in the apostolic mission of the whole people of God," concludes with an acknowledgment that "this is shared with other Churches and traditions beyond this Covenant,"[65] a phrase that is repeated verbatim in 2.1.5.

A careful reading of the entire Covenant text reveals that none of the affirmations required of signatories would be impossible for Christians of other traditions.[66] Further, Section 1.2, where commitments are made about how to live out "this inheritance of faith in varying contexts," a similar pattern is discerned: again, only one reference[67] to the Anglican Communion and one that should raise no problem for non-Anglicans. That is, a non-Anglican church could act "in continuity and consonance" with the catholic faith and order as it has been "received by the Churches of the Anglican Communion," and be "mindful of its common counsels and ecumenical agreements." The ecumenical charism is again explicitly endorsed in the penultimate affirmation: "to seek . . . for the fuller realization of the communion of all Christians."[68]

The clear intention of the Covenant to be another instance of ecumenical law is clear in the opening of Section 4 where the implementing principles and procedures are laid out: "Each Church adopting this Covenant affirms that it enters into the Covenant as a commitment to relationship in submission to God. Each Church freely *offers this commitment to other Churches* in order to live more fully into the ecclesial communion and interdependence which is foundational to the Churches of the Anglican Communion."[69] Later in that same section, the Covenant also gives the authority to the Instruments of Communion to "invite other Churches to adopt the Covenant," while still leaving "recognition by, or membership" in the Instruments in the hands of the Instruments themselves.[70]

65. Covenant, 1.1.8.

66. Though it is worth noting that if a church has rejected the "historic episcopate" (Covenant, 1.1.6), it would at least raise questions about what it means for such a body to adopt the Covenant unless they were to follow something like the course that was followed between the Church of the England and the Church of South India. See Podmore, *Aspects*, 89–91.

67. Covenant, 1.2.1.

68. Covenant, 1.2.7.

69. Covenant, 4.1.1.

70. Covenant, 4.1.5.

CONCLUSION

Christopher Seitz suggests that the "Creed is more than putting out theological brushfires. It is letting Scripture come to its natural, two-testament expression."[71] What I have argued is that the Anglican Covenant lets the Quadrilateral come to its full, ecclesiological expression, one which rejects any distinction between the means for unity *within* ecclesial communities and *between* them by an appeal to catholic norms. This is a completely unique moment in the history of ecumenism. Most of the debates around the Covenant have missed its ecumenical strand,[72] and if the discussion remains in the realm of politics and in the trenches of debates over sexuality, the Anglican Communion may very well observe its own demise, along with its ecumenical charism and any real claim to catholicity, even as some exclaim their faithfulness to a prophetic calling. Only history will tell.

In his final address to the 2008 Lambeth Conference, Archbishop Williams outlined the virtues of a "covenanted future" and said that such a commitment might "even be a prophetic one,"[73] and I believe he is absolutely correct. The most important reason that the Covenant is, in fact, a prophetic act is that it echoes the scriptural witness of the action of the prophets. The prophetic act is never marked by historical innovation. Rather, as Walter Brueggemann argues, it is a recovery of "its tradition of faith" that "permits that tradition to be the primal way out of inculteration."[74] This is the prophetic act to which the Communion is now called, not the ones which threaten to be its undoing.

"To our Communion many gifts have been given, and God wills to give many more if we let him."[75] Archbishop Williams is correct. The Anglican Covenant makes possible both the ecumenical *vocation* that God has laid upon the Anglican Communion and a willingness to be formed in patience, the *virtue* to which God has called it.[76] Soon, the

71. Seitz, *Nicene Christianity*, 19, 20.

72. For a consideration of the idea of a Covenant and the Quadrilateral see Franklin, "The Episcopal Church in the USA and the Covenant."

73. Williams, "Concluding Presidential Address to the 2008 Lambeth Conference," no pages.

74. Brueggemann, *The Prophetic Imagination*, 2.

75. Williams, "Concluding Presidential Address to the 2008 Lambeth Conference," no pages.

76. For a discussion of Anglicanism's call to the virtue of patience, see the Introduction

Communion must decide between the competing vocations. The choice for catholicity is an embrace of the Covenant and the sacrifices necessary for substantive Christian unity.

BIBLIOGRAPHY

Liturgies

BCP 1549. Preface. No pages. Online: http://justus.anglican.org/resources/bcp/1549/front_matter_1549.htm#Preface.

BCP 1979. *The Book of Common Prayer, according to the use of the Episcopal Church.* New York: Oxford University Press, 1990, 876-78.

English Ordinal (1550). No pages. Online: http://justus.anglican.org/resources/bcp/1549/Deacons_1549.htm.

Litany (1544). No pages. Online: http://justus.anglican.org/resources/bcp/Litany1544/Litany_1544.htm.

Lambeth Conference Reports

Lambeth Conference 1948: Encyclical Letter from the Bishops together with the Resolutions and Reports. London: SPCK, 1948

Anglican Ecumenical Dialogue Reports

Anglican-Orthodox Joint Doctrinal Discussion (A/OJDD). *The Moscow Agreed Statement.* 1976. Online: http://www.anglicancommunion.org/ministry/ecumenical/dialogues/orthodox/docs/the_moscow_statement.cfm.

International Commission for Anglican-Orthodox Theological Dialogue (ICAOTD). *The Church of the Triune God: The Cyprus Agreed Statement.* 2006. Online: http://www.anglicancommunion.org/ministry/ecumenical/dialogues/orthodox/docs/pdf/The%20Church%20of%20the%20Triune%20God.pdf.

ARCIC. *Authority in the Church* I. 1976. Online: http://www.anglicancommunion.org/ministry/ecumenical/dialogues/catholic/arcic/docs/authority_in_the_church_I.cfm.

———. *Authority in the Church* II. 1981. Online: http://www.anglicancommunion.org/ministry/ecumenical/dialogues/catholic/arcic/docs/authority_in_the_church_II.cfm.

———. *Salvation and the Church.* 1986. http://www.anglicancommunion.org/ministry/ecumenical/dialogues/catholic/arcic/docs/salvation_and_the_church.cfm.

———. *Church as Communion.* 1990. Online: http://www.anglicancommunion.org/ministry/ecumenical/dialogues/catholic/arcic/docs/church_as_communion.cfm.

———. *The Gift of Authority: Authority in the Church* III. 1998. Online: http://www.anglicancommunion.org/ministry/ecumenical/dialogues/catholic/arcic/docs/gift_of_authority.cfm.

---

to Williams, *Anglican Identities.*

International Anglican Roman Catholic Commission for Unity and Mission (IARCCUM). "Ecclesiological Reflections on the Current Situation in the Anglican Communion in the Light of ARCIC: Report of the ad hoc sub-commission of IARCCUM presented to the Most Reverend and Right Honorable Archbishop of Canterbury, Rowan Williams and to the President of the Pontifical Council for Promoting Christian Unity, Cardinal Walter Kasper." 2004. Online: http://www.anglicancommunion.org/ ministry/ecumenical/dialogues/catholic/iarccum/docs/pdf/iarccum2004.pdf.

———. *Growing Together in Unity and Mission*. 2007. Online: http://www.anglican communion.org/ministry/ecumenical/dialogues/catholic/iarccum/docs/pdf/ Growing%20Together%20in%20Unity%20and%20Mission%20definitive.pdf.

General

Brueggemann, Walter. *The Prophetic Imagination*. 2nd ed. Minneapolis: Fortress, 2001.

Bulgakov, Sergius. *The Orthodox Church*. Rev. ed. Crestwood, NY: St. Vladimir's Seminary Press, 1988.

Chapman, Mark. *Anglicanism: A Very Short Introduction*. Oxford: Oxford University Press, 2006.

Doe, Norman. "Common Principles of Canon Law in Anglicanism." In *A Fallible Church: Lambeth Essays*, edited by Kenneth Stevenson, 86–121. London: Darton, Longman & Todd, 2008.

Episcopal News Service. "Two Provinces Align with Anglican Covenant." No pages. Online: http://www.episcopalchurch.org/81808_128341_ENG_HTM.htm.

Franklin, R. William, "The Episcopal Church in the USA and the Covenant: The Place of the Chicago-Lambeth Quadrilateral." In *Anglican Covenant: Unity and Diversity in the Anglican Communion*, edited by Mark Chapman, 101–22. London: Mowbray, 2008.

Geffert, Bryn. *Eastern Orthodox and Anglicans: Diplomacy, Theology and the Politics of Interwar Ecumenism*. Notre Dame: Notre Dame University Press, 2010

Hilarion of Volokolamsk. Address to Lambeth. No pages. Online: http://community. beliefnet.com/go/thread/view/44071/25863453/Metropolitan_HILARION_to_ Lambeth_address?post_id=466477461.

Huntington, William Reed. "Tract XCI: The Articles of Religion from an American Point of View." No pages. Online: http://anglicanhistory.org/tracts/tract91.html.

Kasper, Walter Cardinal. "The Aim of Our Dialogue has Receded Further." No pages. Online: http://www.zenit.org/article-23385?l=english.

Kiser, John W. *The Monks of Tibhirine: Faith, Love, and Terror in Algeria*. New York: St. Martin's Griffin, 2003

Lubac, Henri de. *Splendor of the Church*. Translated by Michael Mason. San Francisco: Ignatius, 1999.

McPartlan, Paul. *The Eucharist Makes the Church: Henri de Lubac and John Zizioulas in Dialogue*. London: T. & T. Clark, 1993.

———. "IARCCUM: Growing Together in Unity and Mission." No pages. 2007. Online. http://ecumenism.net/archive/iarccum/growing_together_mcpartlan.htm.

Meyer, Harding and Lukas Vischer, editors. *Growth in Agreement: Reports and Agreed Statements of Ecumenical Conversations on a World Level*. New York: Paulist, 1984.

Newbigin, Lesslie. *All in Each Place*. Geneva: World Council of Churches, 1981.

Neill, Stephen. *Anglicanism*. London: Penguin Books, 1958.

Newman, John Henry. "Via Media No. 1." No pages. Online: http://www.newmanreader. org/works/viamedia/volume2/viamedia.html.

Patterson, W. B. *King James VI and I and the Reunion of Christendom*. Cambridge Studies in Early Modern British History. Cambridge: Cambridge University Press, 1997.

Podmore, Colin. *Aspects of Anglican Identity*. London: Church House Publishing, 2005.

Schofield, John. *Philip Melanchthon and the English Reformation*. Aldershot, UK: Ashgate, 2006.

Seitz, Christopher R. *Nicene Christianity: The Future for a New Ecumenism*. Grand Rapids: Eerdmans, 2004.

Solovyov, Vladimir. *War, Progress, and the End of History: Three Conversations, including a Short Story of the Anti-Christ*. Hudson, NY: Lindisfarne, 1990.

Tanner, Mary. "The Ecumenical Future." In *The Study of Anglicanism*, edited by Stephen Sykes, 427–46. Rev. ed. London: SPCK, 1998.

Tavard, George H. *The Church, Community of Salvation: An Ecumenical Ecclesiology*. New Theology Studies 1. Collegeville, MN: Liturgical, 1992.

Tillard, J. M. R., OP, *Church of Churches: The Ecclesiology of Communion*. Collegeville, MN: Liturgical, 1992.

———. *Flesh of the Church, Flesh of Christ: A Source of the Ecclesiology of Communion*. Collegeville, MN: Liturgical, 2001.

Unitatis Reditegratio. No pages. Online. http://www.vatican.va/archive/hist_councils/ ii_vatican_council/documents/vat-ii_decree_19641121_unitatis-redintegratio_ en.html.

Vermigli, Peter Martyr. *The Oxford Treatise and Disputation on the Eucharist, 1549*. Translated and edited by Joseph C. McLelland. The Peter Martyr Library, vol. 7. Kirksville, MI: Sixteenth Century Essays and Studies, 2000.

Williams, Rowan. *Anglican Identities*. Cambridge, MA: Cowley, 2003.

———. "The Challenge and Hope of Being Anglican." June 27, 2006. No pages. Online: http://www.archbishopofcanterbury.org/articles.php/1478/the-challenge-and-hope-of-being-an-anglican-today-a-reflection-for-the-bishops-clergy-and-faithful-0.

———. "Concluding Presidential Address to the 2008 Lambeth Conference." August 3, 2008. No pages. Online: http://www.archbishopofcanterbury.org/articles.php/1350/ concluding-presidential-address-to-the-lambeth-conference.

World Council of Churches. *Christ the Hope of the World*. London: SCM, 1954.

———. *Baptism, Eucharist and Ministry*. Geneva: World Council of Churches, 1982.

Wright, J. Robert (ed.). *Quadrilateral at One Hundred: Essays on the Centenary of the Chicago- Lambeth Quadrilateral 1886/88-1986/88*. Cincinnati, OH: Forward Movement Publications, 1988.

Yates, Nigel. *Eighteenth-Century Britain: Religion and Politics, 1814–1815*. Harlow: Pearson Longman, 2008.

Zizioulas, John. *Being as Communion: Studies in Personhood and the Church*. Crestwood, NY: St. Vladimir's Seminary Press, 1997.

———. *Communion and Otherness: Further Studies in Personhood and the Church*. London: T. & T. Clark, 2007.

9

The Anglican Covenant and
Anglicanorum Coetibus

EVAN KUEHN[1]

IN LATE 2009, TWO ecclesiastical documents of substantial importance for the ecumenical future of Anglicans were published. The Anglican Communion Covenant had been long anticipated and meticulously drafted and revised in light of concerns expressed by the 2004 *Windsor Report* over needed clarification of the principles of inter-Anglican communion.[2] The Apostolic Constitution *Anglicanorum Coetibus*, a document providing for non-geographical jurisdictions of former Anglicans called "Personal Ordinariates," was released in response to petitions made by various traditionalist bodies within Anglicanism for formal recognition by the Roman Catholic Church.

Anglicanorum Coetibus has been controversial within Anglican churches. While the Roman Catholic hierarchy and petitioning Anglicans have praised the document as a milestone of ecumenical reception, other Anglicans have expressed concern that it is a disruption of the ecumenical dialogue that has already been occurring through the Anglican-Roman Catholic International Commission (hereafter, ARCIC) and other inter-ecclesial ventures for decades. The Anglican Covenant has also met mixed

1. I would like to thank Katie Silcox and Anthony Hunt for valuable comments on draft versions of this essay.

2. TWR, Appendix Two, especially Art. 7–8, 15, 24.

responses by Anglicans worldwide. Some see it as a threat (or an ineffective response to existing threats) to venerable Anglican structures such as episcopal oversight or provincial autonomy, although provinces that have accepted the Covenant affirm it as a necessary step towards establishing principles of inter-Anglican unity.

For churches that are part of the Anglican tradition but not currently members of the Anglican Communion,[3] as well as for some Anglo-Catholics and traditionalists within the Anglican Communion, the Covenant and the Constitution present an ecumenical dilemma. Lacking hope for a resolution to inter-Anglican conflict, a growing number of Anglicans are seeking refuge in other churches such as the Roman Catholic Church. Even for those who wish to remain within the Anglican Communion but are troubled by current controversies, the question of whether the Covenant offers a viable ecumenical solution has been difficult to answer.

Since the release of the final text of the Covenant, at least seven primates have declared its inadequacy.[4] It is imperative to assess the viability of the Anglican Communion Covenant for both Anglican and ecumenical relationships. Concerns such as the above have enunciated criticisms of current Anglican structures and require a substantial response. The

3. Concise identification of these bodies is difficult, as there are dozens of churches that identify themselves as Anglican, but not in communion with the Archbishop of Canterbury. The term "Continuing Anglican" refers to churches that broke from the American Episcopal Church and subsequently the Anglican Communion in the 1970s following women's ordination, in particular. I will use the relevant acronyms to describe those bodies that have broken off from the Anglican Communion more recently, most notably the Anglican Mission in America (hereafter, AMiA) and the Convocation of Anglicans in North America (hereafter, CANA). There is no shared point of origin for these latter groups. They are most closely associated with the present dispute over sexuality in the Communion following the consecration of Gene Robinson to the episcopate, although AMiA predates this event. To varying degrees, these groups are working towards creating a new Anglican province in North America, the Anglican Church in North America (hereafter, ACNA). The ACNA is currently in full communion with the provinces of Nigeria and Uganda, but not with the Archbishop of Canterbury. These designations do not exhaust the number of Anglican churches beyond the Anglican Communion, but will suffice for the purposes of this essay. Finally, "Traditionalist Anglican" refers to Anglicans within the Anglican Communion who share many of the sentiments of Continuing Anglicans, the ACNA, etc.

4. Primates Council, *Oxford Statement*, para. 5. Archbishops Venables (Southern Cone) and Kolini (Rwanda) have finished their terms as primates since signing the statement, but their successors (Archbishops Zavala and Rwaje) are on the GAFCON Primates Council. Robert Duncan, primate of the ACNA, was also a signatory.

Apostolic Constitution *Anglicanorum Coetibus* will be considered first, followed by an examination of the Anglican Covenant, particularly those aspects of the Covenant relevant to its feasibility as an ecumenical alternative to the Roman Catholic ordinariates.

ANGLICANORUM COETIBUS

The Ecumenical Status of the Apostolic Constitution

In considering the ecumenical status of *Anglicanorum Coetibus*, it is first necessary to address its ecclesiastical origin. The Constitution was issued by the Congregation for the Doctrine of the Faith (CDF) rather than the Pontifical Council for Promoting Christian Unity (PCPCU), the expected source of documents relating to the ecumenical initiatives of the Vatican. That the Constitution fell under the competence of the CDF is a preliminary indication that its purposes are primarily doctrinal rather than ecumenical in nature.[5]

There is significant disagreement about whether *Anglicanorum Coetibus* was originally intended as an ecumenical measure. William Levada, current prefect of the CDF, has characterized it as "a logical development of the official dialogues between the Anglican Communion and the Roman Catholic Church" and "in continuity with the serious and longstanding engagement with Anglicans exemplified by the ARCIC process."[6] In their joint statement on the constitution, Archbishop Rowan Williams and Roman Catholic Archbishop Vincent Nichols of Westminster acknowledge a relationship, though neither a continuity nor a logical development, between previous ecumenical dialogue and *Anglicanorum Coetibus*. They further note, "the on-going official dialogue between the Catholic Church and the Anglican Communion

---

5. "The proper duty of the Congregation for the Doctrine of the Faith is to promote and safeguard the doctrine on faith and morals in the whole Catholic world; so it has competence in things that touch this matter in any way." *Pastor Bonus,* Art. 48.

6. Levada, "Five Hundred Years." This understanding of the constitution is unlikely. Anglican groups petitioning Rome were in large part disaffiliated from the Anglican Communion and had abandoned the ARCIC process. Further, authorities within the Anglican Communion (including the Archbishop of Canterbury) were unaware of the constitution until immediately before its publication. See also the *Note of the Congregation for the Doctrine of the Faith on Personal Ordinariates.*

provides the basis for our continuing cooperation." [7] This conception of *Anglicanorum Coetibus* presents it as a consequence of the new ecumenical landscape made possible by official dialogue but also separate from the same, which continues to subsist in the official avenues of dialogue between the two communions. Walter Kasper has affirmed a similar stance on the Constitution, arguing that it simply does not contradict ecumenical work.[8]

In contrast, Cardinal Kurt Koch, the current President of the PCPCU, has articulated an "ecumenism of return" whereby true ecumenism is understood as reunion under Petrine primacy (as is the case for former Anglicans under *Anglicanorum Coetibus*).[9] This approach contrasts with most contemporary understandings of ecumenism, and in the case of Anglican-Roman Catholic dialogue it stands in stark contrast with the formula of "L'Église anglicane unie non absorbée" offered by Dom Lambert Beauduin to the Malines Conversations of 1925, an informal though celebrated ecumenical gathering that proposed a reunion of the churches following a reestablishment of the See of Canterbury as an Anglican Patriarchate.[10]

In his 2010 plenary address commemorating the 50th anniversary of the PCPCU, Cardinal Koch argues that Protestants and others have abandoned the ecumenical goal of full visible unity for mutual recognition and table fellowship. He presents the Leuenberg Agreement of 1973[11] as a model of this sort of inadequate ecumenism. Koch's assessment is problematic for a number of reasons. Koch claims that according to the document, ecclesial communion is "essentially a communion of pulpit and altar between various confessional churches."[12] However, "organic union" as an ecumenical goal is simply beyond the purview (rather than in opposition to the vision) of the fellowship established by the Leuenberg Agreement.[13]

7. Nichols and Williams, "Joint Statement," 20.

8. Mattei, "A colloquio."

9. Cf. *Mortalium Animus*, para. 10.

10. Beauduin, "The Anglican Church, United not Absorbed," 35–46.

11. The Leuenberg Agreement followed a decade of ecumenical discussion originating in the work of the WCC and occurring between Reformed, Lutheran, and United churches in Europe.

12. "essenzialmente una comunione di pulpito e di altare tra diverse Chiese confessionali," Koch, "A che punto è il cammino," 30.

13. The Leuenberg Agreement, paras. 44–45.

Koch also claims that the Leuenberg Agreement implies, "Catholics must become Protestant in order to take further steps in ecumenism,"[14] although he offers no clear reference to the document itself. The Leuenberg Agreement understands itself to be a contribution to wider ecumenism, but does not state or imply this sort of Protestant doctrinal criterion for all churches that Koch imagines.[15] The Agreement affirms that unity in Word and Sacrament is "the necessary and sufficient prerequisite for the true unity of the Church," but does not claim that it is anything more than a prerequisite.[16] As such, the statement appears to be in line with numerous Catholic-Protestant ecumenical dialogues pursuing various prerequisites of fellowship along similar lines.[17] In contrast, Koch's own views established in this address work to affirm precisely the stance that he criticizes in Protestants, insofar as he essentially demands that Protestants become Roman Catholic in order to further ecumenical goals. This is likewise the criticism that has been leveled against *Anglicanorum Coetibus* by various Anglicans: that it is not ecumenical progress, but rather an absorption of Anglican groups into the Roman Catholic Church. The Roman Catholic stance becomes explicit in the continued non-recognition of Anglican orders initially defined by *Apostolicae Curiae*.[18] Koch's assessment of ecumenical work with Protestant churches contradicts the assessment of his PCPCU predecessor Walter Kasper, who has claimed, on the one hand, that "all churches engaged in the ecumenical movement" agree that its ultimate goal is visible unity, while on the other hand, that "intermediate

---

14. "noi cattolici dovremmo diventare protestanti per poter compiere ulteriori passi nell'ecumenismo," Koch, "A che punto è il cammino," 30.

15. The Leuenberg Agreement, para. 46ff.

16. Ibid., para. 2.

17. See Sagovsky, "Anglicans and Roman Catholics," 28–29, for an examination of the differences between Anglican-Roman Catholic dialogue and Roman Catholic dialogue with other Protestants.

18. *Apostolicae Curiae* has become more prominent in Roman Catholic declarations during the last decade, beginning with the CDF's *Doctrinal Commentary on the Concluding Formula of the Professio fidei*, §11. *Anglicanorum Coetibus* VI §1 can be contrasted with the Ordinariate established in the Anglican province of the Southern Cone, which recognizes Roman Catholic orders and does not require re-ordination. See Beavan, "Peru Anglicans." For a similar example in a Continuing Anglican context, see the Anglican Catholic Church Canon 14.2.03: "All Priests and Deacons ordained as such in undoubted Catholic and Apostolic Churches may be received in their Orders by any Bishop Ordinary of this Church with the consent of his Council of Advice."

goals" are necessary such that incomplete confessional agreements should not be seen as precluding the ultimate goal of full union.[19]

While the ordinariates established in *Anglicanorum Coetibus* may have been an appropriate pastoral response to the petitions from Anglicans for reception into the Roman Catholic Church, they cannot be considered viable ecumenical structures. Official statements from Anglican and Roman Catholic officials have attempted to present the apostolic constitution as a part of ecumenical dialogue, but the facts of the matter present the ordinariates as a cessation from the process of ecumenical reception. The decree *Unitatis Redintegratio* states, "However, it is evident that, when individuals wish for full Catholic communion, their preparation and reconciliation is an undertaking which of its nature is distinct from ecumenical action,"[20] so that even by Roman Catholic standards *Anglicanorum Coetibus* is distinct from any ecumenical endeavor.

Although ordinariates are in the process of development, many Continuing Anglican groups have responded negatively to the Constitution for these reasons of ecumenical concern. In his official response to *Anglicanorum Coetibus* for the Anglican Catholic Church, Metropolitan Mark Haverland states, "The Note does not imply the union of ecclesial bodies, but rather the conversion of former Anglicans to Roman Catholicism with what amounts to the prior, effective, and complete dissolution of their former ecclesial structures."[21]

For those Anglicans determined to work towards the unity of the churches and currently weighing the choice between *Anglicanorum Coetibus* and the Anglican Covenant, the former is a problematic option. The question of whether and how the Anglican Communion Covenant is an ecumenical document will be considered next, as well as those points within the Covenant that are especially important for consideration by Continuing, ACNA, and other traditionalist Anglican bodies or individuals.

19. Kasper, *That They May All Be One*, 43.

20. *Unitatis Redintegratio* 3.4

21. Haverland, "A Response."

THE ANGLICAN COMMUNION COVENANT

Ecumenical Identity in Anglicanism

The Anglican Communion Covenant is an ecclesiastical document for a particular communion of churches and is not intended to achieve union with non-communing churches; however, it is characteristic of other Anglican documents in that its self-understanding always acknowledges a fundamental ecumenical aspiration. Michael Ramsey offers a standard account of Anglicanism's self-understanding as a contributing structure within the Catholic Church, "while the Anglican church is vindicated by its place in history, with a strikingly balanced witness to Gospel and Church and sound learning, its greater vindication lies in its pointing through its own history to something of which it is a fragment."[22] The Anglican tradition is a genuine witness to the fullness of the faith, but does not recognize itself as the completion of the Church.

The idea of Anglican incompleteness might be traced to the 39 Articles,[23] but the notion took on an increasing sense of "provisionality," during the late-nineteenth and twentieth centuries as the ecumenical movement developed. With the visible reunion of the churches as an end, the fragmentary nature of Anglicanism is penultimate to the eventual unity of the Body of Christ. In his response to the Covenant Design Group, Matthew S. C. Olver (who has also contributed to the present volume) emphasizes the extent to which this stance is unique to Anglicanism, and has traced its origin to the Chicago-Lambeth Quadrilateral.[24] The Introduction to the Covenant likewise recognizes the place of the Anglican Communion amidst a wider family of churches,[25] as well as its current missional status within the context of the Church universal, anticipating though not waiting for the appearance of visible unity to establish the Covenant's ecclesiological ground.[26]

22. Ramsey, *Gospel and the Catholic Church*, 220.

23. 39 Art., Art. 34.

24. Olver, "Ecumenical Burden," 3.

25. Covenant, Introduction, para. 4.

26. Covenant, Introduction, para. 7.

To Nurture and Sustain Eucharistic Communion

In the first section of the Covenant, entitled "Our Inheritance of Faith," each province is expected to affirm its commitment "to seek in all things to uphold the solemn obligation to nurture and sustain eucharistic communion, in accordance with existing canonical disciplines, as we strive under God for the fuller realisation of the communion of all Christians."[27] The obligation of communion should be an especially convicting standard for Anglicans separated from one another by the current crisis of communion. Those in provinces that have transgressed standards of fellowship acknowledged by the Communion, like those provinces which have either declared a state of impairment due to these transgressions or have left the Communion entirely to form continuing Anglican bodies, will need to assess the obligatory status of eucharistic communion under the terms of the Covenant. While disunity among the churches is always a scandal to the Gospel, this clear covenantal explication of the duty of communion will bring the broken state of potential signatories to the fore. Traditionalist Anglicans within the Anglican Church of Canada or The Episcopal Church (USA) who are struggling with the alternatives of either an Anglican or a Roman Catholic future should note that this obligation reaffirms claims made throughout the Windsor Process that provinces must not separate themselves from the Communion by pursuing agendas in contradiction with previous decisions of the Instruments of Communion or without consultation with other provinces.[28]

The commitment to "nurture and sustain eucharistic communion" will present difficulties for a trusting reception of the Covenant by the ACNA, Continuing Anglicans, and similar Anglican bodies. Both

27. Covenant, 1.2.7.

28. Ibid., cf. 3.2.3 –3.2.6. Eucharistic communion is distinct from the bonds of membership in the Anglican Communion, although they are related. Since 2003, provinces opposing the developments in the U.S. and Canada have employed language of "impaired" or "broken" communion between themselves and offending provinces, usually marked by an explicit break in eucharistic fellowship and an implicit suspension of recognition (e.g., of the legitimacy of the U.S. Episcopal Church). Sometimes it is difficult to distinguish these two standards of communion. A good example comes from the recent Primates' Meetings; during the 2007 Tanzania meeting, a number of Primates refused table fellowship with the Presiding Bishop of TEC, while a significant contingent of primates absented themselves from the 2011 Dublin Primates' Meeting out of opposition to the attendance of the Presiding Bishop of TEC. In the Covenant process, then, both table fellowship and Communion membership will be central to the healing of communion.

groups have declared "the dissolution of Anglican and Episcopal Church Structure," or broken communion against North American provinces of the Anglican Communion, and some have declared the same with regard to the See of Canterbury.[29] These groups have not separated from the Anglican Communion as a schismatic act or with any intention of disunity. The decision to break communion was a difficult one of conscience in the face of prior disunity that had not been properly addressed by the Instruments of Unity in accordance with the recommendations of TWR.[30] An obligation to retain fellowship with provinces of the Communion who violate standards agreed upon in TWR, previous Lambeth Conferences, and Primates' Meetings stands at odds with the very standards that the Covenant claims to uphold. While the Covenant is not intended to address past grievances, in accepting the Covenant a province thereby accepts the standards of communal fellowship recognized by the Covenant in the various Anglican structures; but these standards are precisely what have been rejected already!

Fortunately, this solemn obligation of full communion seeks to abrogate neither personal conscience nor obedience to the Christian faith. The Covenant calls adopting churches to "nurture" and "sustain" communion, which artfully conveys the extent to which ecclesial communion is a challenging, sacrificial, and sometimes-uneven process of the mutual pursuit of sanctification. While the assumed, normative status is that of being in communion with all covenanting churches, communal relationships are bonds that must be attended to and are rarely either "full" or "broken." In the language of 3.1.2, the meaning of a covenanting church's solemn obligation is "its resolve to live in a Communion of Churches."

THE ANGLICAN COVENANT AND THE ANGLICAN DIASPORA

Two revisions made to the Covenant text are worth noting on account of their relevance to Anglican bodies beyond the Communion. The first involves the process by which non-Communion churches may adopt the

29. The language of dissolution comes from *The Affirmation of St. Louis*. While continuity of communion with Canterbury and "all faithful parts of the Anglican Communion" was stated in *The Affirmation of St. Louis*, it has since become void.

30. On the failures of the Instruments of Unity and the canonical reform of the Church of Nigeria in response to the present crisis of inter-provincial unity, see Kuehn, "Instruments of Faith and Unity."

Anglican Communion Covenant, and the second involves the decision-making role of the episcopate. In the following section I will consider questions raised by the Covenant for these issues, as well as how best to understand and respond to them.

Adoption by Non-Member Churches

The Ridley Cambridge Draft of the Covenant, following its invitation for all member churches of the Anglican Communion to affirm the Covenant, states that, "It shall be open to other Churches to adopt the Covenant."[31] The final draft of the Covenant, in contrast, reads: "The Instruments of Communion may invite other Churches to adopt the Covenant using the same procedures as set out by the Anglican Consultative Council for the amendment of its schedule of membership."[32] The requirements for adoption of the Covenant by other Churches seem steeper than in the previous draft. The Commentary on Section 4 clarifies that the reason for this change is a concern for due process and an intention of reflecting current practice; the procedure for adoption of the Covenant is based upon that used for amendment of the ACC Schedule of Membership.[33]

How this protocol would apply to non-member churches seeking to adopt the Covenant if they are not currently under consideration as new provinces of the Anglican Communion is unclear. Further, the lack of clarity actually works against the Covenant's effectiveness for including Anglican churches outside of the Communion and preventing the entrance of former Anglicans into communion with Rome under *Anglicanorum Coetibus* or the continued formation of bodies such as ACNA that question the legitimacy of the jurisdiction of current Anglican provinces. While the Working Group encourages commitment to the Covenant from churches outside of the Communion,[34] the procedure delineated in 4.1.5 will make affirmation more difficult for churches that see their relationship with the Anglican Communion as relevant to their own identity, despite the lack of direct communion with the Archbishop of Canterbury. The Covenant and its Commentary do

31. RCDC, 4.1.5.

32. Covenant, 4.1.5.

33. Revisions, 4.1.

34. Ibid., "This sort of endorsement is to be encouraged as contributing to the covenantal life of the Communion"

not explain how such deliberations will play out within the ACC and the Primates' Meeting. Normally the ACC Schedule of Membership simply follows from church membership in the Anglican Communion, which is determined by ACC consultation with, and eventual recognition of, a province. The primary intention seems to be that prior consultation between the ACC and the Primates' Meeting would precede invitation to adopt, but if this consultation is specifically modeled on amendment to the Schedule of Membership, then clarification of the distinction between Communion membership and Covenant adoption as well as its implications for the covenanting process is essential.

The Role of the Episcopate in Inter-Provincial Governance

For many traditionalist Anglicans within and beyond the Anglican Communion, a strong emphasis on episcopal governance is necessary for Anglican identity and the Christian Church more generally.[35] In the past this episcopal focus has been cause for dissent in ecumenical ventures,[36] and dissenting reactions to the current Anglican Covenant have been similar. Under the Covenant, the Primates' Meeting and the Anglican Consultative Council act jointly in an advisory role towards the Standing Committee.[37] The commentary on the Covenant describes the process by which inter-provincial governance was addressed throughout the drafting process, emphasizing the representative status of the Standing Committee for all Instruments of Communion, its derived authority from other Instruments, and its coordinating role.[38]

This may be a point where traditionalists need to accept a broader *sensus fidelium* over their own vision of the episcopate for the Communion. The Covenant includes a role for the Primates in addition to the ACC, each of which is mediated by the Standing Committee;[39] however, the 2011 Dublin Primates' Meeting made clear that the Primates' Meeting

35. See the declaration by the House of Bishops of the American Episcopal Church, 1886, which would become the Chicago-Lambeth Quadrilateral. The four points were asserted as central to all Christian churches.

36. See "Memorandum of Dissent" D.26 in Churches' Council for Covenanting, *Towards Visible Unity*, 89.

37. Covenant, 4.2.2, 4.2.4, 4.2.6.

38. Revisions, 4.2; cf. Covenant, 4.2.6 and 4.2.7.

39. Covenant, 4.2.2.

does not see itself as standing in adequate position to judge these matters.[40] Some may claim that the increasing synodical focus is an abandonment of the episcopal focus of the Chicago-Lambeth Quadrilateral, but a commitment to episcopal governance does not preclude various innovations in response to current circumstances; the Quadrilateral itself speaks of local adaptation, and inter-provincial governance as determined by the Covenant should be viewed as just that. The current role of the ACC does not threaten episcopal authority as practiced within Anglicanism because there is no established episcopal role for inter-provincial governance within the Communion. The bishops gather in council and govern the provinces of the Communion in various ways; while the standards of conciliarity described in the Covenant may not please all parties, they do not usurp an existing episcopal authority. Rather, "the Covenant Design Group did not see its role as inventing new structures for the Communion, but rather explicating and strengthening existing structures."

What will be important to monitor in the future, however, is whether the ACC and the Standing Committee proceed with undue license beyond the confines of their dependence upon the episcopal Instruments of Communion. The resignation of Bishop Mouneer Anis from the Standing Committee in 2010 has brought potential abuses of the Committee to the attention of the Communion. He comments, "I have come to the sad realization that there is no desire within the ACC and the SCAC to follow through on the recommendations that have been taken by other Instruments of Communion to sort out the problems which face the Anglican Communion and which are tearing its fabric apart. Moreover, the SCAC, formerly known as the Joint Standing Committee (JSC), has continually questioned the authority of the other Instruments of Communion, especially the Primates' Meeting and the Lambeth Conference."[41] Amidst the increasingly strong role played by the ACC amongst the Instruments of Communion, the role of the Archbishop of Canterbury as a "focus of unity"[42] amongst the Instruments will also be important to guard. Paul McPartlan writes from a Roman Catholic perspective about the importance of preserving the mutual relationship

---

40. "The unanimous judgement of those who were present was that the Meeting should not see itself as a 'supreme court,' with canonical powers," Williams, *Letter to the Primates.*

41. Anis, *Open Resignation Letter.*

42. TWR, §109.

between primacy and conciliarity in the Covenant. He argues that, "primacy and synodality (or conciliarity) go *together* and are not alternatives. There is no synod without a primate, and no primate without a synod."[43] For Anglicans, the effectiveness of synodical governance depends on preserving the role of the Archbishop of Canterbury; this need not present itself as akin to papal primacy, but Anglican governance should remain balanced among the Instruments of Unity, which find their center in the See of Canterbury as their focus of unity.

It should be noted, however, that a weakening of primacy is not merely the fault of an increasingly influential ACC. *The Windsor Report* states, "the Communion should be able to look to the holder of this office to speak directly to any provincial situation on behalf of the Communion where this is deemed advisable. Such action should not be viewed as outside interference in the exercise of autonomy by any province."[44] In many cases, Archbishop Rowan Williams has been hesitant to speak in such a direct manner to the provinces during the present crisis of unity, and renewed affirmation of his office as the *primus inter pares* will be important for the renewal of the effectiveness of his leadership. Traditionalist bodies of Anglicans within and outside of the Communion are ideally suited for preserving such ecclesiological priorities, and should recognize opportunities for contributing to a covenanted future of the Anglican Communion even as they recognize that their stance on episcopacy will need to embrace developing synodical structures.

Just as the role of the Primates in inter-provincial governance has faced a turning point in the Covenant, the role of the bishop in the Roman Catholic ordinariates breaks from typical geographical jurisdiction. Within the Personal Ordinariate, jurisdiction is not geographical. The situation is an extraordinary one, but not without precedent: analogies have been drawn to the Roman Catholic military ordinariates and the Anglican provincial episcopal visitors. One might also add the examples of AMiA and CANA, where Anglican provinces in communion with Canterbury extended oversight at the request of Anglican churches that had left the Episcopal Church (USA). Ordinaries may or may not be a bishop, and they exercise power jointly with local Diocesan Bishops in certain cases,[45]

---

43. McPartlan, "Towards an Anglican Covenant," 167.

44. TWR, §109.

45. *Anglicanorum Coetibus* V.

although the Ordinary is appointed by the Roman Pontiff.[46] In light of these developments concerning the role of oversight for non-episcopal offices through both *Anglicanorum Coetibus* and the Covenant, it may be that creative developments in the synodical structures of the churches leads to future opportunities for unity.[47] Christopher Hill notes the role of the Governing Council in *Anglicanorum Coetibus*, "The Ordinary will be required to gain the consent of the Governing Council on admission of candidates to orders, the erection or suppression of parishes and in the formation of clergy (Norms 12.2). This goes significantly *beyond* current Roman Catholic requirements and indeed the role of a Bishop's Council and Diocesan Synod in the Church of England."[48] Again, the possibilities for synodical governance are adaptable to circumstance and should not be taken as a threat to the historic episcopate.

CONCLUSION

The dual processes of the Anglican Covenant and *Anglicanorum Coetibus* are complex and mutually informing despite the fact that they work towards opposing ecumenical ends and present a difficult choice for Anglicans committed to ecumenical unity and frustrated by the current state of disunity within the Anglican Communion. We are far from concrete knowledge of how God will use these measures to further the unity of His Church, and critical reflection upon these implications for the Anglican Communion remains warranted. Anglicans that stand outside of mainstream provincial functions—either because they have separated themselves from these provinces, or have voiced dissent from within the Communion, or have pursued fellowship in other Christian churches—cannot be ignored. They have brought to light some of the most intractable problems of church unity that currently threaten the Anglican Communion, and will be a part of any future solution to these problems.

46. *Anglicanorum Coetibus* IV.

47. See Clifford, "Local Church and Its Bishop," 68–71. Clifford notes that it is the episcopal office that remains a primary obstacle to church unity, rather than the local church or the ecclesiology of communion. Present innovations in episcopal oversight in both the Anglican and Roman Catholic communion could contribute to new conceptions of *episcope* that would be more ecumenically constructive.

48. Hill, "What is the Personal Ordinariate?" 206.

BIBLIOGRAPHY

Anis, Mouneer. "Open Resignation Letter from the ACC." 2010. Online: http://www.dioceseofegypt.org/english/sites/default/files/Bishop%20Mouneer%27s%20 Resignation%20from%20the%20ACC.pdf.

Beauduin, Lambert. "'The Anglican Church, United not Absorbed.' Memorandum by a Canonist read by Cardinal Mercier (1925)." In *From Malines to ARCIC: The Malines Conversation Commemorated*, edited by A. Denaux, 35–46. Leuven: Leuven University Press, 1997.

Beavan, Ed. "Peru Anglicans Set Up Own Ordinariate for RC priests." *The Church Times*, February 11, 2011.

Clifford, Catherine. "The Local Church and its Bishop in Ecumenical Perspective." *The Jurist* 69.1 (2009) 59–83.

Churches' Council for Covenanting. *Towards Visible Unity: Proposals for a Covenant*. London: Churches' Council for Covenanting, 1980.

Congregation for the Doctrine of the Faith. *Doctrinal Commentary on the Concluding Formula of the Professio fidei*. 1998. No pages. Online: http://www.vatican.va/ roman_curia/congregations/cfaith/documents/rc_con_cfaith_doc_1998_professio-fidei_en.html.

Congregation for the Doctrine of the Faith. *Note of the Congregation for the Doctrine of the Faith on Personal Ordinariates for Anglicans Entering the Catholic Church*. 2009. No pages. Online: http://www.ewtn.com/library/curia/vpoordinangl.htm.

Congress of St. Louis. *The Affirmation of St. Louis*. 1977. No pages. Online: http://www. anglicancatholic.org/main/who/stlouis.html.

Haverland, Mark. "A Response from the Anglican Catholic Church to Rome's Offer to Former Anglicans." No pages. Online: http://www.anglicancatholic.org/acc -response-to-rome.html.

Hill, Christopher "What is the Personal Ordinariate? Canonical and Liturgical Observations." *EccLJ* 12.2 (2010), 202–8.

Kasper, Walter. *That They May All Be One*. New York: Burns & Oates, 2004.

Koch, Kurt. "A che punto è il cammino." *Il Regno: Quindicinale di Attualità e Documenti* 1 (2011) 23–33.

Kuehn, Evan. "Instruments of Faith and Unity in Canon Law: the Church of Nigeria Constitutional Revision of 2005." *EccLJ* 10.2 (2008) 161–73.

Levada, William. "Five Hundred Years After St. John Fisher: Benedict's Ecumenical Initiatives to Anglicans." Unofficial transcription of address delivered on March 6, 2010 at Queen's University, Kingston, Ontario. No pages. Online: http:// saltandlighttv.org/blog/?p=11055.

Mattei, Giampaolo. "A colloquio con il cardinale Kasper sulla Costituzione apostolica 'Anglicanorum coetibus.'" *L'Osservatore Romano*, 20 November 2009. No pages. Online: http://www.vatican.va/news_services/or/or_quo/interviste/2009/265q07a1. html.

McPartlan, Paul. "Towards an Anglican Covenant: A Roman Catholic Perspective." in *The Anglican Covenant: Unity and Diversity in the Anglican Communion*, edited by Mark Chapman, 157–74. New York: Mowbray, 2008.

Nichols, Vincent and Rowan Williams. "Joint Statement: A Consequence of Dialogue." *L'Osservatore Romano* (English Edition) 28 October 2009, p. 20.

Olver, Mathew S.C. "The Ecumenical Burden of a Covenanted Future: Why the Hope for the Anglican Communion Rests on an Embrace of its Ecumenical Charism." Submission to the Covenant Design Group. Online: http://www.anglicancommunion. org/commission/covenant/docs/G09 13 Matthew.pdf.

Pope Benedict XVI. *Apostolic Constitution Anglicanorum Coetibus.* 2009. No pages. Online: http://www.vatican.va/holy_father/benedict_xvi/apost_constitutions/ documents/hf_ben-xvi_apc_20091104_anglicanorum-coetibus_en.html. Official Latin Publication: AAS 101 (2009) 985–90.

Pope Leo XIII. *Encyclical Apostolicae Curiae.* 1896. No pages. Online: http://www. papalencyclicals.net/Leo13/l13curae.htm.

Pope Pius XI. *Encyclical Mortalium Animus.* 1928. No pages. Online: http://www.vatican. va/holy_father/pius_xi/encyclicals/documents/hf_p-xi_enc_19280106_mortalium-animos_en.html.

Primates Council of the Global Anglican Future Conference (GAFCON). *The Oxford Statement.* 2010. No pages. Online: http://www.gafcon.org/news/oxford_statement_ from_the_gafcon_fca_primates_council/.

Provincial Synod of the ACC. *Canons of the Anglican Catholic Church.* Cleveland, 2007. Online: http://www.anglicancatholic.org/ACC%20Canons%20-%202007.pdf.

Ramsey, Arthur Michael. *The Gospel and the Catholic Church.* 2nd ed. New York: Longmans, Green, 1956.

Sagovsky, Nicholas. "Anglicans and Roman Catholics: A Joint Declaration of Agreement?" In *The Unity We Have and the Unity We Seek,* edited by Jeremy Morris and Nicholas Sagovsky, 27–51. Edinburgh: T. & T. Clark, 2003.

Second Vatican Council. *Unitatis Redintegratio.* 1964. No pages. Online: http:// www.vatican.va/archive/hist_councils/ii_vatican_council/documents/vat-ii_ decree_19641121_unitatis-redintegratio_en.html.

Williams, Rowans. *Archbishop of Canterbury's Letter to the Primates of the Anglican Communion.* 2011. No pages. Online: http://www.anglicancommunion.org/acns/ news.cfm/2011/3/12/ACNS4813.

10

The Anglican Communion Covenant
An Orthodox Response

AUGUSTINE CASIDAY

ANGLICAN-ORTHODOX RELATIONS HAVE DEEP roots.[1] If the anachro-nism can be forgiven, we might trace them back to Sunday, May 27, 669. On that day, Theodore of Tarsus arrived from Rome into Kent where he became the only Greek to serve as archbishop of Canterbury, which he did for precisely 21 years, three months, and 26 days.[2] Although he was accompanied by a North African, Hadrian, who had been spe-cifically charged to "take diligent care lest [Theodore] introduce anything into the church over which he presided that was contrary to the faith, in the manner of the Greeks,"[3] Theodore's legacy is uniformly positive in a way that belies the Venerable Bede's apprehensive and seemingly xeno-phobic note. Theodore was celebrated for bringing order to fissiparous communities, not least through the reform of canon law undertaken at

1. My thanks to Alan Brown for many topical discussions that are reflected in these observations.

2. Bede, *Ecclesiastical History*, IV.2; in Colgrave and Mynors, *Bede's Ecclesiastical History*, 332–33. On Theodore, see now Lapidge, *Archbishop Theodore: Commemorative studies on his life and influence*.

3. Bede, *Ecclesiastical History*, IV.1; in Colgrave and Mynors, *Bede's Ecclesiastical History*, 330; my translation.

the Council of Hertford (673) and through assembling his *Penitential*.[4] In the eyes of one commentator, Theodore's works "established a bond of fellowship with the Eastern Church, which the unhappy controversies of later times could not altogether sever."[5] Thus began the long, sometimes contentious, but generally constructive relationship between the Greek Church and the English Church. The precedent of a Greek hierarch making contributions to the reformation of the churches in England is ponderous. Being mindful of that history, I offer here some remarks on the Anglican Communion Covenant as a lay member of the Greek Orthodox Archdiocese of Thyateira and Great Britain.

My remarks are informed by three perceptions about the contemporary state of Orthodox and of Anglican Christianity, the relevance of which to the Anglican Communion Covenant I attempt to demonstrate in what follows. The first observation is that both Anglicans and Orthodox have inherited a legacy of profound nationalism that in the early years of this century poses distinctive, but comparable, problems for our respective communities precisely in their contemporary *global* settings. The second observation I will make is that attempts at providing overarching and unifying structures are fraught with great difficulties that are, again, typically distinctive but comparable and that in any case are unlikely to be resolved by recourse to platitudes. My final observation is that the Orthodox Churches and the Anglican Communion have in common—sometimes to their disadvantage—a practice of defining themselves in opposition to Roman Catholicism, in ways that limit their abilities to act effectively as global communities.

THE CHURCH "BY LAW ESTABLISHED"

The Covenant rightly recognizes that Christianity is a world-wide phenomenon.[6] But from an Orthodox perspective, it is worth pausing over a preliminary matter. Much of what is considered "World Christianity" was disseminated by missionaries, often a noble response to the Great Commission (Matt. 28:19) but inevitably bearing the good news in cul-

4. Haddan and Stubbs, *Councils and Ecclesiastical Documents Relating to Great Britain and Ireland*, III:173–204.

5. Williams, *The Orthodox Church of the East in the Eighteenth Century*, iii.

6. Covenant, Introduction, paras. 3, 7–8.

tural terms informed by their homeland. The distinctiveness of "World Christianity" can be tracked as the indigenization of Christianity in Africa, South America, and Asia as compared to the characteristic traits of Protestant or Catholic Christian missions.[7] Orthodox Christianity is rarely mentioned in these discussions, perhaps because mission activity by Orthodox Christians is historically unusual. The glory days of Orthodox missionary activity was the conversion of the Slavs in the ninth century, followed by the spread of Christianity into Alaska from the late eighteenth century. More often than as a consequence of deliberate missionary endeavor, Orthodoxy has spread inadvertently through emigration of Orthodox Christians.[8]

Be that as it may, one way or the other Orthodox Christianity has also spread around the world. That fact is easily overlooked if we presume that the Western world is somehow Christian by default, since Orthodoxy has tended to proliferate in lands already Christian rather than amongst heathens. And so Orthodox Christianity no less than Protestant or Catholic Christianity has become established beyond its original boundaries and is currently indigenizing in unfamiliar places. Against the background of Christianity established locally, the processes of indigenization and the factors that inform them are experienced differently by Orthodox Christians. An anecdotal example may help. Often enough, upon identifying oneself as Orthodox to another Christian, the Orthodox Christian will be asked quizzically, "Greek or Russian?"—regardless of how obvious it is that the Orthodox Christian is culturally Western and has a Western surname. Counterintuitive as that question is, it is still meaningful because it corresponds in popular perception to the close linking of Orthodoxy and ethno-national identity. It is generally expected that a person is born into Orthodoxy Christianity, though sometimes a person marries into an Orthodox Church. In my experience it is rare for people to be comfortable without some further descriptor to specify "what kind of Orthodox" I am; without an ethnic marker for completeness, Orthodox Christianity is apparently incomprehensible. Conversations with colleagues who are employed in the academy and who are also Orthodox indicate to me that

7. See now Jacobsen, *The World's Christians*, 346–74.

8. The exception presented by the Orthodox Christian Mission Center (see www.orthodoxmission.org) is arguably more apparent than real, in that it is a North American initiative and as such can be seen as a result of the indigenization of Orthodoxy Christianity within the North American Christian milieu which supports mission activity.

this experience is not unique. One acquaintance remarked that it is easy enough to feel that one is (in this instance) first Bulgarian, then Orthodox, and Christian as nearly an afterthought. In nearly twenty years of being Orthodox, I have only once met someone who identified along the opposite trajectory: she considered herself first Christian, then Orthodox, and finally—almost as a matter of circumstance—Greek.

This integration of identities is not surprising. An interweaving of political identity and religious community in the Orthodox world, or worlds, has reinforced a sense that Orthodoxy is an ethnic form of Christianity.[9] From early days, Orthodox churches grew in close connection with the Christianization of the Roman Empire.[10] Definitions of Christian orthodoxy were sanctioned by law. Conspicuous examples include the decree *Cunctos populos* by the emperors Gratian, Valentinian II, and Theodosius, dated Feb. 27, 380 (*Codex Theodosianus* 16.1.2),[11] which legally defined Christian orthodoxy with reference to the theology of Pope Damasus and Peter of Alexandria, and Emperor Justinian's robust endorsement of Theodosian preferences for Nicene orthodoxy throughout his own legal code. The relationship between civil and ecclesiastical authority could be very cozy. In the letter to Patriarch Epiphanius that serves as the preface to *Novella* 6, Justinian asserted that "God's greatest blessings to humans, granted by divine kindness, are the priesthood and the empire [*imperium*]. Of them, the former serves divine matters and the latter is set over human affairs and cares for them, while both proceed from one and the same source and both adorn human life. Nothing therefore is a greater concern to emperors than the clergy's reputation [*sacerdotum honestas*], who for their part pray to God for them."[12]

Furthermore Justinian himself was a theologian of some note, as indeed were the emperors Constantine V (718–75), whose theological acumen for all its heterodoxy is unmistakable, and John VI Kantakouzenos (c. 1292–1383), who abdicating retired to the Holy Mountain as the monk Joasaph and wrote a history favorable to the theology of his contemporary, Archbishop (now St) Gregory Palamas.[13] After the Byzantine period,

9. For a far more subtle account, see McGuckin, *The Orthodox Church*, 380–98.

10. See Runciman, *The Byzantine Theocracy*.

11. Boyd, *The Ecclesiastical Edicts of the Theodosian Code*; Mousourakis, *A Legal History of Rome*, 151–52.

12. Osenbrüggen, *Corpus juris civilis*, t. III, 34.

13. On Justinian, see Amelotti and Zingale, *Scritti teologici ed ecclesiastici di*

political and religious syntheses continued among the Ottoman subjects in the *millet-i Rûm*,[14] in the Byzantine Commonwealth united in no small measure by the Orthodox practices of prayer and society that gave rise to what Alexandru Elian called the "Hesychast International,"[15] and especially in the emergence of the Russian ideology of the "Third Rome."[16] With Holy Russia, the evolution climaxes of a distinctively Orthodox "chosen people, a holy nation, a royal priesthood."[17]

In sum, for centuries Orthodoxy has informed and consolidated expressions of identity, both personal and social. The resulting consolidated expressions range from a heady blend of faith and civics, to a saccharine endorsement of the spiritual side of life as usual. As Orthodox Christianity has migrated beyond its native lands, this dense network of ethnic identity, social organization, and religious practice has been revealed as a mixed blessing. The generosity with which native Orthodox Christians can share the riches of their cultural inheritance, and rejoice in doing so, is humbling. Other aspects of the integration of ethnicity and belief are ambivalent. In much the same way that the Covenant bears the Latinate name of England as its marker throughout the world, Orthodox parishes frequently carry the demonyms of their founders. In both cases, the respective communities name themselves with names that memorialize the lands of their origins. But in the case of Orthodoxy in the West, exactly that feature of Orthodoxy can unfold into problems. How Greek ought a Greek Orthodox parish to be? (Naturally, this question also goes for a parish that is Russian, or Serbian, or Romanian, or Bulgarian. . .) With unprecedented economic emigration from traditionally Orthodox

Giustiniano; on Constantine V, see Hennephof, *Textus byzantinos pertinentes ad iconomachiam*, 52–57; for Kantakouzenos' part in the Palamite controversies, see my "John XIV (Kalekas), Byzantine politics-*cum*-theology and the early hesychast controversy."

14. Runciman, *The Great Church in Captivity*, 165–85; Papadopoullos, *Studies and Documents Relating to the History of the Greek Church and People Under Turkish Domination*, 2nd ed.

15. I have not had access to A. Elian's original publication, but see Obolensky, *The Byzantine Commonwealth. Eastern Europe, 500–1453*, 302.

16. Laats, "The Concept of the Third Rome and Its Political Implications"; Poe, "Moscow, the Third Rome."

17. Avirentsev, "The Idea of Holy Russia." Wil van der Bercken, *Holy Russia and Christian Europe: East and West in the Religious Ideology of Russia*; Soloviev, *Holy Russia: The History of a Religious-Social Idea.*

lands after the dissolution of the Soviet bloc, that question is urgent. Sometimes, responding to it provokes crises.

Respect for one's heritage and history is a good thing, within measure. Nor is it wrong to want to protect and to enlarge that heritage and to carry that history forward. However, what we are considering here are cases where an ethnic (not to say "state") church has moved abroad. There is often tension—and sometimes there is a demonstrable poorness of fit—between the national legacy of Anglican and Orthodox communities and the modern experience of globalization. Those national legacies are not always exclusivist, of course. But in the case of Orthodoxy, no one can doubt that the concrete expressions of its historical experiences constitute a barrier that defines the community. Znamenny chant and Byzantine iconography, leavened Eucharistic bread floating in the chalice, hirsute clergy and thick incense, bee's-wax tapers glowing in the darkness all serve to set Orthodox Christianity apart. It is through habituation and familiarization with these facets of Orthodoxy that one comes to enter into the Orthodox Church. Such is the primary phenomenon, but there is another. Because the community's identity is secured by its cultural boundaries, Orthodox churches are overwhelmingly unlikely to abandon them regardless of how long they inhabit strange lands. Such resistance to naturalization is not without its problems. It is common enough that, as Orthodox families indigenize over a few generations, the rising generations (for whom local life is natural as breathing) tend to leave the community. In several cases known to me, they have found their way into other churches in the USA or in the UK that are culturally more accessible—in one memorable case, as an Anglican vicar—all the while preserving a sense that they have preserved their Christian identity.

All of this is not to claim that Orthodox Christianity "abroad" remains entirely unchanged. Instead, it is rather to illustrate the profound importance of identity markers for Orthodox churches and to suggest that, across all churches in the Byzantine Orthodox tradition, there is a broad consensus about what those identity markers are. And here once more refinement is needed: it is not enough for there to be agreement that certain identity markers are important. The ways that Orthodox Christians in different parishes relate to those identity markers can be fiercely controversial: which melodies are used, whether the women cover their heads, how often and under what circumstances adults receive the Eucharistic gifts . . . On that basis, problems can arise if (e.g.) Orthodox Christianity as lived in a parish in North America does not correspond with Orthodox Christianity as lived in a parish in Russia. The particulars undoubtedly differ, but even so the dynamic at work in that case is comparable to differences that distinguish, say, Anglican Christianity in Nigeria from Anglican Christianity in England. How precisely the particular churches cope with those difference is a matter of obvious importance.

STRUCTURES AND BELIEFS

For any far-flung organization it is vital that members are able to recognize one another. Shared values and practices facilitate mutual recognition and so reinforce the organization.[18] This holds true for communities of churches, and has since the beginning. The importance of mutual recognition is arguably evident already in the fact that the open letter is the first major genre of Christian literature.[19] The Apostle Paul was adept at developing social networks long before sociologists began to analyze the "weav[ing] of a bond to personalities that lie outside this original circle of association" —viz., the family—"and instead possess a relationship to the individual through an actual similarity of dispositions, inclinations, activities, etc."[20] Indeed, a major concern for apostolic exhortation is the promotion of similar "dispositions, inclinations, activities, etc." amongst believers so that their relationships can, when necessary, supersede claims based on biological kinship. The social structures of Christianity developed in synthesis with its teachings, for, as Mary Douglas has noted, "Culturally shared worldviews are steadied by supporting institutions. [. . .] Ideas and values only become strongly entrenched when they are embedded in institutions."[21]

And we have observed that, in many ways, the institutions of Orthodox Christianity (and, I suggest, of Anglican Christianity—though not being a specialist I am content here to make a suggestion only) were characterized by the social histories of the nations for whom they expressed the people's religion. One way of looking at that phenomenon is

18. Cf. Covenant 4.2.2

19. For the material circumstances and their social consequences in early Christianity, see Leyerle, "Communication and travel."

20. Simmel, *Sociology*, 2: 363–64.

21. Douglas, "A history of grid and group cultural theory."

to see how a Christian community that originates from a single culture is provided by that very culture with a handy set of mutually recognizable tokens of membership. From that perspective, incidentally, the apparent timelessness of Orthodoxy might be attributed as meaningfully to the "artifice of eternity" that Yeats found in Byzantium, as to Heaven drawing near. In any case, Orthodox Christians are not alone in cherishing the cultural legacy that gives definition to their communities. In the Covenant, too, the importance of characteristic forms and practices for a Christian community is signaled by its acknowledgment of the "Thirty-nine Articles of Religion, the 1662 Book of Common Prayer, and the Ordering of Bishops, Priests, and Deacons,"[22] the Apostles' and Nicene Creeds,[23] and the historic episcopate.[24] These forms and practices perform an especially important service for Anglican identity, since churches of the Anglican Communion are bound together "not by a central legislative and executive authority, but by mutual loyalty sustained through the common counsel of the bishops in conference" [Lambeth Conference 1930] and of the other instruments of Communion.[25] We must pause at that statement to consider its implications. In default of a central legislative and executive authority—and, though it is not mentioned here, of a central judicial authority—(which, it should be noted, is a feature of the Orthodox Churches no less than of the Anglican Communion), the implicit structures we have been considering must bear additional weight. By attending to how those structures function, we may learn more about the communities that they support.

The sources prioritized by the Covenant converge on communal prayer and praise as sources for Anglican identity. The Covenant affirms the centrality of worship when it affirms "the shared patterns of our common prayer and liturgy which form, sustain and nourish our worship of God and our faith and life together."[26] Communal worship is the school

22. Covenant, 1.1.2., n. 3.

23. Covenant, 1.1.4.

24. Covenant, 1.1.6. It is by now an old canard that, from an Orthodox perspective, it is baffling for the Anglican Communion to set such emphasis on the historical episcopate and yet to equivocate on whether ordination is a sacrament, which is listed among the "five commonly called Sacraments . . . [that] have not any visible sign or ceremony ordained of God" (39 Art., Art. 25; cf. "Of Ceremonies" in BCP 1662).

25. Covenant, 3.1.2.

26. Covenant, 1.1.7. Cf. NDC n. 5.

of virtue in which habits or prayer and charity are trained. How we live together daily, how we understand ourselves and our place in the world, and how we comfort and support one another as Christians is informed by the ways that we constitute ourselves as communities, most especially when we draw together to partake in the sacrament of communion. One need not go so far as to assert that the Eucharistic chalice is somehow the font of meaning itself in order to appreciate that how we worship impacts how we think and how we live. A far less metaphysically adventurous perspective on this dynamic has circulated since the days of Prosper of Aquitaine (c. 390–c.455): ". . . and so let us consider the sacraments of priestly prayers, which have been inherited from the apostles and are celebrated uniformly in the whole world and in every catholic church, so that *the rule of praying may establish the rule of believing*."[27] Or, in the Latin paraphrase, *lex orandi, lex credendi.* What these prayers teach informs the way Christians behave both within and beyond the walls of a church. Hence, the Covenant affirms that these common ways of praying support common ways of striving for the realization of Christian principles that are socially beneficial.[28]

Even so, the actual persistence within the Anglican Communion of factions that are not obviously reconcilable can lead to questions about whether these forms and practices are sufficient for the coherence of the Communion. An outsider might note that these historical instruments are minimal and doubt whether they have promoted a *consensus fidelium* that unites the Anglican Communion in more than name. By contrast, the Byzantine consensus of the Eastern Orthodox Churches is so entrenched that, for better or worse, the question of coherence simply does not arise. As for the Anglican Communion, a further question arises. How is Anglican consensus evaluated? The Anglican recognition of the ancient Christian faith and its symbols is a salutary extension of what Chesterton memorably called "democracy for the dead,"[29] and allows for the wisdom of ages to inform responses to the needs of the moment. But attitudes toward tradition are not uniform in a communion that

27. Prosper, *De gratia Dei et libero voluntatis arbitrio* 8.11 (PL 51:209): ". . .obsecrationum quoque sacerdotalium sacramenta respiciamus, quae ab apostolis tradita, in toto mundo atque in omni catholica Ecclesia uniformiter celebrantur, *ut legem credendi lex statuat supplicandi*" (emphasis added).

28. Covenant, 2.2.2.d.

29. Chesterton, *Orthodoxy*, 85

(perhaps too simplistically) affirms that its history was "reshaped by the Reformation,"[30] since multiple reforming movements affected the Church in Britain and Ireland and since the reformers were by no means united in their regard for tradition. And indeed the equally significant recognition of "local adapt[ion] . . . to the varying needs of the peoples and places called by God, "[31] stands as a reminder that these ancient traditions can be variously received in different locales. At this point, I would recur to my earlier remarks about a shared legacy and expand them: if a common heritage is presumed, then variations in its expression can easily seem to be the betrayal of something precious.

There is at work, I suspect, a willingness to relocate unity from the sphere of the empirically observable to a more heavenly plane. Emphasis on prayer is consistent with a shift from coherence that is generally visible to coherence that is visible to God and perhaps to the saints. If this is so, then there is something complex at work in the insistence that the life of communion in the church is none other than "the very divine life of God the Trinity."[32] That claim resonates profoundly with the theological anthropology and the ecclesiology of John Zizioulas, Metropolitan of Pergamon, and the mystical theology of Fr Sophrony Sakharov. What it leaves unclear, however, is how the flourishing of this life amongst humans is related to the virtues which serve to edify the community of the faithful.[33] After all, edification can be understood without any particular reference to the transforming consequences that the divine life of the Trinity have upon humans, and regarded instead as a phenomenon adequately attested by political engagement and working for social justice. But how long can any Christian community last if it limits itself merely to considering unity to be an eschatological consolation? Much more could be said about the propensity of Orthodox Christians for thinking in that way, but what is striking is a common tendency to defer to the Holy Spirit any responsibility for institutional shortcomings. A century ago, in his lectures on how Christians were responding to the theory of evolution Henry Drummond identified "gaps which they fill up with God."[34] He

30. Covenant, 2.1.2.

31. Covenant, 1.1.6; cf. 39 Art., Art. 34.

32. Covenant, Introduction, para. 1.

33. Cf. Covenant, Introduction, para. 4.

34. Drummond, *Lowell Lectures on the Ascent of Man*, 333

was describing the practice of invoking God's presence whenever human understanding falls short, in effect, apportioning our ignorance as God's proper place—a reprehensible and faithless habit, but one that is assuredly common. It seems to me that we moderns are similarly disposed to relying upon God when we come up short as a group, thinking perhaps that a degree of irresponsibility is tolerable because God will make up the difference. These shortcomings (and the corresponding abrogation of responsibility) cluster wherever there are systemic failures, but at present let's concentrate on the matter of the unity of the faithful.

It is very difficult to think that, when Jesus prayed to the Father that his followers should be one (John 17:21–23), he intended that his followers should have a casual attitude toward unity since God the Father would see to such things in his own good time. So effortless is it to defer that unity to the eschaton, that one rarely thinks—or anyway I rarely think—about its implications for maintaining (rather than *attaining*) Christian unity. In this connection, the lack of judicial oversight within the Anglican Communion is especially relevant.[35] When the Covenant addresses itself to disputes and their resolution,[36] its emphasis falls squarely on the internal moderation of covenanting member communities.[37] Even when a problem has been referred to the Standing Committee and that committee has issued a decision, or rather a recommendation (the difference might be significant), "Each Church or each Instrument shall determine whether or not to accept such recommendations."[38] The making of real decisions abides with covenanting members. In cases of dispute, the overarching Covenant does not integrate its members into a unity; what it does instead is encourages them to re-affirm the terms of the Covenant. By doing so, each covenanting member necessarily re-affirms its independence from the Covenant.

---

35. For completeness, I would note that the lack of judicial oversight across the Orthodox churches is a similarly grave problem.

36. Covenant, 4.2.

37. Thus, Covenant 4.2.3: "When questions arise relating to the meaning of the Covenant, or about the compatibility of an action by a covenanting Church with the covenant, it is the duty of each covenanting Church to seek to live out the commitments of Section 3.2. Such questions may be raise by a Church itself, another covenanting Church or the Instruments of Communion." Cf. ibid. 4.2.9.

38. Covenant, 4.2.7.

LOCAL CATHOLIC CHURCHES IN GLOBAL COMMUNITIES

Perhaps it is the case that the absence of effective judicial oversight is a cost worth paying, since it could only be viable when integrated with a suite of other mechanism of the sort explicitly disavowed by the Covenant: "not by a central legislative and executive authority, but by mutual loyalty." I cannot fail to detect in the rejection of central authority of whatever kind a preoccupation with rejecting the Papacy. What motivates my comment is the observation that, down the centuries, Anglicans and Orthodox have frequently recognized one another and identified features in common— liturgical worship, high regard for the Church Fathers,[39] the Christian *imperium* (at least, for Russian Orthodox and Anglican interactions)—while explicitly contrasting themselves to the Roman Catholic Church. Indeed, when Anglicans and Orthodox alike profess their belief in "one, holy, catholic and apostolic church," one can almost hear in the way the word is pronounced that "catholic" takes a miniscule. To gives some substance to these claims, let me return to my first remarks about the dealings between Anglicans and Orthodox.

I was willful in identifying Archbishop Theodore as I did, of course. It is more accurate to come forward by about 950 years. In 1617, as the result of a venture between King James VI and I and Archbishop Abbot on the one hand, and Cyril Lukaris, Patriarch of Constantinople on the other, the priest Metrophanes Kritopoulos arrived in Oxford to study there.[40] The measured success of Kritopoulos's scholarship led to the establishment of a college in Oxford for Greek Orthodox students.[41] The impetus for this fascinating, though short-lived, experiment in education was the establishment in 1577 of the Collegio Sant' Atanasio in Rome—since neither party wanted to allow the Roman Catholic Church an advantage in education, with all the sinister possibilities that education entails. That suspicions against Rome did not quickly wane can be glimpsed from the terms used by Archbishop Tenison in relating commendations for Neophytos of Philippopolis, who in 1701 received doctorates of divinity from Oxford and Cambridge during his visits to those universities, on

---

39. See now Quantin, *The Church of England and Christian Antiquity*. A comparable analysis of Orthodox recourse to Christian antiquity is much to be desired.

40. Davey, *Pioneer for Unity: Metrophanes Kritopoulos (1589–1639) and Relations between the Orthodox, Roman Catholic and Reformed Churches*.

41. Doll, *Anglicanism and Orthodoxy 300 Years after the 'Greek College' in Oxford*.

grounds of "his wise behaviour at Paris in avoiding the Pope's Nuntio and forebearing everything that might carry with it an appearance of being latinized."[42] On occasion, the attempt at building up mutual recognition through disavowing the Catholic Church is overt, as with the Encyclical to the Eastern Churches, promulgated by the Lambeth Conference of 1888, which states *inter alia*:

> We reflect with thankfulness that there exist no bars, such as are presented to communion with the Latins by the formulated sanction of the Infallibility of the Church residing in the person of the Supreme Pontiff, by the doctrine of the Immaculate Conception, and other dogmas imposed by the decrees of Papal Councils. The Church of Rome has always treated her Eastern sister wrongfully. She intrudes her Bishops into the ancient Dioceses, and keeps up a system of active proselytism. The Eastern Church is reasonably outraged by these proceedings, wholly contrary as they are to Catholic principles; and it behoves us of the Anglican Communion to take care that we do not offend in like manner.[43]

It was the cordial relations between the Community of the Resurrection in Mirfield with the Romanian Orthodox Church, and above all the emigration of Orthodox from Russia and elsewhere in Eastern Europe into England in the early decades of the twentieth century, that set Anglican-Orthodox relations on their current trajectory. No organization exemplifies those relations so neatly as the Fellowship of St Alban and St Sergius.[44] The Statement of Aims and Basis of that society, published in 1933, celebrated liturgical worship as the "centre of the work of the Fellowship," noted that "it has been by entering into the riches of the Catholic tradition, as represented in the two Churches concerned, that both the individual life of members have been enriched and a spiritual unity discovered, which is deeper than some of the points of difference," and stipulated as a minimal requirement for membership the "desire to understand the Catholic tradition, on which the work is based."[45] This

---

42. Thomas Tenison to John Covel, Sept. 6, 1701, in Williams, *The Orthodox Church of the East in the Eighteenth Century*, lix.

43. LC 1888 Encyclical Letter, in Davidson, *The Lambeth Conferences of 1867, 1878, and 1888*, 273–74 at 274.

44. Geffert, *Easter Orthodox and Anglicans*, 143–83.

45. The Executive of the Fellowship of St Alban and St Sergius, "Statement of Aims and Basis."

stipulation is explicitly made with a view to "a smaller group" of "Free Churchmen" or low-church Anglicans who might wish to participate. It is odd enough in a statement just over a page long that the Fellowship executive would recur to the term "Catholic" four times to characterize the aims and basis of an Anglican-Orthodox ecumenical group, but it is all the more curious that the statement does not so much as envisage participation by Catholic Christians.

What I wish to demonstrate from these examples is that Anglican and Orthodox Christians have—or have had—an established habit of self-identifying as catholic, or even Catholic, and adopting that term in more or less explicit contrast to the Roman Catholic Church. In the past, Anglicans and Orthodox have indulged in speculation about the Roman Catholic Church that verges on the paranoid. It is significant, particularly when we recall that both the Orthodox Churches and the Anglican Communion lack effective means for resolving internal disputes, that such speculation repeatedly returns to the institution of the Papacy. The image of the Supreme Pontiff reducing all Christendom to his infallible will seems as potent now as ever it was. That is lamentable, because it obscures the facts that not all Catholics are Roman, that the Catholic Church is plural in its rites and heritages,[46] that the plurality of the Catholic Church cannot be attributed solely to the wily schemes of Dominicans or Jesuits or whomever,[47] and that eastern Christians can legitimately and in good conscience be in communion with the Pope in Rome regardless of how that effects the sensibilities of other Christians. More to the point for our purposes, the vilification of the Papacy is also insidious insofar as it bolsters any sense that administrative oversight of Christians is somehow the handiwork of the devil. Supposing with Lord Acton that absolute power corrupts absolutely, we might try to justify the absence of anything more than honorary leadership by claiming that it is the prudent course. But why think that all arrangements of Christian authority must inevitably tend toward papal monarchy? It is hard to imagine how problems among the Orthodox Churches and within the Anglican Communion can be resolved for as long as Christians in those respective communities perpetuate resistance to co-ordination, administration, and

46. See especially the Decree *Orientalium Ecclesiarum* 3.

47. The examples of the Italo-Greeks and the Maronites are relevant here. Note, however, that I am not denying that there were wily Dominicans or Jesuits. See, for instance, Santich, *Missio Moscovitica*.

appeals by caricaturing such things as the detestable excesses of Rome. Lord Acton's concerns about the corrupting effects of power, especially in matters of religion, remain valid; even so, entrusting the well-being of Christians around the world to be maintained by the good will and honesty of local leaders acting in harmony seems perilously like tempting God to work miracles.

BIBLIOGRAPHY

Amelotti, M. and L.M. Zingale. *Scritti teologici ed ecclesiastici di Giustiniano*. Milan: Giuffrè, 1977.

Avirentsev, Sergei S. "The Idea of Holy Russia." *History Today* 39/9 (1989) 37–44

Bercken, Wil van der. *Holy Russia and Christian Europe: East and West in the Religious Ideology of Russia*. London: SCM, 1999.

Boyd, William K. *The Ecclesiastical Edicts of the Theodosian Code*. New York: Columbia University Press, 1905.

Casiday, Augustine. "John XIV (Kalekas), Byzantine Politics-cum-Theology and the Early Hesychast Controversy." In *Le Patriarcat œcuménique de Constantinople aux XIVe – XVIe siècles*, Edited by D. Mureşan, 19–35. Paris: Centre des Études Byzantines, Néo-Helléniques et Sud-Est Européennes, 2007.

Chesterton, G. K. *Orthodoxy*. London: Bodley Head, 1909.

Colgrave, Bertram and R. A. B. Mynors, editors. *Bede's Ecclesiastical History*. Oxford: Clarendon, 1969.

Davey, Colin. *Pioneer for Unity: Metrophanes Kritopoulos (1589-1639) and Relations between the Orthodox, Roman Catholic and Reformed Churches*. London: British Council of Churches, 1987.

Davidson, Randall, editor. *The Lambeth Conferences of 1867, 1878, and 1888: With the Official Reports and Resolutions, Together with the Sermons Preached at the Conferences*. London: SPCK, 1889.

Doll, Peter M., editor. *Anglicanism and Orthodoxy 300 Years after the 'Greek College' in Oxford*. Oxford: Lang, 2006.

Douglas, Mary. "A History of Grid and Group Cultural Theory." 2007. Online: http://projects.chass.utoronto.ca/semiotics/cyber/douglas1.pdf.

Drummond, Henry. *Lowell Lectures on the Ascent of Man*. 14th ed. New York: Pott, 1908.

Executive of the Fellowship of St Alban and St Sergius. "Statement of Aims and Basis." *Journal of the Fellowship of St Alban and St Sergius* 19 (March–April, 1933) 34–35.

Geffert, Bryn. *Easter Orthodox and Anglicans: Diplomacy, Theology, and the Politics of Interwar Ecumenism*. Notre Dame: University of Notre Dame Press, 2010.

Haddan, A.W. and W. Stubbs (eds.). *Councils and Ecclesiastical Documents Relating to Great Britain and Ireland*. Oxford: Clarendon, 1871.

Hennephof, Herman. *Textus byzantinos pertinentes ad iconomachiam*. Leiden: Brill, 1969.

Jacobsen, Douglas G. *The World's Christians*. Oxford: Wiley-Blackwell, 2011.

Laats, Alar. "The Concept of the Third Rome and Its Political Implications." In *Religion and Politics in Multicultural Europe: Perspectives and Challenges*, edited by Alar Kilp and Andres Saumets, vol. 1, 98–113. Tartu: Tartu University Press, 2009.

Lapidge, Michael, editor. *Archbishop Theodore: Commemorative Studies on His Life and Influence*. Cambridge: Cambridge University Press, 1995.

Leyerle, Blake. "Communication and Travel." In *The Early Christian World*, edited by Philip F. Esler, vol. 1, 452–74. London: Routledge, 2000.

McGuckin, John Anthony. *The Orthodox Church: An Introduction to Its History, Doctrine and Spiritual Culture*. Oxford: Blackwell, 2008.

Mousourakis, George. *A Legal History of Rome*. London: Routledge, 2007.

Obolensky, Dimitri. *The Byzantine Commonwealth: Eastern Europe, 500–1453*. London: Weidenfeld & Nicholson, 1971.

Orientalium Ecclesiarum. 1964. Online: http://www.vatican.va/archive/hist_councils/ii_vatican_council/documents/vat-ii_decree_19641121_orientalium-ecclesiarum_en.html.

Osenbrüggen, E., editor. *Corpus juris civilis*, t. III. Leipzig : Baumgärtner, 1865.

Papadopoullos, Theodore H. *Studies and Documents Relating to the History of the Greek Church and People Under Turkish Domination*. 2nd ed. Aldershot, UK: Variorum, 1990.

Poe, Marshall. "Moscow, the Third Rome: the Origins and Transformations of a 'Pivotal Moment.'" *Jahrbücher für Geschichte Osteuropas* 49 (2001) 412–29.

Quantin, Jean-Louis. *The Church of England and Christian Antiquity: The Construction of a Confessional Identity in the 17th Century*. Oxford: Oxford University Press, 2009.

Runciman, Steven. *The Great Church in Captivity*. Cambridge: Cambridge University Press, 1968.

———. *The Byzantine Theocracy*. Cambridge: Cambridge University Press, 1977.

Santich, Jan Joseph. *Missio Moscovitica: The Role of the Jesuits in the Westernization of Russia, 1582–1689*. New York: Lang, 1995.

Simmel, Georg. *Sociology: Inquiries into the Construction of Social Forms*. 2 vols. Translated by Anthony J. Blasi et al. Leiden: Brill, 2009. German ed., 1908.

Soloviev, Alexander. *Holy Russia: The History of a Religious-Social Idea*. 's-Gravenhage: Mouton, 1959.

Williams, George. *The Orthodox Church of the East in the Eighteenth Century*. London: Rivington, 1868.

11

The Necessity of Expediency

John Henry Newman's Preface to The *Via Media of the* Anglican Church *and the Anglican Covenant*

NEIL DHINGRA

IN HIS 1877 PREFACE to the third edition of *The Via Media of the Anglican Church*, a revision of his 1837 *Lectures on the Prophetical Office of the Church*, written while he was still an Anglican, John Henry Newman distinguished three "functions, aims, and interests" in the Church that would always exist in tension—the sacred ministry of pastors, which appeals to our emotional nature and can lead to superstition and enthusiasm,[1] the teaching of the Schools, which tends towards rationalism, and the governance of the papacy and curia, which is inclined to ambition and tyranny. These offices are the sacerdotal or mystical, the intellectual or prophetical, and the regal or political, respectively. They correspond to and originate in Christ's offices as Priest, Prophet, and King and take institutional form in the three aforementioned "centres of action."[2]

The discordance between these three offices explains why the ideal stability of official Roman Catholic theology seems to differ from the

1. Here meaning "fanaticism," with connotations of "the delusion or imposture of those who falsely believe or profess that they are or have been possessed by the Spirit." See Pocock, "Enthusiasm," 10.

2. Newman, *Via Media,* 21.

popular and political manifestations of Roman Catholicism, a dissimilarity that had been significant for Newman in 1837. ("[I]t was the latter which the Author had chiefly in mind when he spoke of Romanists and Romanism," the 1877 Newman recollects.)[3] At times, for instance, the political office might collide with the prophetical office, and we have the strange sight of the Emperor Constantine fighting a war under the banner of self-sacrificing love. Confusion is also possible. In the contemporary Roman Catholic Church, according to theologian Nicholas Lash, the acceptance of a teaching is often really mere obedience to an order, and disagreement with a teaching is quickly labeled as a failure of loyalty, or "dissent." This misperception is not the inevitable result of central authority. It comes from the *confusion* of two of Newman's "functions, aims, and interests," namely teaching and governance. Lash follows the Jesuit Robert Murray, who points out that the term "magisterium" referred to authorized teaching in the Church until the anti-Modernist controversy of the early twentieth century, when "Magisterium" began to refer to episcopal and papal governance.[4]

It can be imagined that the Anglican Covenant will cause a similar confusion between teaching and governance. To be sure, the Covenant distances the Anglican Communion from Roman Catholic polity, affirming that the churches of the Covenant are bound together "not by a central legislative and executive authority" but "mutual loyalty."[5] It only grants a Standing Committee the authority to make recommendations to churches about the recognition of impaired or limited communion.[6] But the Covenant is still a historical development from the Lambeth Conference, which, as Mark Chapman notes, "claimed no power," merely a "persuasive authority" based on office and "shared ethos and history." Chapman asks whether "moral advice," aiming at persuasion, will now become simultaneously a command, demanding obedience. And, then, as Chapman suggests, might the Covenant represent an overreach, its toxic blend of teaching and governance ironically resulting in "some sort of messy new Reformation?"[7]

3. Ibid., 18.
4. Lash, "Teaching," 18–19.
5. Covenant, 3.1.2.
6. Covenant, 4.2.7.
7. Chapman, "Dull Bits," 95, 98.

Of course, merely asserting the dangers of governance presents no solution at all to the present Anglican crisis. As Ephraim Radner points out, denying the importance of politics in the Church can have its own disastrous consequences. For one thing, "by separating church politics from the Gospel, one can lay open the door to allowing those politics a kind of free rein within historical experience—they are after all, not that important."[8] So, then, what can be done about governance in the Church? Must governance always arrive as a necessary but destructive form of "Magisterium"?

The solution, this essay will argue, is found in separating the teaching and governing offices of the Church. It should be made clear that the now apparently needed instruments of the Anglican Communion—namely, the Archbishop of Canterbury, the Lambeth Conference, the Anglican Consultative Council, and the Primates' Meeting, represent only the governing office, with its own guiding principle of expedience. On Newman's model, these instruments will, like the papacy, also exhibit a tendency towards ambition and tyranny. But governance means that the instruments cannot simultaneously set forth Anglican theology *and* issue commands and instructions to implement such a theology.[9] They can and must act when governance is necessary for the unity and peace of the Church. But, as mere governors, they must tolerate a difference between what might appear to be a theologically fully developed "official" Anglicanism and its incomplete reception in the United States or Nigeria or elsewhere. The instruments cannot be coercive educators. As the language of this paragraph intimates, John Henry Newman is oddly relevant to efforts at Anglican conciliarism.

|

Paul Avis, in his recent *Beyond the Reformation?*, affirms Newman's schema as a way to examine the history of conciliarism, of which the Anglican Covenant is surely now part. The conciliarists, after all, can be seen as

8. Radner, "Wheels Within Wheels," 5.

9. The distinction was made by Archbishop Rowan Williams in an interview with the *Times* regarding his 1989 essay, "The Body's Grace," "That's what I wrote as a theologian, you know, putting forward a suggestion. That's not the job I have now." Davies, "Archbishop," no pages.

positioning the mystical and intellectual offices of the church against the political office—pastors and schools against the papacy—in the interests of reform. But Avis does not find Newman to be very promising for thinking about an Anglican Covenant. For Avis, Newman is still too much of a centralist, elevating "particularly the pastoral or governing office."[10] Avis's conclusion is not that unusual for an Anglican reviewer. In 1877, the reviewer of Newman's third edition of the *Via Media* for the *Contemporary Review* had written that, although Newman had acknowledged that Church authorities, motivated by expedience, act in rather embarrassing ways and are "specially liable to failure and mistake," Newman still somehow believed that God "laid such a tremendous burden of responsibilities upon frail human shoulders."[11] The *Church Quarterly Review*, for its part, held in 1877 that Newman's admission of ecclesiastical failures and mistakes was meant to ironically show that the popes were "right after all" or simply committed "mere errors of judgment as to the limits of conflicting duties, on which no person of candid mind will hereafter found a charge."[12]

It is true that Newman says in his preface that God promised the Church "infallibility in her formal teaching" and protection from "serious error in worship and political action," whatever collisions between offices, with their different functions, aims, and interests, may occur. It is also true that Newman says that the Pope as "chief part of the Body" of Christ inherits the three offices and can act for the Church in them.[13] In 1877 Newman is definitely a Roman Catholic. But his relevance to conciliarism, of which he himself probably knew little,[14] and, consequently, the Anglican Covenant, is clearer if we imagine Newman trying to *limit* and *recontextualize* a centralized Church authority.

Besides the simple fact that Newman, in his Preface, did admit papal failures and mistakes—"a concession which can never be made except

---

10. Avis, *Reformation*, 3–4, 10.

11. *Contemporary Review*, 1097–98.

12. *Church Quarterly Review*, 233.

13. Newman, *Via Media*, 36, 35. For a view of how primacy might not be, in itself, un-Anglican, see McPartlan, "Toward an Anglican Covenant," 166–67. Nevertheless, this essay will simply suggest authority that is more than consultative and advisory, leaving the specific question of primacy aside.

14. Avis, *Reformation*, 15, and Misner, *Papacy*, 36.

for the sake of argument,"[15] argued the Jesuit *Month* in 1877—it must be recognized that Newman wrote against the backdrop of Ultramontanism and both the intellectual and institutional decline of Roman Catholic theological schools. As Eamon Duffy has recently written, Newman was clearly worried about "centralization . . . established at head-quarters." More specifically, he was concerned with papal or curial fiat replacing theological debate in the aftermath of the First Vatican Council. The significance of Newman's model of three dissimilar offices in tension is that it replaces such a "monolithic understanding of the church" with a "dialectical process, rich and life-giving, but consequently messy, in which the tensions between the conflicting claims of truth, expediency, and ardor would not be resolved this side of the eschaton."[16]

Although the papacy could theoretically reconcile the three offices, it is difficult to imagine how this would realistically take place. Newman describes the offices as "several departments of duty"—each of the three "has its own separate scope and direction," with its "own interests to promote." It is "arduous" to administer one office, but "much more arduous are they to administer when taken in combination."[17] Newman provides only a single example of a "papal exercise of the Prophetical Office." Here Pius IX had "warned the faithful" against dubious prophecies and miracles and forbade "some new and extravagant" Marian titles. Tellingly, Newman never provides an example of the "papal exercise of the Prophetical Office"[18] *against* the interests of the regal office. Ordinarily, the pope, whom Newman clearly states is within the Body of Christ "not himself the Body of Christ,"[19] is immersed within what Duffy called a messy "dialectical process"—he does not transcend it.

In his 1877 Preface to the *Via Media*, Newman also gives very high place to the theological schools whose role now seemed to be eclipsed by the papacy. Newman closely relates the prophetical offices to these schools. And, to Newman, the prophetical office, associated with "the Schools," *created* the regal and sacerdotal offices. Thus, theologians should be "in employment in keeping within bounds both the political

15. *Month*, 373

16. Duffy, "That Was Then," 171, 173. The Newman quote is from a letter to Robert Ornsby, 26 March 1863, *Letters and Diaries* XX:425–26.

17. Newman, *Via Media*, 27, 26.

18. Ibid., 30.

19. Ibid., 25.

and popular elements in the Church's constitution"[20] which are always seeking to wildly "liberate" or "emancipate" themselves from restraints.[21] This is significant. Earlier, Newman had used a more general concept of an *ecclesia docens* [teaching church] in his controversial 1859 article on the consultation of the faithful.[22] The *ecclesia docens* existed in a multiplicity of channels, diminishing the clear distinction between the offices and the relative importance of the theological schools. The term *ecclesia docens* is not used in the 1877 Preface at all. Even earlier, in the 1837 first edition of the *Via Media*, Newman had spoken of a very expansive "prophetical tradition" that existed, among other places, in "legend and fable," even "popular prejudices, in local customs."[23] Here, in 1877, the prophetical office is *clarified*—most of the channels of the *ecclesia docens* and the "local customs" are now exiled to the priestly office.[24] Newman does not even mention the liturgy, which would tend to cloud things, crossing the boundary between the prophetical and sacerdotal offices. (As Duffy notes, Newman tends to reduce the "sacral dimension of Christianity to religious emotion or even popular superstition."[25]) The role of the schools, and, more specifically, the prophetical office's jurisdiction over the other offices, is set in very clear relief. As Newman had written to his friend Emily Bowles a decade earlier about how theological controversy had been conducted before his century, "If the controversy grew, then it went to a Bishop, a theological faculty, or to some foreign University."[26] The sad events of the nineteenth century—"national and international troubles,"[27] as Newman writes in his Preface—had changed all that, enabling a papal centralization in its place. As Fergus Kerr writes, "Perhaps Newman is nostalgic, even fanciful, about 'the schools.'"[28] Newman may even go too

---

20. Ibid., 29.

21. Ibid., 41.

22. Newman, *Consulting*, 76, 77, 86, 106.

23. Newman, *Via Media*, 268.

24. See the critique in McDade, "Episcopal and Prophetic," 18–19.

25. Duffy, "That was Then," 173. Dulles notes the absences as well: Dulles, "Threefold Office," 382. For a discussion of Newman's entire usage of the three offices, see Yakaitis, *Office*. For instance, note the greater emphasis on the kingly office as an "organizing principle" in Newman's earlier *Essay on the Development of Christian Doctrine*, 136–37.

26. Newman to Emily Bowles 19 May 1863, *Letters and Diaries* XX:448.

27. Newman, *Via Media*, 29.

28. Kerr, "Tradition and Reason," 42.

far in the high place he now gives to the schools. "[N]or is religion ever in greater danger than when, in consequence of national or international troubles, the Schools of theology have been broken up and ceased to be."[29]

Thus, for Newman, the regal office is not at all meant to supplant the theologians. "Under secular inducements," he tells us, some popes, including Boniface VIII, had tried to do this, venturing "beyond the lines of theology." They were "unsuccessful." Newman does not mean to collapse teaching into governance. Such a dissolution would be especially perilous, since governance, as political, is especially liable to "excess and corruption," and must be kept "within bounds" by theologians. The regal office is meant to act under its own guiding principle—expedience. On the other hand, the theologians cannot themselves assume this office, because theology is "too hard, too intellectual, too exact."[30] Theologians are likely incapable of the equity and compassion required to make truces and compromises. (In any case, Newman tends to think that theologians are not ambitious.) The offices must be kept *distinct*.

II

Newman's recognition of the need to limit central governance, according to this principle, is precisely why his thought is useful for analyzing the Anglican Covenant. What might it mean for the governing instruments of the Anglican Communion to act with the guiding principle of expedience? Clearly, these instruments[31] are not meant to supplant divinity schools nor to supply, much less replace, popular sentiment, both of which presumably can be maintained in the Anglican Communion in their familiar dispersed or distributed forms. But the instruments must act to secure "independence and self-government" for the Anglican Communion—to "keep up and to increase her various populations in this ever-dying, ever-nascent world" and to "strengthen and facilitate the intercourse of city with city, and race with race so that an injury done to one is felt to be an injury to all." They must be on the "watch-tower."[32] This is

29. Newman, *Via Media*, 29.

30. Ibid., 29–30.

31. Here I am less concerned with the specific forms of the institutions than the institutions representing a "way of life." See Radner, "Wheels within Wheels," 7.

32. Newman, *Via Media*, 48–49.

political, insofar as it requires identifying what the Covenant says "could threaten the unity of the Communion and the effectiveness or credibility of its mission"[33] (3.2.5), even if clarity on these matters should always be sought in prayer and through the preservation of the bonds of affection and the love of Christ.[34]

There is always risk in governance, in the exercise of the regal office. As Newman writes about the "regal autocracy" of the Church: "It is easy to understand how from time to time such serious interests and duties involve, as regards the parties who have the responsibility of them, the risk, perhaps the certainty, at least the imputation, of ambition or other selfish motive, and still more frequently of error in judgment, or violent action, or injustice." The awareness of this "risk" itself presents another check on centralization, because it places direct scrutiny upon the instruments, even as it makes their mistakes both understandable and even forgivable. The question to ask about controversial actions of the instruments—and Newman's examples of governance can be presently seen as both provocatively conservative (Gregory I puts away the "diversified traditional forms of ritual" in various parts of the Church) and controversially liberal (Liberius and Honorius evince a "personal want of firmness or of clear-sightedness in the matter of doctrine")—is whether the actions are "absolutely and undeniably necessary for the unity, sanctity, and peace of the Church." If they are so judged, they can never really be theologically self-destructive, because falsehoods can never "be necessary for those blessings."[35] This concern for peace and especially unity, it should be said, also happens to align Newman with the history of conciliarism.

An ecumenical, if somewhat selective, reading of Newman gives more specific criteria for the action of the instruments. Newman claims that the canonization of Roman Catholic saints and the validity of the Sacraments must be infallible acts. This is because the canonization of a damned man or woman would be a "damnable error" (Aquinas) of huge implications, and a decisive break in apostolic succession would mean that Christ was effectively no longer present with the church. In "The Gift of Authority," the Anglican-Roman Catholic International Commission has stated that "In specific circumstances, those with this ministry of

33. Covenant, 3.2.5.

34. Covenant, 3.2.6, 3.2.7.

35. Newman, *Via Media*, 50.

oversight (*episcope*), assisted by the Holy Spirit, may together come to a judgment which, being faithful to Scripture and consistent with apostolic Tradition, is preserved from error." Otherwise, the Church would no longer be "maintained in the truth so that it may continue to offer its 'Amen' to the glory of God."[36] The Anglican instruments of unity act properly, and thus under the principle of expediency, when if they act to protect the Church's indefectibility.[37]

For instance, they can act to secure the continued existence of the priestly office, which is necessary for the proclamation of the gospel. Newman notes that in 1049 Pope Leo IX held a "solemn Council" in which simoniacal orders were judged to be invalid. The consequence, according to St Peter Damiani, was "serious tumult and resistance," because it meant that Masses might altogether cease in Rome. One can judge that there really should not be simoniacal ordinations, but it would be inexpedient if their elimination would mean an actual ceasing of liturgical worship. Put more generally, then, the instruments of the Anglican Communion act property if they act according to the principle that none of the Church's functions "should be the *destruction* of another."[38]

The Church chose to recognize schismatic ordinations, as well as heretical baptisms, out of a concern for unity. Regarding the latter, in the third century, "Pope Stephen took this side then in a memorable controversy, and maintained it against almost the whole Christian world." But, as Newman writes, he was ultimately correct. "To cut off such cautious baptism from the Church was to circumscribe her range of subjects and to impair her catholicity."[39] Likewise, the popes allowed for more lax penance, since "the kingdom of heaven should be a net, gathering fish of every kind.[40] Newman is careful to suggest that these developments must be received. "Expedience is an argument which grows in cogency with the course of years," and he notes that only after 150 years after Stephen, was his decision acknowledged by "the School of the Theologians." Turning

---

36. ARCIC, *The Gift of Authority*, 42.

37. ". . . failures cannot destroy the Church's ability to proclaim the gospel and to show forth the Christian life; for we believe that Christ will not desert his Church and that the Holy Spirit will lead it into all truth. That is why the Church, in spite of its failures, can be described as indefectible." ARCIC, *Authority in the Church* I, 18.

38. Newman, *Via Media*, 52; emphasis added.

39. Ibid., 54.

40. Ibid., 55.

then to the Anglican Communion, we can gather that the instruments have acted properly if they clearly are acting for the sake of catholicity. Additionally, we can gather that the instruments have properly acted if their claims are received in time, either immediately by theologians or what Newman would call the "instinct, or [*phronema*], deep in the bosom of the mystical body of Christ,"[41] or, more likely, by a more labored process of theological debate and discussion, formal action, and increased consultation "to see whether the formal action settles down and makes itself at home," as suggested by *The Windsor Report*.[42]

III

Besides presenting us with ways to evaluate the actions, expedient or inexpedient, of the regal instruments of the Anglican Communion, Newman provides us with ways to diagnose the Communion's present ills. While each of the three offices will "influence and modify" each other, when left to their own devices, "reasoning tends to rationalism; devotion to superstition and enthusiasm, and power to ambition and tyranny."[43] In the absence of governance in the Anglican Communion, has reasoning tended towards "rationalism" or devotion towards "superstition and enthusiasm"? *The Windsor Report* enumerated six "deeper symptoms" of "illness" in the life of the Anglican Communion. Two had to do with governance itself—namely, the absence of ecclesiastical procedures and governance at a Communion-wide level. But four concerned problems with theological reasoning. Most importantly, it was alleged that ECUSA had not made a "serious attempt to offer an explanation to, or consult meaningfully, with the Communion" regarding the consecration as bishop of V. Gene Robinson in 2003,[44] presumably because the Episcopal Church prematurely considered his partnering to be *adiaphoron* and itself "free to take decisions on matters" which affected the entire Communion.[45] The

---

41. Newman, *Consulting*, 23.

42. TWR, §68.

43. Newman, *Via Media*, 25.

44. TWR, §33.

45. Ibid., §39

Anglican Communion, said TWR, has been affected by political "over-simplification and a polarization of many issues."[46]

On the one hand, we see the problem of rationalism. While it would be unfair to generalize from polemics, it does seem that theology in the Anglican Communion has suffered from an absence of the regal office. The Archbishop of Canterbury, Rowan Williams, has publicly stated his concern that arguments against the present Anglican moratoria regarding same sex-unions have tended to be based on the "fundamental human rights dimension of attitudes to LGBT people," rather than "solid theological grounding" or any theological consensus.[47] After the Lambeth meeting in 1998, Ben Quash wrote that two methods of exegesis were prominent. The first extracted "clear and definitive indicative ('descriptive') statements and . . . binding imperative ('ethical') ones" from an authoritative Bible, and a second was based on a concept of experience "that was meant to stand as unquestioned and unassailable as the authority of Scripture."[48] Each of these methods, like the reduction of "theological grounding" to the question of human rights in the secular, civil sphere, veers dangerously close to what Newman would have called rationalism.

While still an Anglican, Newman wrote, "[T]he Rationalist makes himself the center, not his Maker; he does not go to God, but he implies that God must come to him." Both the reliance on an unassailable Scripture and an unassailable "experience" show impatience with the "notion of half views and partial knowledge, of guesses, surmises, hopes and fears, or truths faintly apprehended and not understood, of isolated facts in the great scheme of Providence, in a word, the idea of mystery is discarded."[49] This is, for instance, quite clear in the strong claims for an authoritative Bible. This stance, as Quash notes, eliminates many of the Bible's less immediate or imperative "moods and possibilities," and is rooted in a very human need—"We need an anchor in the storm."[50] The problem with such strong claims, mirrored in certain claims for the authority of experience or the postwar human rights movement, is that

---

46. Ibid., §40.
47. Williams, "Communion," no pages.
48. Quash, "Damascus," no pages.
49. Newman, "Rationalism," 34.
50. Quash, "Damascus," no pages.

the felt need for an anchor forces God to come to us in immediate clarity and transparency.

On the other hand, we must ask, has the priestly office in the Anglican Communion also suffered from the lack of a regal office, perhaps approximating "superstition" or "enthusiasm"? Again, it is unfair to generalize from polemics, and "superstition" and "enthusiasm" are somewhat vague terms. (In the decade before Newman wrote his Preface to *The Via Media*, he himself was again accused of being an enthusiast in at least one review of the *Apologia Pro Vita Sua*.[51]) But if we follow J.G.A. Pocock and define "enthusiasm" as the mistaken belief that one has been "possessed by the Spirit," it is then related to antinomianism, which tends to disregard both the Law and the Church through which the Spirit is ordinarily mediated. With such a definition, we can say that ECUSA might be seen as "enthusiast." This is "enthusiasm" in a distinctively American antidogmatic manner—focused on identifying the experience of God with the liberty of inquiry concerning God.[52] Ephraim Radner has claimed that ECUSA exhibits "pneumatic universalism," which can be defined as the belief that individuals might escape from history and sin through "personal religious scrutiny and discovery" to "seek some immediate reconstitution of the immediate 'face of God.'" Episcopal Catholicism is constituted and "ever renewed" through the "sheer desire and will" of these seeking individuals, these American "enthusiasts."[53] The priestly office, subject to what Newman calls "popular elements," is always liable to "excess and corruption." Here, perhaps, we see an American "intemperate devotion."[54]

An office focused specifically on governance might check the tendency of the prophetical office towards rationalism, and the priestly office towards enthusiasm—in the United States, enthusiasm in the form of "pneumatic universalism"—by creating a counterforce. This office would permit neither theology nor spirituality to stand in distorted isolation. As Newman reminds us, historically the prophetical office has existed in some tension with the regal office. If the prophetical office has been solely concerned with what might be considered immediately authoritative, and is biased towards those facts, the regal office must concern itself

51. See Turner's introduction to Newman, *Apologia*, 108.

52. Pocock, "Enthusiasm," 10, 24.

53. Radner, "Children of Cain," 48, 45.

54. Newman, *Via Media*, 29.

with ecclesial unity, and following the principle of "Economy," insist upon temporary "concealment" and a process of gradual "accommodation." For example, such practices were needed to minimize the "disorder and dismay, which the Galilean hypothesis would cause the good Catholics."[55] Similarly, the regal office can "approve and praise the devotional enthusiasm of the people," when it focuses on the dubious "length of a miracle attached to a certain crucifix or picture," but only while keeping "our Lord's parable of the wheat and the cockle" very firmly in mind.[56] The regal office prevents the other offices from following their natural tendencies to either rationalism or enthusiasm.

IV

The application of force and counterforce between the three offices does not lead to an easy harmony. The Church will be "crossed and discredited now and then by apparent anomalies."[57] Based on historical examination, there is no real possibility of a triumphalist account of an ecclesial history of perfect cooperation, or of one office exercising a benevolent hegemony other the others. Instead, the introduction of a regal office into Anglicanism to replace the present reality of a dispersed authority should be the introduction to a *tragic* view of ecclesial history. Newman concludes his Preface with a brief and disturbing mention of "the collision and the adjustment" of the regal office at the expense of the sacerdotal in the person of the Emperor Constantine. "The sacred symbol of unresisting suffering, of self-sacrificing love, or life-giving grace, of celestial peace, became in the hands of the first Christian Emperor, with the sanction of the Church, his banner in fierce battle and the pledge of victory for his sword."[58] Earlier, Newman had spoken of the regal office similarly colliding with the prophetical office, which had been "dissuasive of using force in the maintenance of religion." Christianity survived, even flourished, but there was a spiritual and theological price. Something of the "sacred symbol" and "early tradition"[59] was lost. But it is difficult to imagine how

55. Ibid., 36, 34.
56. Ibid., 39.
57. Ibid., 57.
58. Ibid.
59. Ibid., 49.

it could have been otherwise. There is, apparently even for ecclesiastical tradition and symbols of unresisting suffering, self-sacrificing love, life-giving grace, and celestial peace, no history without loss.

One might imagine a harmonious church history by overemphasizing one principle, whether that of expedience, truth, or devotion. Such a picture may conceal tyranny, as we saw with Nicholas Lash's description on contemporary Roman Catholicism that began this essay. Perhaps it will obscure superstition and enthusiasm, or perhaps mask cold rationalism. The reality of church history is one of economy, accommodation, acts that are intelligible for peace and unity but at first glance "simply unjustifiable." Finally, there are "incongruities," because the three offices are always in some degree of tension with one another. This means that there will always be the problematic distinction between the "official" Church and its "popular and political manifestations" that disturbed Newman.[60] The Church in history is always locked in tension.

The Anglican Covenant, by introducing a political or governing office, represented by the various "instruments," cannot and should not hope to solve the problems in the Anglican Communion. (It may not even solve the dilemmas of individual Anglicans—one suspects that, on the neuralgic issue of homosexuality, Rowan Williams the theologian will not necessarily be reconciled with the Archbishop Williams, who as a bishop, must act for unity.) But, at the very least, it should make the problems themselves more intelligible, and perhaps manageable.

This does not make the problems any less painful. Newman can be accused of making ecclesial inconsistencies seem quite natural, but we can suggest that, especially with the discussion of Constantine, his portrayal of Church history lends itself to the tragic. For Donald MacKinnon, the tragic occurs in the conflict between the claims of truth and the claims of the victims of the process of the enactment of that truth.[61] The Gospel narratives at once transmit faith in the paschal mystery, but also remind us of the "destructive force" of "moral evil" in the "somber events which they describe." At once, the death of Christ led to the truth, "the unmasking of human motives," *and* "provided inevitably an excuse for [Christ's] followers in later years to fasten responsibility for the crucifixion upon the Jewish people and their descendants." The death of Christ, MacKinnon

60. Ibid., 23.

61. For this, see Devanny, "Truth, Tragedy and Compassion," 36.

controversially suggests, makes two claims upon us—hope for humanity and "the unmentionable horror of an anti-Semitism whose beginnings can perhaps be traced in the New Testament itself."[62]

There is no action, then, without failure and defeat. What MacKinnon called the "ultimate contradictions of life" are more present in the death of Christ, but there have been and will be contradictions in the fact that, if the Church is to witness to the truth of God, it must be also able to exist and draw humanity to itself, two quite different pursuits that are at times incommensurable. These contradictions can be resolved if, as in the situation that Nicholas Lash described, we simply collapse truth into expedience. But that situation that Lash described is disastrous. Alternately, we could suggest that the Church's witness to the truth—its professions of the Creeds and the works of learned theologians—should itself guarantee its existence in peace and unity. But the present crisis in the Anglican Communion makes it clear that this suggestion is also disastrous. We cannot collapse expedience into truth.

The non-solution that I would humbly suggest is to recognize all three offices in the Church by enacting the Covenant and creating a regal office, most realistically in conciliar form. This would expose the Anglican Communion to the very real dangers of ambition and tyranny. But acknowledging the existence of these dangers would in turn minimize the equally real dangers of rationalism and enthusiasm. The strengthening of a regal office should also mean that the Anglican Communion embraces the "contradictions of life" that are part of ecclesial history—such as Constantine. We are called to trust that, through it all, Christ who saved the world through the "sheer waste" of failure, is still with us, present in what appears to be our own "sheer waste."[63]

If this is even remotely possible, John Henry Newman can be even more of a blessing to both the Roman Catholic Church and the Anglican Communion. This is because he presents us with a vision of the Church "crossed and discredited now and then by apparent anomalies which need, and which claim, at our hands an exercise of faith."[64] This is the Church of Galileo, dubious miracles, overly extravagant Marian titles, Constantine, *and* painful disputes about sexuality. But even in dispute,

---

62. MacKinnon, "Atonement and Tragedy," 103.
63. Ibid.
64. Newman, *Via Media*, 57.

even with a Church wounded by division, this is not cause for despair but rather a more chastened, sober, and realistic hope.

BIBLIOGRAPHY

Anglican-Roman Catholic International Commission (ARCIC). *The Gift of Authority: Authority in the Church* III. No pages. Online: http://www.anglicancommunion.org/ministry/ecumenical/dialogues/catholic/arcic/docs/gift_of_authority.cfm.

Avis, Paul. *Beyond the Reformation? Authority, Primacy and Unity in the Conciliar Tradition.* New York: T. & T. Clark, 2006.

Chapman, Mark D. "The Dull Bits of History: Cautionary Tales for Anglicanism." In *The Anglican Covenant: Unity and Diversity in the Anglican Communion*, edited by Mark D. Chapman, 81–99. New York: Mowbray, 2008.

Davies, Matthew. "Archbishop Says There's 'No Problem' with Celibate Gay Bishops." *Episcopal News Service*, 27 September 2010. No pages. Online: http://www.episcopalchurch.org/81808_124764_ENG_HTM.htm

Devanny, Christopher. "Truth, Tragedy and Compassion: Some Reflections on the Theology of Donald MacKinnon." *New Blackfriars* 78/911 (1997) 33–42.

Duffy, Eamon. "'That Was Then, This Is Now': Some Comments on Newman's 1877 Preface to the Via Media and the Modern Church." *New Blackfriars* 92/1038 (2011) 170–75.

Dulles, Avery, SJ. "The Threefold Office in Newman's Ecclesiology." In *Newman after a Hundred Years*, edited by Ian Ker and Alan G. Hill, 375–99. Oxford: Clarendon, 1990.

Kerr, Fergus. "Tradition and Reason: Two Uses of Reason, Critical and Contemplative." *International Journal of Systematic Theology* 6 (2004) 37–49.

Lash, Nicholas. "Teaching or Commanding? When Bishops Instruct the Faithful." *America* 203/18 (2010) 17–20.

MacKinnon, Donald M. "Atonement and Tragedy." In *Borderlands of Theology and Other Essays*, by Donald M. MacKinnon, edited by George W. Roberts and Donovan E. Smucker, 90–96. Philadelphia: Lippincott, 1968.

McDade, SJ, John. "Episcopal and Prophetic Traditions in the Church." *New Blackfriars* 92 (2011) 18–19.

McPartlan, Paul. "Towards an Anglican Covenant: A Roman Catholic Perspective." In *The Anglican Covenant: Unity and Diversity in the Anglican Communion*, edited by Mark D. Chapman, 157–74. New York: Mowbray, 2008.

Misner, Paul. *Papacy and Development: Newman on the Primary of the Pope.* Leiden: Brill, 1976.

Newman, John Henry. *Apologia Pro Vita Sua and Six Sermons.* Edited by Frank M. Turner. New Haven: Yale University Press, 2008.

———. "The Introduction of Rationalistic Principles into Revealed Religion." In *Essays, Critical and Historical*, 30–99. Vol. 1. London: Pickering, 1872.

———. *Letters and Diaries, Volume XX: Standing Firm Amid Trials July 1861 to December 1863.* Edited by C. S. Dessain. London: Nelson, 1970.

———. *On Consulting the Faithful.* Translated by John Coulson. New York: Sheed & Ward, 1961.

————. *The Via Media of the Anglican Church.* Edited by H. D. Weidner. Oxford: Clarendon, 1990.

Pocock, J.G.A. "Enthusiasm: The Antiself of Enlightenment." *Huntington Library Quarterly* 60/1–2 (1997) 7–28.

Quash, Ben. "Theology on the Road to Damascus." *Journal of Scriptural Reasoning* 7/1 (2008). No pages. Online: http://etext.lib.virginia.edu/journals/ssr/issues/volume7/number1/ssr07_01_e01.html.

Radner, Ephraim. "Children of Cain: The Oxymoron of American Catholicism." In *The Fate of Communion: The Agony of Anglicanism and the Future of a Global Church,* by Ephraim Radner and Philip Turner, 25–58. Grand Rapids: Eerdmans, 2007.

————. "Wheels Within Wheels: The Promise and Scandal of Anglican Conciliarism." Inaugural Lectures at Wycliffe College, Toronto, SEAD Conference, Toronto, October 9, 2007. No pages. Online: http://www.wycliffecollege.ca/documents/Conciliarism.doc.

"Reviews and Notices." Review of *The Via Media of the Anglican Church,* by John Henry Newman. *The Month* 31 (1877) 368–73.

"A Self-Refutation." Review of *The Via Media of the Anglican Church,* by John Henry Newman. *Contemporary Review* 30 (1877) 1093–98.

"Short Notices." Review of *The Via Media of the Anglican Church,* by John Henry Newman. *Church Quarterly Review* 5 (1878) 232–36.

Williams, Rowan. "Communion, Covenant, and Our Anglican Future: Reflections on the Episcopal Church's 2009 General Convention for the Bishops, Clergy and Faithful of the Anglican Communion." Unpublished essay. No pages. Online: http://www.anglicancommunion.org/acns/news.cfm/2009/7/28/ACNS4641.

Yakaitis, Michael T. "The Office of Priest, Prophet, and King in the Thought of John Henry Newman." PhD diss., Pontifical Gregorian University, 1990.